D0059774

THE JAPANESE WAY
OF POLITICS

Studies of the East Asian Institute
Columbia University

THE JAPANESE WAY
OF POLITICS
Gerald L. Curtis

COLUMBIA UNIVERSITY PRESS
New York   1988

Columbia University Press

New York   Guildford, Surrey

Copyright © 1988 Columbia University Press

Printed in the United States of America

Hardback editions of Columbia University Press books are Smyth-sewn and are printed on permanent and durable acid-free paper

Curtis, Gerald L.
    The Japanese way of politics / Gerald L. Curtis.
        p.   cm.—(Studies of the East Asian Institute)
    Bibliography: p.
    Includes index.
    ISBN 0-231-06680-5
    1. Political parties—Japan. 2. Japan—Politics and government—1945–
    I. Title. II. Series.
JQ1698.A1C868   1988
324.252—dc19   87-27651
                                                                        CIP

THE EAST ASIAN INSTITUTE
OF COLUMBIA UNIVERSITY

The East Asian Institute is Columbia University's center for research, education, and publication on modern East Asia. The Studies of the East Asian Institute were inaugurated in 1962 to bring to a wider public the results of significant new research on modern and contemporary East Asia.

CONTENTS

PREFACE

In a matter of just a few years the world has suddenly awakened to the importance of Japan. This nation of more than 120 million people squeezed into a land area that is smaller than the state of Montana produces almost 15 percent of the world's GNP, has the second-largest economy in the noncommunist world, and is the world's largest capital exporter. Japan is already a major actor on the stage of world economic affairs and an ally of the United States whose importance in terms of American political, economic, and security interests is second to none.

In the United States the growing awareness of Japan's importance has created a veritable boom in interest in things Japanese, from sushi to quality control circles. Books purporting to reveal the secrets of Japanese economic success now fill bookstore shelves that until just a few years ago rarely held anything at all about Japan, and newspapers and magazines provide a steady stream of articles about the Japanese economy, about trade frictions with the United States, and about various aspects of Japanese life.

But despite this heightened interest and increased flow

of information, knowledge of Japan is far from adequate. Indeed, mesmerized by Japan's economic success, Americans have had a strong tendency to look for shortcuts to understanding, for neat and easily grasped theories of a Japan Incorporated, of an all-powerful bureaucracy, or of a social structure in which individual desires are suppressed in order to serve the interests of the group.

It is sometimes mentioned that Japan is a democracy, but the complexities, contradictions, dynamism, and political compromises inherent in democratic politics are usually missing from the powerful image that has emerged of an economy that operates according to long-range government plans and visions, and of a society that dutifully accepts the priorities and policies of a homogeneous and unified establishment. Fortunately the perception of Japan as a nation of imitators, retarded in its economic and political development by the society's failure to discard its feudal values in favor of more "modern" western ones, is no longer prevalent. But in its place have arisen new stereotypes and clichés that distort reality just as seriously.

Nowhere is this more true than in respect to Japanese politics, where misconceptions, partial truths, outmoded ideas, and obsolete information predominate. The Liberal Democratic party, in power ever since its creation in 1955, is usually portrayed as being a rural-based party that is able to remain in power because of an election district system that overrepresents farmers. And LDP politicians are widely thought to be interested in issues of public policy only to the extent that they provide opportunities to protect this rural electoral base. A political opposition that has never been in power is usually dismissed as being almost irrelevant to what happens in Japanese political life. In reality, not one of these propositions is entirely true.

There is relatively little solid information available to people interested in contemporary Japan about how that country's political system actually does work. There are several excellent monographs available on highly specialized topics, but few broad-gauged studies and surprisingly little that relates the development of the political system since the end of the Second World War to the momentous changes that have occurred in the Japanese economy and in Japanese society during that time. This book was written in the hope that it might help fill that gap.

It is a book that is primarily about the evolution of Japanese politics over the more than three decades of Liberal Democratic party rule. It is in large part a story of how the political system absorbed, responded to, and helped promote and channel the enormous social and economic changes that occurred during this time. Accordingly, it is a book about the dynamics of a political system that has combined stability in terms of party power with a remarkable capacity for flexibility and change.

This emphasis on change and on party politics is quite different from the more conventional focus on Japan's extraordinary political stability and on Japanese bureaucratic power. Yet the three decades of stable LDP rule constitute anything but a static system. LDP dominance is best seen as providing an umbrella under which the party system, and Japan's politics more generally, have undergone a fundamental transformation.

Moreover, the importance of bureaucratic institutions, or the political role of the big-business community, are not adequately explained by reference to theories of party reign and bureaucratic rule, or by the notion that political power resides in the hands of a triumvirate of big business, the bureaucracy, and the LDP—the political scientist's version of Japan Incorporated. The role of the bureaucracy is best understood in the context of its relationship with the nation's elected leadership, whose participation in government decision making has itself been changing over the years. And the role of big business, and of other organized interests, needs to be seen in the context of an increasingly pluralistic society, one characterized by a growing fragmentation in the representation of political interests and by a growing autonomy of the economy and of the society vis-à-vis the state.

This book is about the Japanese way of politics. Much of what it has to say will have a familiar ring, because there are many similarities in the way politics is practiced in any modern democracy, no matter how different the cultural contexts of those politics. Respect for civil liberties, competitive elections, responsible government, even the high cost of election campaigns will strike a chord of instant recognition. But Japan has used the threads of democratic politics to weave through its social structure, constitutional order, political traditions, and value systems a distinctly Japanese pattern. A better understanding of this pattern should contribute to a deeper appreciation of this enormously vibrant, successful, and endlessly interesting country.

This study draws heavily on Japanese language sources, as will be apparent from the footnotes and bibliography. As is the case with other democratic countries, there is available in the Japanese public record—in government and party publications, newspapers, and scholarly works—an enormous amount of information and analysis about Japanese politics and government. Indeed, it is quite remarkable how much one can learn about the details of government decision making and political developments from a perusal of the Japanese press, as every serious student of contemporary Japanese society soon learns. The Japanese decision-making system is not impenetrable, and information about Japanese politics is not difficult to come by for those who have the language skills to see what the Japanese are saying and writing about themselves. Training a much larger number of Americans in these skills, incidentally, is essential if we are to develop better public understanding of Japan and if American business and government are to be able to deal with Japan more effectively.

But the major sources for the information and the analysis in this volume are the practitioners of politics in Japan themselves, from Diet members to village assemblymen, from Liberal Democrats to members of the political opposition with whom I have met over the past two decades and more. With rare exception, these politicians have been extraordinarily open about their vocation, indeed eager to explain in detail what they do and how they do it. I have spent countless hours talking with them in Tokyo and many enjoyable and interesting times visiting their constituencies. There is no way that I can publicly acknowledge my sense of gratitude to all of them, nor to the staff people, the local politicians, the journalists, scholars, bureaucrats, business leaders, and many other people from all walks of life in Japan who have gone out of their way to help me.

But I do want to take special note of the political leaders to whom I owe a particularly profound debt of gratitude for the generosity they showed me over the years of research that went into producing this book. These include Satō Bunsei, Minister of Posts and Telecommunications in the second Nakasone cabinet in 1986, whose first successful campaign for the lower house in 1967 was the subject of my *Election Campaigning Japanese Style.* He has been as enthusiastic in helping me understand the Japanese way of politics in the years since that first election victory as he was during the year that I lived in his home and gathered the information for that earlier study.

I was introduced to Satō in 1966 by Prime Minister Nakasone Yasuhiro, who was a "new leader" at the time and who has been unfailingly generous with his time and insights in the years since. So too has been former Prime Minister Miki Takeo, who has been a member of the Diet for fifty years and with whom I have had the distinct pleasure of spending many hours discussing Japanese politics. I also want to take this opportunity to express my gratitude to Takeshita Noboru. Takeshita, who became prime minister in November 1987, is one of Japan's new "new leaders," but prior to obtaining that appellation he was known in LDP circles as a "god of elections." Over the twenty years or so that I have known him he has been extremely generous in sharing with me his knowledge and insights about LDP organization and the functioning of the Japanese election system. Ezaki Masumi, Fukuda Takeo, Hatoyama

Iichirō, Kakizawa Kōji, Katō Kōichi, Kōno Yōhei, Kōsaka
Tokusaburō, Kōsaka Zentarō, Kujiraoka Hyōsuke, Miyazawa Kiichi, Nikaidō Susumu, Sakamoto Misoji, Yamaguchi
Toshio, and Yamashita Ganri have also been particularly
helpful. To them, and to the many other LDP politicians I
have not mentioned here, I want to express my deepest appreciation.

In the process of doing the research for this book I
spent a great deal of time talking with members of the Socialist party and visiting local Socialist party headquarters
in Hokkaidō, Kanagawa, Niigata, Fukushima, Ōita, and Ya-
magata prefectures. I want to extend a collective thank you
to all the Diet and local politicians in the JSP, and to the
staff members both in party headquarters in Tokyo and in
local branches around the country who gave me so much
of their time and their knowledge.

I particularly want to express my gratitude to Socialist
party Diet member Kawakami Tamio, whom I first met in
1963 when I was a graduate student and he a young pro-
fessor of political science spending the year as a visiting
scholar at Columbia University. Kawakami ran for the lower
house after returning to Japan, being elected from the same
district in Kobe that his father, Kawakami Jōtarō, the former
chairman of the JSP, had served for many years before him.
Kawakami not only shared with me his own keen insights
into Japanese politics but went out of his way on many occasions to arrange meetings for me with other Socialists and
with union leaders.

I also owe a deep debt to two Socialist leaders who
have passed away. One is Eda Saburō, whom I met on many
occasions in the last year or two of his life and from whom
I learned a great deal. The other is Miyake Shōichi, who not
only had a distinguished career in the prewar tenant farmer
union movement and in the postwar JSP, but who was a
wonderful raconteur and with whom I spent a number of
particularly interesting days in his district in Niigata prefecture (the district that also elects to the Diet former Prime
Minister Tanaka Kakuei). Other Socialist Diet members to

whom I owe special thanks include Asukata Ichio, Hori Masao, Ishibashi Masashi, Kawasaki Kanji, Sasaki Kōzō, and Yokomichi Takahiro, who has since been elected as governor of Hokkaidō.

I also want to acknowledge the help of politicians in other parties. Democratic Socialist party Diet member Nagasue Eiichi has given me many insights into Japanese politics over the years. Discussions with DSP Diet members Sasaki Ryōsaku, Tsukamoto Saburo, and Itō Eisuke also have been very helpful. I also want to thank Den Hideo and Kan Naoto in the Social Democratic League, and Yano Junya and Kuroyanagi Akira in the Kōmeitō.

At the risk of failing to mention others to whom I am equally indebted, let me express my gratitude for the special kindnesses and important assistance given to me by Andō Jinbei, Akuto Hiroshi, Atsumi Keiko, Chūma Kiyofuka, Isaac Eisenlohr, Fukai Taeko, Ishikawa Masumi, Kamiyu Fuji, Kase Hideaki, Katsumata Hideko, Kobayashi Shōichi, David C. Klein, Kunihiro Masao, Nagai Yonosuke, Obi Toshio, James and Shirley O'Cain, Satō Seizaburō, Shinohara Hajime, Tomita Nobuo, Torii Keiichi, Fay Willey, and Yamamoto Tadashi. My wife and my children deserve a special note of thanks and affection for bearing with me, and without me, during the many research trips I made to Japan, and during the time I spent alone wresting the material I had collected down onto paper and getting the book into shape.

The manuscript benefited immensely from comments on earlier drafts given to me by Michael Blaker, David Halberstam, Kamiya Fuji, Kobayashi Katsumi, James Morley, Herbert Passin, Hugh Patrick, and Ezra Vogel. It also profited from the able research and secretarial assistance provided by Deborah Bell, Charles Curtis, Douglas Durham, Kamiya Matake, Sheila Smith, and Robert Uriu.

I also want to gratefully acknowledge the financial support I received from the Japan Society for the Promotion of Science and the Japan Foundation; from the Toyota Research Program of the East Asian Institute of Columbia University; and from the Ford Foundation and Thyssen Foun-

dation. A joint grant from the last two organizations enabled
me to spend several months at the Royal Institute of International Affairs (Chatham House) in London where, with
the enthusiastic encouragement of the late Andrew Shon-
feld, I had the opportunity to increase my understanding
of contemporary European politics and develop a broader
perspective within which to approach the analysis of Japanese political democracy presented in these pages.

Let me close with the usual but nonetheless entirely
genuine admonition that while people who have helped me
in the course of researching and writing this book share the
credit for what is worthwhile in it, only I am responsible
for its errors and shortcomings.

THE JAPANESE WAY
OF POLITICS

1.

THE TRANSFORMATION OF THE JAPANESE POLITICAL PARTY SYSTEM

In contrast to the frenetic pace of economic and social change that has accompanied Japan's rise to economic superpower status, one of the hallmarks of Japan's political system has been its profound stability. For more than thirty years now, government power has been in the hands of the Liberal Democratic party (LDP). Created in 1955, the LDP has never faced a serious challenge to its dominant position. In the late fifties and in the 1960s it enjoyed large majorities in both houses of Japan's bicameral legislature, the Diet. Its majority of seats grew smaller in the 1970s, but even then its ability to control the premiership and the government was never threatened. And in an election held in 1986, a simultaneous election of both houses of the Diet, the LDP returned a majority as large as it had enjoyed in the early sixties. There are other countries with competitive party systems that have experienced long periods in which one party has retained governmental control. But in none has the possibility of an alteration of the party in power has been as remote as in Japan.

Nonetheless, the history of Japanese politics under LDP rule is as importantly a story of political change as it is of continuity and stability. There is a world of difference between the political party system that exists today and the one that was created in 1955. The LDP's dominant position has served as a kind of umbrella under the cover of which Japan has experienced vast political as well as economic and social change.

When the Liberal Democratic party came into existence, Japanese society was profoundly divided ideologically and politically. There was a huge cultural chasm, on one side of which were ranged the conservatives with their electoral roots in the agricultural work force and small business leadership. On the other side stood the Socialists and other progressives (*kakushin*) who spoke for the modern, urban, and young electorate. Distrust and hostility were the hallmarks of relations between these two politically warring camps, in what one author referred to as the "cultural politics" of the time.[1]

Japanese society by the late 1980s, by any comparative measure, was remarkably free of wrenching social cleavages. Extremists of the left and the right had been pushed to the sidelines of political life. And the antagonism between mutually suspicious camps that characterized the country three decades earlier had given way to a competition to secure a footing in the political center.

The LDP itself has changed in fundamental ways during the years of its rule. In 1955 it was little more than a loose coalition of factions, the glue holding it together being the fear that division would give the Socialists the chance to take power. Thirty years later the LDP had become a complex and differentiated organization whose whole had become greater than the sum of its factional parts. On the other hand, its nemesis, the Japan Socialist party, had become a mere shell of its former self, enfeebled by years of internal party squabbling over ideology and the distribution of party power.

Equally striking is the transformation of the political agenda over these years of the Japanese economic miracle. In the early years of its rule, the LDP engaged in bitter battles with the opposition over foreign policy and over rearmament. The Socialists' call for unarmed neutrality—which neatly combined in one slogan opposition to both rearmament and alliance with the United States—enjoyed considerable public support. Opposition to American military bases and to the building up of the Japanese Self-Defense Forces was widespread. And in 1960, Prime Minister Kishi's determination to obtain Diet passage of a revised U.S.-Japan Security Treaty precipitated the largest public protest in Japan's political history.[2]

In the 1950s and 1960s the LDP was the champion of rapid GNP growth, a policy that was as marked for the broad public support it enjoyed as the policy of alliance with the United States and a moderately paced rearmament was noted for the public controversy it engendered. The LDP's focus on economic growth became particularly sharp following the resignation of Prime Minister Kishi immediately after the revised Security Treaty came into effect in 1960. The new government of Prime Minister Ikeda Hayato opted for a "low posture" on foreign affairs and concentrated its attention on a double-the-income policy that was to signal the blossoming of Japan's economic miracle. Moreover, LDP policy in these years was characterized not only by an emphasis on growth, but by the energetic use of the government purse to dispense benefits to the party's traditional, and loyal, supporters.

By the late 1970s, however, the same party whose earlier survival as the party in power seemed so inexorably linked to the handing out of ever-larger slices of the government pork barrel was championing the virtues of fiscal restraint and administrative reform. After 1980 the government imposed a virtual budget freeze in almost all areas.

The major exception has been defense, the former object of intense political conflict, where annual spending increases of 6 to 7 percent now provoke little more than ritualized political protest.

All of these changes were part of a more general transformation of Japanese politics during these years. The result has been a political system characterized by striking contrasts: of political change and stability, of one-party dominance and intense interparty competition, of adaptability in the face of new circumstances and profound continuity.

The Pre-1955 Political System

Political parties are not new to Japanese politics. The first modern parties were founded in the 1870s and 1880s, and the first parliamentary elections were held in 1890. But with political power formally fragmented among several civilian and military elite groups, parties faced a constant struggle to establish their centrality in the political system. Considerable progress was made in the 1920s toward establishing the practice of party government, but in the context of growing militarism in the 1930s the conservative parties lost their tenuous hold on political power while socialist parties, known in Japanese as proletarian parties (*musan seitō*), which had grown in popularity in the years following the adoption of universal manhood suffrage in 1925, were subjected to increased repression. In 1940 all political parties were dissolved.

During the Second World War many conservative and socialist leaders joined the government-created Imperial Rule Assistance Association (IRAA, *taisei yokusankai*) and actively supported the wartime government. But wartime totalitarianism in Japan was never quite total, and some of the old party leaders continued to be politically active outside the IRAA. In the one wartime parliamentary election, held in 1942, several of these former party leaders were elected to the Diet without the recommendation of the IRAA. These included a number of men who were to become leaders of the postwar parties: Hatoyama Ichirō, the LDP's first prime minister; Miki Takeo, prime minister from 1974 to 1976; Kōno Ichirō, one of the LDP's early faction bosses and the political mentor of Prime Minister Nakasone Yasuhiro; and Nishio Suehiro, postwar Socialist party leader and the founder in 1960 of the Democratic Socialist party.

No sooner had the war ended than prewar politicians—those who had supported the militarists and those who had not—began to reorganize political parties. In October 1945, leaders of all the noncommunist parties in the prewar proletarian movement agreed to join forces in a single political party, the Japan Socialist party (JSP). Less than a month later Hatoyama, who had been chief cabinet secretary from 1927 to 1929, minister of education from 1931 to 1934, and who had led a faction in the prewar Seiyūkai party (one of the two major conservative parties at the time), organized the Liberal party (Nihon Jiyūtō). Its members were mainly Seiyūkai politicians and other conservatives who had not been part of the IRAA. Shortly thereafter, another conservative party, the Progressive party (Nihon Shinpotō), was formed mainly among politicians who had been active in the IRAA. In December a third conservative party, the Japan Cooperative party (Nihon Kyōdōtō), was created.

These last months of 1945 also saw the emergence of the Communist party as a legal entity. The JCP—the only postwar party to retain its prewar name—had led an illegal existence ever since its founding in 1922, with most of its leaders who survived the wartime years doing so either in jail or abroad. On October 4, 1945 the American Occupation authorities ordered the release of all political prisoners, including Communists, some of whom had been imprisoned for nearly two decades. The party immediately resumed publication of its party newspaper, *Akahata* (Red Flag), for the first time in eleven years, and in December held its first party congress in eighteen years. Thus, within just a few months of the end of the Second World War, Japan's prewar politicians had picked up the pieces of the prewar party movement and organized new or revived political parties.

But these fledgling parties had no sooner been formed when in January 1946, SCAP (the Supreme Commander for the Allied Powers, i.e., General MacArthur; but commonly used to refer to the Occupation authorities in general) implemented the order titled "The Removal and Exclusion of Undesirable Personnel from Public Office."[3] Among those ousted in this purge were nearly 35,000 people who had held public office at the national and local level. This number included all Diet members elected as recommended candidates of the IRAA in the 1942 election and whoever else in the judgment of Occupation authorities had "by speech, writing, or action . . . shown himself to be an active exponent of militant nationalism and aggression."[4]

This latter criteria was used to purge Liberal party leader Hatoyama on the eve of his appointment as prime minister in 1946. It also was used against Ishibashi Tanzan, former editor of an influential economics journal, the *Tōyō Keizai Shinpō* (Oriental Economist), whose purge seems to have had more to do with his unpopularity among SCAP officials than with anything he did during or before the war.[5] Ishibashi later returned to political life and succeeded Hatoyama as the LDP's second prime minister, a post that illness forced him to relinquish after only two months.

The purge virtually wiped out the Progressive party. Of its 274 lower house members, only 27 survived the purge. The purge took 10 of the Liberal party's 50 Diet members and 10 of the Socialists' 17 members. Even the cabinet of Prime Minister Shidehara, which was responsible for implementing the purge order, was not left unscathed. Five of his cabinet members were forced to resign and leave political life.

The purge of politicians had two important consequences. One was to provoke a bewildering series of party splits and mergers among conservative politicians and help create or reinforce cleavage lines—between purged and nonpurged politicians, between professional politicians and former bureaucrats, and between men deeply hostile to one another for personal reasons—that were later to manifest themselves in factional alignments within the LDP.

The other was to create a leadership vacuum that opened the way for a new generation of political leaders. Prominent among these new leaders were men who had risen to high positions in the national bureaucracy. Since the American Occupation was an indirect occupation that worked through the existing Japanese government structure, the bureaucracy was left relatively untouched by the purge. In July 1948 the Liberal party announced that it was being joined by twenty-five high-ranking bureaucrats. Included in this group were two later LDP prime ministers, Ikeda Hayato, who at the time was the vice minister of the Ministry of Finance, and Satō Eisaku, the vice minister of the Ministry of Transportation. These Liberal party bureaucrats became the core of what came to be known as the "Yoshida School," bureaucrats-turned-politicians who were handpicked by Prime Minister Yoshida and who were to be a dominant force in conservative politics thereafter.

But the purge opened the door to high political office to many other politically ambitious people as well. This included a large number of local politicians, some of whom ran as surrogates for purged politicians. By 1951 SCAP was allowing the Japanese government to release selected individuals from the purge, and in April 1952, when the peace treaty came into effect and the Occupation ended, all those who had been purged were allowed to reenter political life. Many purged politicians tried to make a political comeback only to find that their old local political organizations were either no longer loyal to them or else not strong enough to oust the new incumbents from office.

All told, 91 former Diet members recommended by the IRAA in the 1942 election eventually were elected to the lower house in the postwar period. This amounted to some 24 percent of the 381 candidates the IRAA recommended in the 1942 election.[6] Whether one considers this to be a lot or a little depends on how one assesses the responsibility of these politicians for Japan's wartime policies. The point that is germane to our discussion is that the purge effectively excluded from postwar Japanese politics more than 70 percent of the politicians who had been in the Diet before 1945.

The purge had one other impact worth noting. In June 1950 the purge directive and a 1946 government order aimed at curbing right-wing elements by prohibiting militarist and other political organizations whose aims ran counter to those of the Occupation were used as vehicles to purge all twenty-four members of the Communist party central committee and seventeen executives of the party newspaper.[7]

The purge directive had been designed to exclude from public life those who had been leaders of Japan's war effort, an accusation that could hardly be leveled against the Communists. But by 1950 the Occupation authorities and the Japanese government were engaged in a frontal assault on the Communists, and on their power in the burgeoning labor movement in particular. The purge of the JCP leadership was followed by a so-called Red Purge instituted by the Yoshida government to drive "Communists and their sympathizers," as the Prime Minister himself put it, "from Government posts, press and industries."[8] This purge took eighteen months to complete and led to the dismissal of over ten thousand industrial workers, several hundred journalists, and thousands of government workers. In all, some 22,000 people were discharged from their jobs during the Red Purge.[9]

The attack on the Communists was led not only by SCAP and the conservative Japanese government. It also came from within the labor movement itself. A democratization movement (mindō) emerged within the large Communist-dominated labor federation Sanbetsu (Zenkoku Sangyōbetsu Kumiai Kaigi, National Congress of Industrial Unions) and received the enthusiastic support of SCAP. This helped bring about the end of Communist power in the labor movement and led to the formation in 1951 of Sōhyō (Nihon Rōdō Kumiai Sōhyōgikai, General Council of Japanese Trade Unions). But Sōhyō rather than becoming the moderate labor union federation that SCAP had hoped for, quickly came under the control of elements aligned with the left wing of the Socialist party. The labor movement's right wing formed an organization in 1954 called Zenrō (Zen Nihon Rōdō Kumiai Kaigi, All-Japan Trade Union Congress) which later became Dōmei (Zen Nihon Rōdō Sōdōmei Kumiai Kaigi, Japan Conferation of Labor). Sōhyō and Dōmei have dominated the labor movement ever since, with Sōhyō aligned with the JSP and Dōmei with the Democratic Socialists.

In July 1946 the last election under the Meiji constitution was held. The Liberal party secured a plurality and prepared to form a coalition government with Hatoyama as prime minister. But as a result of Hatoyama's purge, Yoshida Shigeru, a career diplomat who had become foreign minister in September 1945 and was neither a member of the Liberal party nor a member of the Diet at the time, became president of the Liberal party and prime minister. In later years Hatoyama claimed that he and Yoshida had agreed that Yoshida would turn power back to him when the purge decree was lifted.[10] Yoshida's alleged betrayal of this understanding,[11] coupled with the fact that Hatoyama and his supporters were mainly political professionals while Yoshida's followers were primarily men drawn from the national bureaucracy, led to a deep division within the Liberal party that was for many years reflected in the factional alliances and animosities within the LDP.

The major task of the first Yoshida government was to have the Diet adopt a new constitution that had been drawn up by the previous cabinet under the close guidance of the American Occupation authorities. The new constitution—referred to as the "MacArthur constitution" by the right, and the "Peace constitution" by the left—came into force on May 3, 1947. It remains Japan's constitution, unamended, to the present day.

The postwar constitution replaced the Meiji constitution's fragmentation of governmental power with a system in which the Diet was formally established as the su-

preme organ of state power and in which the prime minister
and a majority of cabinet ministers must be Diet members.
In practice, all twenty cabinet ministers (in addition to the
prime minister) are almost always members of the Diet,[12]
and by convention only three of them are chosen from the
less powerful upper house.[13]

Centralizing formal political power in the Diet did not
suddenly make the Diet powerful. For many years the Diet
did little more than rubber stamp policies designed largely
by bureaucrats. What the new constitution did do was insure that the party, or coalition of parties, that controlled a
majority of Diet seats would control the premiership and
the cabinet. This was a fundamental, and a fundamentally
important, change in the rules of the political game. It established the parties as the ultimate arbiters of political power,
and it changed the nature of party-bureaucratic relations,
drawing politically ambitious bureaucrats into the parties and
forcing the bureaucracy to collaborate closely with politicians in the ruling party.

The first lower house election under the new constitution was held in April 1947. It was conducted under an
election law that reintroduced the prewar single-entry ballot, multimember district system that had been first adopted
in 1925. Under this system, the lower house that was elected
in 1947 consisted of 466 members chosen from 117 multimember districts. Each voter was given one ballot and, depending on the size of the district, victory went to the
candidates obtaining the top three, four, or five votes. This
system remains in effect today, though with some modifi-
cations. The total number of seats has been increased to 512,
the number of districts to 130, and there are now one six-
and four two-member districts in addition to the traditional
three- to five-member ones.[14]

Japan's first election under the new constitution gave
the JSP a plurality of seats and resulted in the establishment
of Japan's only Socialist-led government, with Katayama
Tetsu, leader of the JSP's right wing, as prime minister. But
he ruled a coalition government that was dominated by

conservatives. This put the Socialists in the position of having to accept conservative policy positions or risk having the government collapse. This, combined with the fact that Katayama was a weak and vacillating leader, had a lot to do with the government's dismal performance during its nearly ten months in office. It fell in February 1948, brought down in the end by the JSP's own left wing when Suzuki Mosaburō, the leader of the party's major left faction and the chairman of the lower house Budget Committee, led his supporters in that committee to vote with the Communists in defeating the government's proposed budget.

The Katayama government was succeeded by another coalition government that included the Socialists but was led by conservative Ashida Hitoshi. The JSP's right wing was represented by Nishio Suehiro, who became vice premier. Kato Kanjū, an important leader on the party left, served in the cabinet as labor minister.

But this government, coming into power at a time when the Occupation was shifting its emphasis from political reform to economic reconstruction, became responsible for implementing a severe anti-inflation policy, loosening some of the antimonopoly restrictions that had been adopted earlier in the Occupation and, of particular agony to the Socialists, depriving workers in public corporations of the right to bargain collectively and to strike.[15] The government was brought down in October 1948 by postwar Japan's first, but by no means last, major corruption scandal, involving alleged political payoffs by the Shōwa Denkō company.

The fall of the Ashida government marked the end of Socialist participation in government. What the public thought of the JSP's governmental performance was made clear at the next lower house election in 1949, when Socialist representation was reduced from 143 to 48 seats. This election was followed by a "reconstruction congress" that became the setting for a fierce ideological debate between right-wing leader and former Education Minister Morito Tatsuo and the left's Inamura Junzō.[16] Finally, in 1951, the JSP split into two parties, the Right JSP and Left JSP.

The major issue precipitating this split involved the question of whether or not the party should support the San Francisco Peace Treaty and the U.S.-Japan Security Treaty, the former having been signed on the morning of September 8, 1951, and the latter signed later on the same day, also in San Francisco. The left opposed the peace treaty because it provided for a peace that left Japan formally in a state of war with the Soviet Union, which refused to sign the treaty; and it opposed the Security Treaty because it violated the party's commitment to neutrality and its opposition to rearmament.

Most of those on the right, reflecting the depth and breadth of pacifist views in the party, also opposed the Security Treaty. But they favored acceptance of the Peace Treaty as the only realistic way to regain Japan's sovereignty. Only a few on the right, however, were prepared to recognize that calling for acceptance of the one but rejection of the other treaty was itself unrealistic, given the international politics of the time.

When a vote was taken in the JSP's central executive committee in October 1951 to decide the party's position, those who favored acceptance of the Peace Treaty and rejection of the Security Treaty (known as the "A Plan") defeated the left-supported "B Plan" (i.e., opposition to both treaties) by a vote of 16 to 14.[17] But in the party congress which convened later that month, the left outnumbered the right. Knowing that it would be rejected by the congress, the CEC never submitted its recommendation. Instead, on the night of October 24, the party's right wing met and adopted the A Plan, while the left wing met separately to approve the B Plan. Thereupon the JSP entered upon a period of formal division that lasted until October 1955.

Party politics on the right were no less volatile than they were on the left. But there was one enormous difference. While the Socialists, for whatever reasons, had been incompetent at governing, Prime Minister Yoshida, nicknamed "one man" for his autocratic ways, proved himself to be a master statesman, master politician, and a master bargainer with Occupation authorities. He retained a firm grip on both the government and what came to be known as the mainstream of the Liberal party. And in the process he seemed to convince the public that whatever "storm in a cup" (*koopu no naka no arashi*)—the Japanese rendering of "a tempest in a teapot"—conservative politicians might brew by their factional fighting, their leaders could be relied upon to govern competently. Needless to add, this legacy proved to be an enormous asset for the LDP and a terrible handicap for the Socialists.

In November 1954, Hatoyama, who had been trying to recapture the presidency of the Liberal party from Yoshida ever since his depurge in 1951, led his supporters out of the Liberal party to form a new party called the Japan Democratic party (Nihon Minshutō). He was joined by another group from the Liberal party loyal to Kishi Nobusuke, who had been minister of commerce and industry in the wartime Tōjō cabinet and spent the first three years of the postwar period in Sugamo prison awaiting trial as a suspected war ciminal. He was never tried, and after being released in December 1948, he embarked on a new political career that ten years later would bring him the prime ministership. The other group to join Hatoyama's new party was the Reform party (Kaishintō), which had been formed in 1952 by depurged politicians who had been active in the prewar Minseitō and by Miki Takeo and others who represented the liberal wing of the conservative camp. The composition of this new Democratic party, bringing together as it did people who were regarded as representing both the right-wing and liberal elements in the conservative camp, offers an excellent example of the extreme degree to which ideological differences have been subordinated to personal rivalries and factional power struggles in postwar Japanese conservative politics.

In December 1954, Yoshida, at the urging of Ogata Taketora and other leaders in his Liberal party who wanted to begin negotiations looking toward a merger of the conservative Democratic and Liberal parties, resigned the premiership, allowing Hatoyama to become premier, a position that he would have obtained in 1946 had he not been purged. After a general election that Hatoyama called in February 1955 and in which his Democratic party secured a plurality, negotiations seeking a merger of the Liberals and the Democrats began in earnest. They were spurred in part by growing evidence that the Left and Right Socialists were about to attempt another effort at unified action. These negotiations were also encouraged by business leaders whose worries about the prospects for political stability were heightened by the eruption of a major political scandal involving the shipbuilding industry. Finally, they were consummated by the poltical skill of Miki Bukichi (no relative of Miki Takeo), a wily elder statesman and Hatoyama ally who had negotiated the details with Ōno Bamboku and other Liberal party leaders.

The Socialist party reunified on October 13, 1955. One month later, on November 15, the Liberal and Democratic parties were dissolved and a new Liberal Democratic party was formed. Initially unable to decide who the LDP's first president should be, the leaders agreed that Hatoyama should form a new cabinet, that the party presidency should be left vacant until a party congress the following spring, and that in the interim Hatoyama, Ogata (Yoshida's successor as head of the Liberal party), Miki Bukichi, and Ōno Bamboku should comprise a kind of ruling council. An agreement was apparently made at the time that Hatoyama should become the party's first president and be succeeded by Ogata. Ogata, however, died the following January, and in April Hatoyama was made party president. He was to resign that post along with the prime ministership on November 2 that year, the day after his return from the Soviet Union where he had concluded a normalization treaty that brought formal peace (but no formal peace treaty) to relations between the two countries. Hatoyama was succeeded by another purged politician, Ishibashi Tanzan, who in turn was replaced two months later by Kishi Nobusuke.

The Three Phases of LDP Rule

Given the volatility of party politics in the decade from 1945 to 1955, the stability of the political system since 1955 is all the more striking. The LDP, as was noted at the outset, has ruled Japan uninterruptedly since it was formed. There is no evidence that suggests that the LDP's position as Japan's only government party will soon end.

This unending panorama of LDP rule makes Japan the world's preeminent example of what is often referred to as a predominant or dominant party system. But such party systems can in theory and do in fact differ from one another, particularly in respect to the number of parties they contain and the ideological distance that separates the dominant party from the others. There is a world of difference between the functioning of a political system in which the dominant party confronts a vigorous unified opposition that embraces an ideology and policy positions antithetical to its own and that of a system in which the opposition is fragmented among several ideologically diverse parties, some of which advocate policy programs that put them closer to the ruling party than to other parties in the opposition. Differences between predominant party systems, moreover, need not only be cross-national differences. As Japanese politics since 1955 shows, it is entirely possible for a predominant party system within one country to undergo fundamental change in its format and in the ideological positioning of the parties within it.

In 1955 the LDP faced an opposition that was unified, unalterably opposed to what the LDP stood for, and ready to resort to extraparliamentary tactics to influence the policy process. By dint of the intensity of the opposition's support among a large minority of voters, it was able to prevent the LDP from realizing many of its policy goals and to force it to accomplish others only by resorting to what was widely referred to as a tyranny of the majority.

More recently the LDP has faced a fragmented opposition at odds with itself over policy goals and political tactics, with elements eager to make deals and win some concessions from the party in power. Ideological polarization has weakened, and policy differences between most of the parties have tended to become matters of degree or approach more than of fundamental alternatives. The LDP has remained dominant for more than thirty years, but the Japanese party system, as well as the dominant party itself, have been fundamentally transformed.

Indeed it would be hard to imagine how this situation could have been otherwise, given the rapidity of economic and social changes during these three decades. These changes greatly weakened the salience of a conservative-progressive cleavage in Japanese politics; they forced the LDP to alter its political program to become responsive to the demands of an increasingly urbanized, pluralistic, affluent electorate in order to retain its dominant position; and they created an environment conducive to the emergence of new opposition parties seeking the support of social groups dissatisfied both with the policies being pursued by the LDP and with the alternatives being proposed by the Socialists.

Under the umbrella of LDP rule, the Japanese political party system has moved through three distinct phases. The first lasted roughly a decade, to the mid-sixties. The second carried Japanese politics through the 1970s. And the third emerged in the last years of that decade and has characterized Japanese politics in the 1980s.

THE FIRST PHASE

The first phase of Japan's predominant party system was characterized by a two-party format and by intense ideological polarization. In the 1958 general election, the first lower house election following the 1955 party mergers that created the LDP and a reunified JSP, these two parties together polled 91 percent of the popular vote and won 97 percent of the lower house seats. (The LDP won 57.8 percent of the popular vote and 61.5 percent of the seats, while the Socialists received the support of 32.8 percent of those voting and obtained 35.5 percent of the seats.) The Communist party received only 2.6 percent of the vote, with the remaining 6 percent or so going to minor parties and to independents aligned with the LDP.

Relations between the LDP and the JSP during this first phase were characterized by a deep ideological polarization that imparted to Japan many of the features of what Sartori has termed a system of "polarized pluralism."[18] In Japan ideological polarization took the form of a two-bloc competition rather than following Sartori's model of multiple parties representing opposing and plural ideological positions. But his fundamental condition for classification as a polarized polity—the existence of an avowedly antisystem party that challenges the legitimacy of the existing regime— was very much characteristic of Japanese politics in this period. Indeed, many writers have been struck by the apparent similarities between postwar Japanese party politics and politics in Italy, which provided one of Sartori's primary cases of polarized pluralism.[19]

But Sartori's belief that polarized systems tend to be unstable, that they manifest centrifugal tendencies since the parties in competition disagree not only on policy but on basic principles, was not entirely borne out by the Japanese case. It is true that an atmosphere of tension and discord was brought about by mass demonstrations over issues of rearmament and constitutional revision, the Socialists' resort to physical force to prevent the LDP from ramming through legislation in the Diet, a student movement in the universities that was dominated by the Communist party, and an ideological cleavage so deep between the conservative camp (hoshu jin'ei) and the progressive camp (kakushin jin'ei) that it seemed perfectly natural to use the language of warfare to describe their relations.

But much of this tension was created by opposition to the LDP's avowed objective of overturning the constitutional order established during the American Occupation.

As it turned out, it was the dynamic tension created by the standoff between an "antisystem" JSP which made up for its weakness in numbers by the intensity of its opposition and by the support it received from mass movements loosely affiliated with it, and an LDP that was in its own way also an antisystem party, that kept the postwar system on center, so to speak. Constitutional revision was prevented, the adoption of a single-member district system was thwarted,[20] and defense spending was kept limited. In the real world of Japanese politics at the time, the antisystem JSP defended the postwar constitutional order, while the ruling LDP pressed hard for system change.

Japanese scholars coined the expression "the 1955 structure" (55 nen taisei) to designate this two-party system and what many thought was going to be the beginning of a new period of competition between two governing-oriented parties. But this phase of one-party dominance was fairly short lived. The LDP's determination to retain political power pulled it more and more away from its formal program. At the same time the left wing's power in the JSP effectively prevented that party from exploiting any opportunity to move to the political center; instead, it produced a fissure that within four years of the establishment of the 1955 structure led to a break in the two-party format, with the formation of the Democratic Socialist party in 1960.

THE SECOND PHASE

The formation of the Democratic Socialist party marked the beginning of the end of the first phase of LDP rule, but the conclusion of this phase of polarized politics in an essentially two-party system was symbolized not so much by the creation of the DSP as by the establisment in 1964 of the Kōmeitō. This entirely new party was not produced by a split in an already existing party, but by new social forces that had been set in motion by Japan's drive toward rapid industrialization. With the creation of the Kōmeitō, Japan moved into a new period characterized by an increase in the number of relevant parties and a contraction in ideological polarization. Political stability in this second phase of LDP dominance increasingly came to rest not on the balance created by political forces pulling in opposite directions, but on the competition between multiple parties seeking more and more to occupy the political center.

Both the LDP and the JSP steadily lost support through this period. The LDP's share of the popular vote in lower house elections went down from a peak of 57.8 percent in the 1958 election to 41.8 percent in the election held in 1976. Electoral support for the JSP slid from 32.9 percent to 20.7 percent in the same period.

The JSP decline was particularly steep in the most urbanized parts of the country. Its share of the popular vote in Tokyo went from 27.1 percent in 1967 to 17.2 percent in the election held nine years later, in 1976. Back in 1963 the JSP and the LDP had split the total of Diet seats in Tokyo almost equally between them; in 1976 the JSP won less than a fifth of the seats at stake in Japan's capital, while the LDP won about a third.[21] Nationwide, a third of the electorate that voted in the 1976 election cast its ballots for candidates who were supported by parties other than the two parties that two decades earlier had commanded over 90 percent of the vote.[22]

LDP electoral performance in this second phase of Japan's dominant party system belies the notion that the LDP has been able to remain in power mainly because of the popularity of its high growth economic policies. Its support declined most precipitously during the years of rapid growth. High growth policies were popular with the public to be sure, but they did not necessarily redound to the LDP's benefit. For one thing, these policies drew more and more people to sprawling urban centers, where they were beyond the reach of the kinds of social networks that the LDP had traditionally utilized to mobilize support. Moreover, pollution, urban congestion, and other social ills that rapid industrialization brought in its wake had created by the end of the 1960s an impressive array of urban protest movements and of local government leaders backed by the opposition parties.[23]

The Socialist party, however, was unable to capitalize on opposition to the LDP. The JSP was slow, for example, to make opposition to industrial pollution a major plank in its program, in no small part because labor unions that backed the party often sided with management in resisting demands for pollution control or compensation for pollution victims that might compromise an industry's economic viability and threaten jobs. Furthermore, the Socialist party, like the LDP, depended to a considerable degree on the ability of its candidates to tap into extensive social networks to mobilize support. The JSP was little better prepared to reach out to the swelling ranks of urban voters who were not enveloped in these kinds of networks than was the LDP. The massive transfer of population from rural to metropolitan areas that made rapid industrialization possible thus took a toll on both major parties.[24]

By the end of the 1960s a third of Japan's population lived on the 1 percent of Japan's total land area encompassed within thirty-mile radii of the three Pacific coast cities of Tokyo, Nagoya, and Osaka. These crowded urban centers offered fruitful territory in which new parties such as the Kōmeitō and a revitalized Communist party could expand support. They also provided the voters who supported the New Liberal Club (NLC), an offshoot of the LDP formed in 1975. While politics in rural Japan remained characterized by an essentially one-and-a-half-party system in which only the Socialists provided any degree of meaningful competition to the LDP, urban Japan had by the mid-1970s produced a system in which six parties (the LDP, JSP, DSP, Kōmeitō, JCP, and NLC) were in active competition.

As competition intensified between these parties, and as the LDP's share of the popular vote and proportion of Diet seats declined, speculation grew that Japan would not only experience conservative-progressive parity (hokaku hakuchū), but a reversal of the influence of the progressives and conservatives (hokaku gyakuten) and the entry of the progressives into the government. But this language of politics came to assume a rather ironic tone, inasmuch as the second phase of LDP dominance was characterized both by a scuttling of progressivism by most of those supposedly in the progressive camp, and by the inability of any of the new challengers—the Kōmeitō, Communists, DSP, and New Liberal Club—to develop into anything more than minor parties, their major function in system terms being to help the LDP retain power by fragmenting the opposition to it. By the end of the 1970s these four parties (and the tiny Social Democratic League) together polled close to 30 percent of the vote, but no one of them received more than 10 percent of it, nor were any doing better at the end of the decade than at its beginning.

The inability of these minor parties to develop into major parties stands in considerable contrast to the expectations, or worries, that each generated when it first came into existence—or in the case of the JCP, when it was revitalized in the late 1960s. Each of these four minor parties enjoyed a boom of sorts for a short period, only to see its support level off or decline. To understand why this should have been the case requires a brief overview of what happened to each as it tried to secure a position for itself in the political system.

The Democratic Socialist Party. Reunification of the JSP in 1955 did not resolve the ideological and policy disputes that had split the party in 1951. Rather, it saddled the JSP with sharp internal differences over whether it should be a class or a mass party, and over national security policy. When Japan in the late 1950s moved into a period of rapid economic growth and toward a revision of the Security Treaty with the United States, these differences became more intense, reinforced by bitter conflict between the Marxist and reformist wings of the labor union movement, each of which underwrote one wing of the JSP.

Although the party's left wing looked as though it were more aggressive and powerful than the right in the late 1950s, economic, social, and political developments had in fact thrown it very much on the defensive. Increases in the standard of living were weakening the interest of blue-collar workers in the militant rhetoric of Sōhyō and initiating a process that was to lead the majority of private sector unions to affiliate with Dōmei, leaving Sōhyō dependent mainly on unions in the public sector. Revision of the Security Treaty promised to make the United States–Japan relationship more equitable from a Japanese point of view, removing the vestiges of Occupation control that were part of the original treaty that had been signed a decade earlier. At the same time, of course, it promised to draw Japan more deeply into military alliance with the United States. The left's response to these changing realities was to try to drive out of the party those who openly argued that the party should move to the right to meet them and to beat down those who advocated "structural reform" as a way to modernize the program of the party's left wing.

Nishio Suehiro, the party's former secretary-general and one of its major faction leaders, became the target of the left's attack on right-wing revisionism. At a party congress convened in September 1959, the left demanded that something be done about the "Nishio Problem."[25] A motion to expel him from the party was defeated, but another, proposing that his case be referred to the party's disciplinary committee and that the committee be given the authority to decide on the appropriate punishment, was adopted.

With the passage of this motion, members of the Nishio faction resigned their party posts and withdrew from the congress. The other large non-Marxist faction in the party, led by Kawakami Jōtarō, also decided to boycott the congress in opposition to the effort to drive Nishio out.

But long-standing personal feuds, factional jockeying for power, and policy differences were not only manifested in a right-left split. They characterized relations between the Nishio and Kawakami factions as well. Within three days of walking out of the congress, the Kawakami faction decided to abandon its policy of cooperation with Nishio, to return to the congress, and to back away from the brink of a party split.

The following month, a few days after the disciplinary committee voted to censure him, Nishio announced his decision to leave the JSP to form a new party, one, he boldly claimed, that would "come to power within five years."[26] In all, fifty-three JSP members—thirty-seven from the lower and sixteen from the upper house—bolted the JSP and participated in the DSP's first party congress on January 24, 1960.

The fact that the division took this truncated form had unhappy consequences for both parties. The Socialist party remained locked in an internal struggle between its Marxist (and Marxist-Leninist) and non-Marxist wings. And the DSP, unable to claim exclusive possession of the mantle of democratic socialism, distinguished itself from the JSP mainly by the virulence of its anticommunism. It was very similar in orientation to the Saragat socialists who bolted the Italian Socialist party early in the postwar period to form the Italian Social Democratic party (PSDI), and it experienced a similar dismal electoral fate. In its first lower house contest in 1960, the DSP saw only 17 of its 105 candidates win seats, collecting between them three and a half million votes, 8.8 percent of the total valid vote. The party's vote share declined to 7.4 percent in the next election in 1963 and has fluctuated little in the elections since then. Tighter candidate endorsement policies have enabled it occasionally to win more seats with essentially the same vote, the high point being the 39 seats it captured in the 1983 election. The party was a major casualty of the LDP landslide of 1986, returning only 26 members and obtaining 6.4 percent of the vote.

In a sense the DSP was formed too early to obtain broad support from the Japanese electorate. In 1960 Japan was still very much in the first phase of LDP dominance, with its deep cleavage between a conservative and a progressive camp. The DSP did not fit easily into either. It claimed that it was a progressive party—its protestation to this effect itself an indicator of the extent to which pro-

gressive credentials were seen as necessary to legitimize opposition to the LDP—while its policy positions put it closer
to the LDP than to the other progressive parties, the JSP
and the Communists. The DSP fell between the two camps,
able to attract neither the support of voters who wanted to
register an unambiguous protest against the LDP, nor the
support of those who were inclined to favor the LDP's policies. Moreover, its leader Nishio did not project a popular
image of new leadership, being widely known as an old-
line powerful party boss who had come out of the prewar
anti-Marxist Sōdōmei labor movement.

The DSP boom proved evanescent, and after the par-
ty's dismal performance in its first election in 1960, it turned
almost entirely to unions in the Dōmei federation for candidates and for organizational backing and financial support. It faced formidable obstacles in trying to reach a broad
constituency under the best of circumstances, but after several years of riding Dōmei's shoulders it essentially gave up
the effort. By the 1970s it was too enfeebled and captured
by a leadership too beholden to Dōmei unions to exploit the
new opportunities that had been created for a centrist opposition.

The Kōmeitō. Four years after the formation of the DSP,
an entirely new party, one that did not draw on any of the
existing parties for its Diet members or organization, was
created. The emergence of the Kōmeitō provides an important benchmark in the evolution of the Japanese party system toward a multiparty format and beyond a conservative-
progressive paradigm. In terms of ideology, basic policy orientations, and in its social bases of support, the Kōmeitō
defies classification in conventional conservative-progressive terms. It has no roots in the labor movement, and its
ideology is grounded on religious principles and not in a
theory of class conflict.

Its religious orientation makes it a party without parallel and without precedent in Japan. While Christian democratic and other denominational parties are commonplace

in Europe, there was no religious-based party in Japan until the Sōka Gakkai, a lay organization of the Nichiren Shōshū sect of Japanese Buddhism, created the Kōmeitō. The Sōka Gakkai, founded in the early 1930s, experienced phenomenal growth in the postwar period.[27] It concentrated its aggressive proselytizing efforts on urban dwellers who were being left behind in Japan's race for double-digit GNP growth: nonunionized workers in small factories, marginal small businessmen, shop clerks, bar hostesses—uprooted and unfortunate people who were promised health and wealth in this world in return for their faith. By the end of the 1960s, Sōka Gakkai had a nationwide membership of some six and a half million families, an estimated 10 percent of the total population.

The Sōka Gakkai had never shied away from political involvement. Its founder, Makiguchi Tsunesaburō, died in prison, where he was sent in 1943 for opposing the government's policy of making Shintō the state religion. From early in the postwar period, the Gakkai ran its own candidates for local public office. It first entered national politics in 1956, when it successfully ran three candidates in the upper house election. Six more were elected in 1959, and nine won in the upper house contest held in 1962. It created the Kōmeitō in 1964, which went on to score impressive political gains through the rest of the decade. By 1969 the Kōmeitō had surpassed the JSP in Tokyo, securing a position in the Tokyo Metropolitan Assembly second only to that of the LDP. It won twenty-five seats in its first lower house contest in 1967 and nearly doubled that number in the election held two years later, when forty-seven of its candidates were elected.[28]

Initially the Kōmeitō stressed its progressive credentials, taking positions similar to those of the JSP on Japanese rearmament and military alliance with the United States, the litmus test of progressivism in Japan. Nonetheless, it was viewed with apprehension by parties in the opposition camp who were worried that the combination of the Gakkai's proselytizing zeal and the Kōmeitō's appeal to nonunion workers and the lower middle class would make this new party a formidable competitor, and who were suspicious, its protestations to the contrary notwithstanding, that it constituted a new right-wing movement.[29] The LDP also viewed it with considerable alarm, given the Kōmeitō's pacifist stance, its anti-LDP posture, and its impressive gains in its first few electoral outings.

In 1969 the Kōmeitō bore the brunt of a major political storm when it became known that it had tried to stop publication of a book critical of its religious patron.[30] Criticism of the party over the book incident led the Kōmeitō to a 1970 decision to break its official ties with the Sōka Gakkai. In spite of the official break, however, the party continued to rely on the Gakkai for its candidates and election campaign machinery. But it set out on a new search for ways to extend its reach beyond the Gakkai's supporters.

This effort took it on a somewhat meandering course away from a position close to the JSP and brought it nearer, both in policy terms and in Diet strategy and general political tactics, to the DSP and the LDP. In the mid-seventies the Kōmeitō advocated close coordination with the DSP and the right wing of the JSP, then led by Eda Saburō. By the end of the decade it was indicating its willingness to join a LDP-led coalition and seemed seriously interested in the possibility of merging the Kōmeitō into a more broadly based centrist party. It also backed away from its early support for the abrogation of the Security Treaty with the United States. At the party's seventeenth congress in January 1980, it adopted a position that called for the "eventual abrogation of the Security Treaty by mutual consent" but also for its continuation "until the world situation changes." At the nineteenth congress in December 1981, the party accepted the treaty in its present form and dropped demands for its abrogation. It also became more supportive of current Japanese military policy, though it has retained a pacifist orientation that contrasts quite markedly with the DSP's enthusiasm for greater Japanese military efforts.

The effort to increase the party's appeal among the

non-Gakkai electorate proved largely unsuccessful. It remained almost entirely dependent on the electoral support of Gakkai members, with the result that the party's share of the popular vote in Diet elections was virtually the same in the mid-eighties as it was in the early seventies.[31] Along with the Communists, the Kōmeitō has the dubious distinction of being the party the Japanese dislike most.[32]

But the stability of its support, and the fact of its being the second-largest opposition party, made the Kōmeitō an important actor in the politics of the second phase of LDP dominance. It became the only opposition party since 1955 other than the JSP to have more than the fifty lower house seats needed to submit budget-related legislation and motions of nonconfidence in the Diet. It succeeded to a considerable extent in overcoming earlier criticisms of its alleged antidemocratic tendencies and, whether liked or not, both the JSP and the LDP sought its cooperation.

The Communist Party. The other party to emerge with new strength in the latter half of the 1960s was the Communist party. Although an insignificant force in electoral politics after its purge in the last years of the American Occupation,[33] the JCP contributed to the ideological polarization of the first phase of LDP dominance by its considerable influence over intellectuals and the student movement, and it was a more important political actor than its meager representation in the Diet would suggest.

Then in the late 1960s, the JCP began to make fairly significant electoral gains, doing so by drawing largely on the support of the same social groups that were being attracted to the Sōka Gakkai and its political arm, the Kōmeitō. The JCP tripled the number of its Diet seats between the elections of 1967 and 1969, and more than doubled their number again in the next election, winning thirty-eight seats and 10.5 percent of the popular vote in 1972. Some LDP leaders at the time spoke of a coming age of confrontation between the LDP and the JCP and tried to shore up their own party's sagging support by raising the specter of a serious internal communist threat. The Communists for their part tried to maintain the momentum of their seemingly growing popularity by pushing further and faster party reforms intended to give the party a moderate Eurocommunist look.

This effort led the JCP to emphasize its independent and nationalist credentials and to mute its ideological positions. Along with its customary attacks on the U.S.-Japan Security Treaty and its claim that Japan was a semicolony of an imperialist America, it took to attacking both the Soviet Union and China. In the early 1960s, when the JCP sided with Peking in the growing conflict in Sino-Soviet relations, the JCP regularly accused the Soviet Union of being guilty of "big power chauvinism" in its dealings with foreign Communist parties.[34] In the mid-1960s, relations deteriorated with China as well and led to total estrangement between the two parties later in the decade, when China was caught up in the throes of the Cultural Revolution. Even though there have been improvements in relations with Moscow and moves toward restoring relations with Peking in more recent years, the JCP still regularly criticizes "some socialist countries, especially the Soviet Union and China, [for] following foreign policies that are incompatible with the principles of scientific socialism, the cause of world peace, and national self determination."[35]

In the early Occupation years, the JCP welcomed the American occupiers as liberators and tried to project an image of a "lovable" JCP. Then in 1951 it adopted a strategy of armed struggle which lasted until 1955, when it began its return once again to support for peaceful and legal political activity. From that point on, the JCP increasingly stressed its readiness to play by the rules of the parliamentary game and to respect the values enshrined in the postwar Japanese constitution. In 1973 it took a first somewhat halting step toward eliminating reference in the party platform to the Leninist concept of proletarian dictatorship. Arguing that use of the word "dictatorship" provoked unwarranted fears about political life in the aftermath of the socialist revolution, the party changed the expression to what translates roughly as "proletarian rule" (substituting the rather archaic word *shikken* for the offensive *dokusai*). There was no break, however, with the concept itself, as critics of the party were quick to point out.

The new Eurocommunist thrust came to a head in the party congress held in July 1976. A number of further changes in language were adopted: all reference to Marxism-Leninism was eliminated from the party program, with "scientific socialism" substituted in its stead. And a new expression was devised for the ill-favored "proletarian dictatorship." Now the party spoke of establishing "workers' power" (*rōdōsha no kenryoku*).

Along with these lexical changes, the party adopted a new Manifesto of Freedom and Democracy. The Manifesto declared that the JCP in power would respect civil liberties and permit the continued existence of a multiparty system, that it would not nationalize small industry or agriculture, and that it would establish a truly autonomous foreign policy. These commitments were referred to as the "Three Freedoms"—namely, freedom from want, political liberties, and freedom from foreign control. They were an attempt to offer a vision of a party accepting of bourgeois political freedoms, committed to an egalitarian economic structure, and strongly nationalistic in foreign policy.[36]

But Communist party hopes that its new look would draw more voters did not materialize. The decline in the popularity of Marxism in the intellectual community gravely weakened the JCP's influence in the student movement and among intellectuals more generally. Moreover, its moderate stance did nothing to widen its appeal among those voters who saw a vote for the JCP as a way to lodge a protest. Neither was a Communist party that tried to stress its fidelity to conventional values particularly appealing to those voters who saw a vote for the Communists as a way to express individualistic, nonconformist values. As is noted in chapter 6, a higher percentage of people who vote for the Communist party express support for attitudes identified with individualism than do supporters of any other party. For a significant number of Communist voters, it was not the collectivist vision of the party's program but the fact that the party rejected conventional mores that made it appealing. The JCP's Eurocommunist look weakened this appeal without increasing the party's popularity among other voters.

The Communist party has been unable to increase its share of the popular vote in national elections beyond the 10 percent level that it reached in 1972.[37] Opposition by the Kōmeitō and the DSP to cooperation with the JCP rendered the prospects for an all–opposition party coalition, or Communist participation in any kind of coalition government, entirely fanciful. And the emergence of near parity in LDP and opposition party strength in the Diet resulted in increased cooperation between the LDP and the noncommunist opposition that left the Communist party increasingly isolated.

The New Liberal Club. By the mid-1970s the process of fragmentation in the opposition camp had all but run its course. There were now three significant opposition parties—the DSP, the Kōmeitō, and the JCP—in addition to the JSP. In 1977 yet another small party, now known as the Social Democratic League (Shakai Minshu Rengō), was formed. But this group's prospects were bleak from the start. It had no major union backing or other source of significant organizational support, and its leader, Eda Saburō, died shortly after bolting the JSP.

The transformation of Japan's party system from a two-party to a multiparty format was accomplished almost entirely by fragmentation on the left. Though factional conflict in the LDP had periodically threatened to split the party, it remained united for the first two decades of its existence. In July 1976, however, a break occurred in the ranks of the post-1955 conservative coalition when one upper and five lower house members of the LDP left the party to form the New Liberal Club.

Lower house member Kōno Yōhei and the other leaders of this group were energetic, irrepressibly optimistic, and seemed to typify for many people the new, modern, "post-ideology" generation. The NLC's criticism of the LDP for failing to come to grips with the problem of political corruption, and the seeming courage of these mainly young and upcoming politicians in bolting the ruling party, struck a responsive chord in the electorate that led to a veritable nationwide boom.

At the height of its popularity several months after being formed, the party had the support of some 13 percent of the electorate, according to public opinion polls.[38] Moreover, this support came mainly from voters whom the LDP had not been able to attract and whom the Socialists had long ago lost, namely, the young, educated, urban middle class.

But the boom went bust in a great hurry. In the upper house election held in the summer of 1977, the NLC ran thirteen candidates but elected only three. Two years later its representation in the lower house was cut back from eighteen to four seats. It had difficulty raising political funds, recruiting attractive candidates, enticing local politicians away from the LDP to help it to build a strong local organization, and extending its support beyond a few prefectures that were mainly in the Tokyo area.

Also, to the extent that the NLC's initial appeal was rooted in its maverick image and its criticisms of the ways the established parties operated, it stood to reason that its support would sag as the NLC itself became established and the memory of the drama of its emergence faded. There was a parallel with the formation of the DSP in 1960. In a poll taken in October 1959 some 10 percent of JSP supporters indicated support for the new Socialist Club (Shakai Kurabu) that Nishio had formed that year. But by January 1961 the Socialist Club, now reconstituted as the DSP, had lost 80 percent of these early supporters.[39]

The NLC was handicapped also by taking so few Diet members out of the LDP with it. The new party was not created by a disaffected LDP faction. The Dietmen who were involved in its formation came from all major factional groups, many of them close to each other by virtue of their being from the same "class" of members who were first elected in 1967. Initially, twelve or more people were involved with Kōno in discussing the possibility of bolting the LDP, but in the end only six left with him. Kōno apparently hoped that others would follow, as criticism of the LDP over the Lockheed scandal continued to mount. But they never did, one important reason being that two months after the NLC was formed, former Prime Minister Tanaka Kakuei was arrested on suspicion of having received illegal funds provided by the Lockheed Corporation, weakening the argument that the LDP would never disclose the full dimensions of the scandal.

Some political observers at the time thought that other LDP politicians would follow Kōno as the NLC strengthened its position as a conservative party of middle class urban voters, leaving the LDP to be more and more identified with rural interests. One veteran political reporter predicted that not only would LDP politicians from metropolitan constituencies join the NLC, but that politicians from other districts experiencing rapid urbanization would find it to their interests also to be in this new urban-based second conservative party.[40] But such predictions failed to recognize the extent to which the LDP was already adjusting its policy priorities to respond to the demands of city dwellers and to expand its support among the same urban groups that were providing the base for NLC support.

The NLC under Kōno's leadership was never able to fix on a clear sense of what the party's objectives were or how it should go about trying to achieve them. Kōno was unable to make up his mind whether the NLC should try to develop into a major second conservative party, seek enough seats to negotiate a return to the LDP on its own terms, or form an alliance with other parties in the opposition. The results were bitter arguments within the party and an erratic policy of cooperation with other parties.

In 1979 controversy between Kōno and the party's

secretary-general Nishioka Takeo burst into full public view when the Nishioka group forced Kōno to rewrite an action plan that called on the party to adopt a middle-of-the-road line. A few months later Nishioka quit the party. According to Nishioka, discussions between the NLC and other parties looking toward an eventual merger were well under way. "There was a two-stage plan," Nishioka revealed later, "first to effect a merger between the NLC and the DSP and between the Kōmeitō and the Social Democratic League and then to bring the two together. This is the absolute truth. . . . What I had been looking for was not that but the reform of conservative [politics] by making the NLC into a fifty [Diet] member party and merging it with the LDP."[41]

After the October 1979 election that reduced the NLC to four seats and deprived the LDP of its Diet majority, the Ōhira faction approached the NLC for its support in Ōhira's battle to retain the prime ministership against a challenge from former Prime Minister Fukuda, as discussed later in this chapter. Its four lower house votes suddenly loomed large, given the almost equal division of the LDP's Diet members between supporters of Ōhira and of Fukuda. The NLC gave Ōhira its support, apparently believing that it had a commitment from Ōhira to appoint one of the NLC's leaders, Tagawa Seiichi, to the cabinet.[42] When it became evident that the new cabinet would not include any representative of the NLC, Kōno resigned as party leader. In 1981 the party again swung away from the LDP and toward alliance with other centrist parties, forming a united parliamentary group in the lower house with the miniscule Social Democratic League.

After the 1983 election, when the LDP once more failed to return a majority with its endorsed candidates, the NLC was again approached for its support. These negotiations resulted in the NLC decision to align officially with the LDP, in return for which it received one portfolio in the cabinet. This went first to Tagawa, who became home minister, then in the next cabinet reshuffle to the party's secretary-general Yamaguchi Toshio, who became labor minister, and then to

Kōno (who had been reappointed head of the party in June 1984), who was made director of the Science and Technology Agency. There was no lack of irony in the fact that the NLC—created at the height of the Lockheed scandal supposedly out of despair that the LDP would ever come to grips with the problem of political corruption and the influence of Tanaka Kakuei—supported Prime Minister Ōhira, who owed his position to the support of the Tanaka faction and then joined a government so dependent on Tanaka's backing that it had been mocked as the "Tanakasone" government.

The history of the NLC came to a close in August 1986, ten years after the party's founding. The fractious quality of relations among the few people who ran the party was evident to the very end. Kōno and the party's secretary-general Yamaguchi argued publicly over Yamaguchi's recommendation that the NLC align with the LDP in the Diet but remain formally independent. Kōno maintained that the NLC should not align with the LDP at all. Then after reluctantly accepting Yamaguchi's demand—under the threat that if he did not, Yamaguchi would quit the party—Kōno decided, apparently on his own and without discussing it with anyone else in the NLC, to dissolve the NLC and have its members enter the LDP.[43] Yamaguchi evidently wanted to keep the party formally independent in the hope that future events would give it some power to negotiate terms for its return to the LDP. All Kōno was able to obtain from Prime Minister Nakasone in exchange for a decision to close this particular chapter in Japan's political history was a commitment to welcome all NLC members into the LDP.[44]

The major role performed by the NLC in its ten-year history was to deprive the opposition of the opportunity to benefit from public antagonism toward the LDP over the Lockheed scandal and the so-called Tanaka problem. Almost the entire decrease in the LDP's share of the popular vote in the 1976 lower house election, for example, was accounted for by the NLC.[45] The NLC challenge probably also contributed marginally to making the LDP more responsive to urban voters, though this process was well under way before the NLC was created and would have continued to gather force in any event. Otherwise the party's record of achievement was thin. There could hardly be a sharper contrast between the enthusiasm and excitement that surrounded the party's formation in 1976 and the utter dejection and frustration that accompanied its demise in the aftermath of the LDP's landslide victory in 1986.

THE THIRD PHASE

By the mid-1970s it was becoming increasingly obvious that the fragmented political opposition would not be able to mount an effective challenge to LDP dominance. But just as in the late 1950s few observers anticipated the shape of the party system that evolved in the mid-1960s, so in the mid-1970s few people thought that a decade later the LDP would recover a position of unassailable dominance.

The evidence of LDP recovery was there, however. The party made steady progress throughout the decade in regaining control over local governments in Tokyo and other metropolitan areas. Its share of the popular vote in the 1979 lower house election increased for the first time ever. Its share went even higher in the next election, in 1980. In 1983 its popular vote slid slightly but still remained higher than in 1979. And its heavy loss of seats in that election was due in part at least to the tactical error of running too many candidates—339 in this election compared to 310 in the previous one. The party's popularity ratings as measured by public opinion polls rose steadily from the late 1970s on. On the eve of the party's 1986 election victory, these ratings had reached a level not seen since the early 1960s.

As the decade of the eighties began to unfold, it became increasingly clear that Japanese politics had entered a new, third phase characterized by a resurgence of LDP support to levels it had enjoyed during its first decade in power, but now in the context of a continuing decline in ideological polarization. Not only did the ideological controversies of the 1950s not reappear, but the appeal of Marxist ideology continued to decline, a factor that contributed substantially to the decision by the Socialist party in 1986 to adopt a new declaration of party principles, the purpose of which was to finally put its Marxism behind it.

Thus the LDP's electoral resurgence in the 1980s marked not a return to an earlier phase of one-party dominance but the emergence of a new phase, and one that importantly implied a basic change in the Japanese system of checks and balances. In the first decade of its rule, the LDP was constrained from implementing some of its most radical policy proposals by the intensity of the minority's opposition to them. Then in the late 1960s and in the seventies, the narrow margin by which it controlled a Diet majority forced the LDP to compromise with opposition parties to facilitate the legislative process. But after the 1986 election, the LDP found itself not only in command of a large Diet majority, but facing an opposition that was almost uniformly demoralized. This left the ruling party seemingly freer than at any earlier point in its history to act in disregard of opposition party views.

But in the 1980s the LDP was no longer the party it had been in the 1950s, nor were Japanese voters divided over basic policy issues concerning defense, rearmament, or constitutional revision as they had been in those earlier years. While some LDP leaders saw the party's new commanding majority as an opportunity to resuscitate a drive for constitutional revision or to press for a major expansion in Japan's military efforts, the party was hardly unified on these issues. Even Prime Minister Nakasone, an avowed advocate of constitutional revision and of increased Japanese military power, refrained from raising the constitutional revision issue, opting instead to call more vaguely for a "settlement of postwar political accounts." He did break with the policy established by Prime Minister Miki in 1976 of keeping defense spending within 1 percent of the GNP, but a budget that provided for spending 1.004 percent of the GNP on defense hardly amounted to a quantum jump in Japanese military expenditures or a fundamental change in Japanese defense policy.

By the time Japan had entered the third phase of LDP dominance in the 1980s, the LDP itself had become so dependent on the support of a diverse social coalition that the need to avoid alienating any significant element within this coalition itself acted as a powerful check on LDP policies. And whatever hopes the LDP's leadership had for being able to use its majority to get unpopular legislation through the Diet were quickly dashed by the enormous public backlash created by its efforts in 1987 to introduce a national sales tax.

The Diet's Changing Role

The evolution of party politics since 1955 brought about significant changes in the operations and role of the Diet. Having served mainly as a rubber stamp for LDP policies and as an arena for opposition party protests during the first phase of one-party dominance,[46] the Diet came to play an important policymaking role in the late 1960s and particularly throughout the 1970s, as ideological confrontation declined and the party system became more competitive.

The need for the LDP to compromise with the opposition to facilitate the Diet's functioning was due in part to Diet rules that require a party to have considerably more than a simple majority of seats in order to control the committees that process legislation.[47] The LDP did not have this so-called secure majority (*antei tasū*) through a good part of the 1970s. It had lost it in the upper house as early as 1968.[48] As a result of the 1972 lower house election, it had to relinquish the chairmanships of several special committees for the first time;[49] then as a result of the 1976 lower house election, it had to give up the chairmanships of four of the sixteen standing committees and seven of the nine special committees, and it lost the majority of seats on seven standing committees. Despite the fact that it held a majority of lower house seats, the LDP in 1977 controlled both the majority of seats and the chairmanships of only four of the sixteen standing committees.

One of the committees in which the LDP lacked a majority was the important Budget Committee. When the government's budget came to that committee in February 1977, the opposition parties refused to let it pass unless the government agreed to provide more money for social welfare and a trillion-yen tax cut. Since 1955 the budget submitted by the cabinet had never been substantively revised by the Diet. The LDP and the Ministry of Finance were determined this time, too, to find a way to avoid having the budget actually rewritten in committee. In the end the LDP refused to formally revise the budget but accepted a separate bill that provided for a ¥300 billion tax cut and made a separate supplementary appropriation for social welfare programs.[50] But in fact, if not in form, this amounted to the first substantive revision of the government's budget since the LDP came to power.

In 1979, unable to work out a compromise with the opposition parties, the government's budget was defeated in the Budget Committee. It was then passed in plenary session, marking the first time in thirty-one years that a committee decision had been reversed on the floor. But the LDP, in response to opposition pressure, also made concessions, increasing the budget by ¥11 billion. A similar pattern of LDP dominance coupled with compromises with the opposition characterized the budget process the following year, when the LDP made revisions in a budget that was again rejected in committee and passed in plenary session.

The need for the LDP to make compromises to enable the legislative process to proceed and the new opportunities for the opposition to participate in shaping legislation were reflected in the sharp decline in the number of bills passed unilaterally by the LDP in the late 1970s and in the equally impressive increase in the number of bills that were adopted with the support of most of the opposition parties. The percentage of bills passed with the support of the LDP alone declined from a high of about 20 percent in some years to less than 5 percent in the 1977–1980 period.[51] During these years of near parity in the Diet between the LDP and the opposition, the Socialists and the Kōmeitō voted for more than 80 percent of all successful legislation and the DSP and NLC for more than 90 percent. Even the Communist party, which prior to 1976 generally supported less than half of the legislation that passed the lower house, voted for more than 60 percent of these bills in 1976 and 1978 and over 70 percent in 1977 and 1979.[52]

The need for closer coordination with opposition parties to facilitate the legislative process increased the importance of party and Diet posts that involved planning Diet strategy and negotiating Diet operations. The lower house Diet Management Committee, for example, became a focal point for interparty negotiation. After 1973 the LDP appointed only senior Diet members to chair this committee.

Closer coordination among the parties also resulted in the virtual disappearance of many obstructionist tactics that had earlier been used by the opposition. Attempts to prevent legislation by resort to physical protests, usually involving an attempt to occupy the speaker's chair and thus prevent a session from being called to order, declined through the 1960s. This form of protest has not been used since 1969.[54] Other delaying tactics and the frequent submission of nonconfidence motions also ended.[55]

On the other hand, tactics that are not in other countries considered part of normal parliamentary procedure became accepted elements in the management of Diet affairs in this second phase of LDP dominance. As resort to physical protest declined, the opposition's use of Diet boycotts, for example, increased. This practice came to be accepted by the LDP and the opposition alike, often with prior agreement as to how long it would last and what compromises would have to be reached to bring it to an end. A similar

pattern of prior agreement became fairly common with regard to the so-called railroading of bills through the Diet by
the LDP. As Satō and Matsuzaki note, these two tactics had
"become part of the rules by which the game of democracy
is played in the Diet."[56]

The dynamics of the party system set in motion by
increased competitiveness and by the existence of middle-
of-the-road parties that had moved close to the LDP on major policy issues also began to change the arithmetic of coalition building. In the first phase of one-party dominance,
all potential coalition partners were in the LDP. But in the
mid-1970s it became possible for LDP faction leaders to look
outside as well as inside their own party for possible partners.

As a result of the general elections held in October
1979, the LDP fell eight seats short of obtaining a majority
and was able to put one together only by bringing into the
party several newly elected members who had run as independents. But LDP factions opposed to Prime Minister
Ōhira, led by former Prime Minister Fukuda, demanded that
Ōhira resign to take responsibility for the LDP's "defeat."
When the lower house convened in November to elect a
new prime minister,[57] the LDP was split almost exactly between those who supported Ōhira and those who wanted
to replace him with Fukuda. The LDP had in effect divided
into an Ōhira LDP and a Fukuda LDP. Unable to reach a
compromise, both men stood for election, the first time in
the history of the Japanese Diet that two men from the same
party had run against each other for prime minister.

The opposition parties then had to decide whether or
not to throw their support to one LDP leader or the other.
Apparently both the Fukuda and Ōhira forces explored the
possibility of obtaining the support of one or more of the
opposition parties. But in the end only the NLC entered the
LDP fight, giving its four votes to Ōhira. The other opposition party members cast their votes for leaders of their own
parties. In the balloting, Ōhira received 135 votes to Fu-

kuda's 125. The leading opposition party candidate, JSP chairman Asukata Ichio, received 107 votes.

Since no candidate received a majority, there was a second round of voting limited to the two candidates obtaining the most votes, LDP leaders Ōhira and Fukuda. There was some speculation that Fukuda might obtain the support of the DSP which, had it occurred, might have made him prime minister in a coalition government. But in the end the DSP and other opposition parties remained neutral, and Ōhira won on the second ballot with 138 votes to Fukuda's 121.

Six months later, on May 16, 1980, the Ōhira government fell when a motion of nonconfidence submitted by the Socialist party passed the lower house. This was only the third time in the postwar period, and needless to say the first time since the LDP was formed, that a nonconfidence motion had carried. It did so because sixty-nine LDP members, mainly from the Fukuda and Miki factions, abstained on the vote. The vote was 243 in favor of the motion to 187 opposed. Rather than resign, however, Ōhira called new elections and set the election date for June 22, when it would coincide with the triannual election of members of the upper house,[58] thus making possible Japan's first "double election."[59]

Had the LDP done as poorly in this election as it had in the previous one eight months earlier, factional divisions almost certainly would have intensified and the possibility of a party split would have increased. But the LDP did surprisingly well in the election, in part because Prime Minister Ōhira's death from a heart attack in the middle of the campaign drew a sympathy vote to the LDP, and more importantly because the party's poor performance in the election six months earlier and the novelty of the double election brought out to the polls LDP voters who had abstained in the previous race.

The LDP came out of the election with 284 lower house seats, 35 more than it had won in the election held the previous October. Suzuki Zenkō, who had succeeded to leadership of the Ōhira faction, was made party president and became prime minister. Two years later he was succeeded as prime minister by Nakasone Yasuhiro.

Through this period of leadership turmoil within the LDP, the opposition parties acted like spectators to the struggle for political power. Their leaders could not agree on whether or not to try to exploit the LDP's internal rivalries or how to to so. Some worried that a failed effort to form a coalition government with LDP factions would be repaid by a loss of votes at the next election; others with long Diet careers remembered the JSP's sorry experience in the Katayama and Ashida cabinets, when it was outnumbered by the conservatives; still others could not bring themselves to support an LDP leader for prime minister after they had spent their entire political lives opposing the LDP and the conservative parties that preceded it.

But this hesitation on the part of opposition parties to openly advocate coalition with elements within the LDP or with the LDP itself in the event it fell short of a Diet majority was already in the process of disappearing. In 1984, when Prime Minister Nakasone's first term as LDP president was coming to an end and the question of his reappointment to a second term arose, Nikaidō Susumu, the LDP secretary-general and one of the Tanaka faction's leading members, negotiated an agreement with the Kōmeitō and the DSP to form a coalition government with himself as prime minister. His gambit failed in the end not because these opposition parties vacillated, but apparently because Tanaka would not agree to have his faction desert Nakasone.[60]

There is every reason to believe that had the situation of near parity in LDP and opposition party strength continued, the pressures to split the LDP would have grown as factional struggles for power spilled over to encompass the centrist opposition. The likelihood of that happening in a period when the LDP is as dominant as it has become in the late 1980s is minimal, but a decrease in the size of the

LDP majority would once again increase the possibility of such interparty alliances.

Playing to Win

Whatever the future might hold in terms of the cohesion of the LDP, the single most impressive characteristic of this ruling party over the past thirty years has been its total commitment to the goal of winning Diet majorities and retaining political power. And this determination to win, more than anything else, defines the most important difference between this perennially governing party and its perpetual opposition.

The JSP throughout its history has been ambivalent about the electoral process, torn between the goals of winning elections, being true to its ideology and cherished revolutionary traditions, and serving the interests of the wing of the labor movement that gives it sustenance. Like the Socialists, many LDP leaders embrace visions of a desirable future quite different from what prevails now. But unlike the Socialist party, the LDP has never let its vision get in the way of the primary goal of winning elections and staying in power.

Through the changing phases of the post-1955 political system, the LDP has demonstrated an impressive capacity to adapt to rapid social and economic changes in order to perpetuate its dominance. And its doing so has resulted in important changes in the party's policies, in its social bases of support, and in the organization of political power itself. The LDP's total commitment to winning Diet majorities has pulled it—in spite of itself, as it were—steadily toward the political center and away from many of the political programs to which it had committed itself when it was founded. However reluctantly on the part of some of its leaders, the party has adjusted to the reality of public support for the present constitutional order, and, as it has adapted to a changing environment, it has become increasingly identified in the public mind with defense of the status quo. Over the thirty years of its rule, this conservative party has become Japan's preeminent party of the center.

2.

THE LIBERAL
DEMOCRATIC PARTY:
PERPETUATING DOMINANCE

Many factors have contributed to the LDP's ability to retain power through decades of rapid economic and social change. To some extent its strength has been a reflection of the inflexibility of the political opposition in the face of change and of the steadfast support the party continues to receive from rural voters, who are overrepresented in the Diet. But these are at best only partial explanations of LDP success. And they implicitly suggest a static quality to the LDP's response to change that could not be more at variance with the party's actual behavior.

The LDP's success in retaining power owes a great deal to its ability to closely track changes in its social and economic environment and to adjust its policies accordingly. It has used all of the resources at its command as Japan's only governing party to perpetuate its dominance, its ultimate control over the government budget being among the most important of these resources. Popular stereotypes of bureaucratic dominance in Japanese policymaking notwithstanding, the Liberal Democratic party has energetically used the government purse to reward its supporters, to cultivate new support, and to reorder the government's policy priorities.

Spending government money to make itself popular with the voters that kept it in power was not a difficult task in the 1950s and 1960s, when the economy was booming, government revenues were increasing, and the LDP's majority was produced mainly by farmers, merchants, and owners of small businesses and their employees in provincial Japan. But in recent years the LDP has become dependent on more diverse constituencies for its electoral majority, and it has had to respond to wide-ranging public demands for government expenditures that far exceed what the government is able to raise in tax revenues, a problem that governing parties in virtually all industrialized democracies face.

The LDP found no easy solution to this problem of having to balance responsiveness to constituent demands with a sense of responsibility for the nation's overall well-being. Its first response was to allow expenditures to move far out in front of revenues. Only after the LDP had permitted budget deficits to reach a level where it could plausibly claim that the country faced a fiscal crisis was it able to build a national consensus that permitted it first to slow, and then virtually to stop, the growth in government spending.

The contrasts between LDP spending policies in the eighties and those of the previous decade—and even more so with those of the 1960s—could hardly be sharper. During the first decade and a half of its rule, the LDP pursued a policy of positive-sum politics in a high-growth economy. A rapidly growing economic pie made possible the steady expansion of the national budget, enabling the LDP to respond to public demands without making many hard choices about priorities. Through public works and other subsidy programs it lavished support on farmers and other rural dwellers, whose representation in the Diet was not reduced to reflect the rapid population movements from countryside to the city that were occurring in this period. And it largely left to the bureaucracy the task of implementing the broad national consensus that existed in favor of rapid industrial growth.

By the early 1970s, however, LDP policy priorities had changed considerably. The national consensus on the desirability of higher GNP figures over and above everything else had begun to unravel, as the public more forcefully than before demanded increased government spending to improve social welfare programs and to address problems of pollution and other social ills that were the by-products of rapid industrialization.

In the economic environment of the 1970s, however, particularly after the oil shock of 1973, the LDP was able to respond to these demands only by pursuing a policy that amounted to a game of positive-sum politics in a low-growth economy. This was only in part the result of the government's support for Keynesian economic policies to stimulate domestic demand; it was more importantly the product of political imperatives generated by the LDP's determination to remain the party in power. It resulted not only in continued high levels of subsidy support for farmers and for public works programs in rural Japan, but in rapidly expanded programs of health care, social security, and other features of the modern welfare state.

Given the economic environment of the seventies, the result of these policies was spiraling government budget deficits. Until 1965 the government was committed to a balanced budget policy and then, for the next decade, ran only small deficits as a result of issuing construction bonds. But beginning with the compilation of the supplementary budget for fiscal year 1975, it started to issue deficit financing bonds that in a few years made the Japanese government deficit the largest in share of GNP among all major industrialized countries. By the end of the decade well over a

third of expenditures in the general account budget were
being financed by borrowed money.

In the 1980s, however, the LDP put a firm brake on
public spending increases. Under the slogan of "fiscal consolidation without tax increases" (zōzei naki zaisei saiken), it
pursued a policy of retrenchment that within a few years
brought to a complete stop the double-digit increases in year-
to-year budget expenditures that had characterized government spending through the 1970s. In the fiscal year 1978
budget, for example, the increase in general expenditures
was 19.2 percent over the previous year. But two years later,
the year-to-year increase was reduced to 5.1 percent, and
in 1982 it was 1.8 percent. The 1986 budget was the fourth
in a row to provide for no increase in net government expenditures whatsoever. Similarly, subsidy expenditures,
which increased by 29 percent in 1972, 27 percent in 1974,
and 17 percent in 1978, were down to a 7.5 percent increase
in 1980, a 4.7 percent increase in 1981, and no increase in
1983.

Throughout the 1980s the hallmark of Japanese policy
was administrative reform, privatization, and a general effort to reduce the role of the government in the economy.
So successful was the LDP in convincing the public of the
desirability of small government and "administrative reform without tax increases" that by the end of the decade
it found itself under intense criticism from its own voters
for violating its strictures against a tax increase by proposing the introduction of a national sales tax, and from the
United States for not using government spending more aggressively as a means to stimulate the domestic economy.
The national consensus on behalf of fiscal austerity was not
easy to achieve, but once reached it proved even harder to
dislodge.

As it pursued these changing spending priorities, the
LDP itself changed. It became less a party of farmers and
of their supporting businesses and much more a "catch-all"
party in which farmer interests were considerably less powerful than they had been in earlier years when high growth,

increasing government revenues, and a large and secure Diet majority had meant that the LDP could afford to engage in "subsidy politics" without much concern for the potentially adverse effects on the overall economy. Indeed, public works programs and other subsidies had been a major positive feature of the government's economic policy, spreading industrialization and employment opportunities in the manufacturing sector and raising the standard of living of people in Japan's poorest regions.

The LDP that emerged in the 1970s, however, was less solicitous of farmer demands, because—despite rural overrepresentation in the Diet—demographic changes made it essential that the party secure the support of other constituencies if it hoped to retain power. That the LDP was able to do so in a manner that not only kept it in power but increased its popular support is testimony to the party's adaptability and skill at mobilizing public support for its policies and its politicians. That it did so by adopting policies that scrupulously tried to be equitable to all bidders on the public purse, and thus avoided the politically difficult issues inherent in redistributive politics, is indicative of the unwillingness of the LDP to make hard political choices even in an economic environment in which they would seem to be unavoidable.

The LDP and the Farmers

The evolution of government spending policies is reflected in a particularly interesting and meaningful way in the changing relationship between the LDP and the farmers who have provided its bedrock base of support, and well as in the government's price support policies for rice, Japan's major agricultural commodity.

The conventional view holds that the LDP is a party of farmers that has been able to remain in power by over-representing rural constituencies in the Diet and showering them with subsidies and other forms of government largess. It is a view that is partly out of date and partly based on false premises to begin with.

Rural voters continue to be overrepresented in the Diet, to be sure. But some adjustments in district representation have been made to reduce the gross inequalities that were created by rapid urbanization. In 1967, 1972, and 1976 the number of lower house seats was increased to permit the creation of new constituencies in heavily populated metropolitan areas to give urban voters greater representation. This approach to reapportionment had the advantage for the LDP of increasing urban representation without eliminating any seats in rural constituencies where the LDP was particularly strong. But it did not substantially reduce the gross disparities in the weight of the vote of urban and rural voters. In 1985, for example, there were 4.4 times as many voters per lower house seat in Chiba prefecture's most populous election district as there were in Hyōgo prefecture's least populated one.

These disparities led to a July 1985 Supreme Court ruling that declared the existing distribution of lower house seats unconstitutional and warned that the results of the next election might be declared invalid if held under current districting arrangements. As a result of this landmark decision, the Diet passed a bill early in 1986 that increased representation in eight urban districts by one seat each and reduced it by one seat in each of seven rural ones. This increased the total number of lower house members by one, to 512, and created for the first time a six-member district (in Hokkaidō) and four two-member districts, in a system that until then had had only three-, four-, and five-member districts.

While rural areas remain overrepresented, the disparities are not as great as they were earlier and they do not explain the LDP's success. Urban voters are better represented in the Diet now than ever before, and the LDP has more seats than before. In the 1986 election, its support among urban voters increased substantially, continuing a trend that had been evident for a decade. According to public opinion polls, only about a quarter of LDP supporters live in towns and villages. The great majority are city dwellers, with nearly half of the total living in metropolitan areas and other large cities.[1]

The overrepresentation of rural areas in the Diet is a contributing factor in the LDP's electoral strength, but it is no longer a convincing explanation of it. Historically, however, this overrepresentation did play a crucial role in cushioning the impact of rapid demographic change on this ruling party. It gave the LDP time, as it were, to adjust to the social and economic changes that its own policies had helped produce. In the process, rural Japan itself has become increasingly industrialized. There are today few truly rural constituencies. According to the formula used by the *Asahi Shinbun*, only 22 of the lower house's 130 districts (electing 76 of 512 members) qualify as rural districts. The *Mainichi Shinbun's* slightly different formula provides for 24 rural districts electing 91 members.[2]

Industrialization spread rapidly into provincial Japan during the 1970s, as indicated in table 2.1. In metropolitan areas and cities, employment in the secondary—primarily manufacturing—sector actually declined in percentage terms between 1970 and 1980, the slack being taken up by increased employment in service industries, the tertiary sector. But in the provinces and counties, employment rose steadily throughout the decade both in manufacturing and in the service sector. In 1970 there was a nearly eleven-point spread in the percentage of the labor force employed in the secondary sector in cities as opposed to counties. By 1980 this had been reduced to little more than a one percentage point difference.

In Japan the term "counties" (*gunbu*) is still usually considered synonymous with "rural," but there is now a larger percentage of the labor force employed in the secondary sector of the economy in this "rural" Japan than in the primary sector of farming and mining. This urbanization of rural Japan has had major political ramifications. It has made "rural" LDP politicians more responsive to what

TABLE 2.1. Composition of the Labor Force by Sector and Type of Region, 1970–1980 (In Percent)

	Primary Sector	Secondary Sector	Tertiary Sector
Metropolitan regions			
1970	8.8	41.3	49.9
1975	5.9	38.8	55.3
1980	4.6	36.8	58.6
Provincial regions			
1970	29.1	27.5	43.4
1975	21.5	29.7	48.8
1980	17.0	30.4	52.6
Cities			
1970	10.4	37.3	52.3
1975	7.5	35.6	56.9
1980	5.9	33.9	60.2
Counties			
1970	40.9	26.5	32.6
1975	32.6	29.9	37.5
1980	25.9	32.3	41.8
Nationwide			
1970	19.3	34.1	46.6
1975	13.9	34.2	51.9
1980	10.9	33.5	55.6

SOURCE: Keizai Kikakucho, *Kokumin Seikatsu Hakusho* (Tokyo: Keizai Kikakucho, 1982).

Notes: **Metropolitan regions** includes Saitama, Chiba, Tokyo, Kanagawa, Aichi, Mie, Kyoto, Osaka, and Hyōgo prefectures. **Provincial regions** includes all other prefectures.

are often thought of as urban concerns, and it has had a major impact on the structure of the agricultural work force and the LDP's relationship to it.

Economic analyses of the evolution of the Japanese political economy invariably depict the LDP as totally committed to protecting Japanese agriculture and to resisting the market forces that have been modernizing the industrial structure. The conventional wisdom is well represented by Imai Ken'ichi, who has argued that Japanese agricultural employment declined *"despite* substantial government protection. Although social and political forces . . . tended to distort market forces in the Japanese economic structure, innovative forces were strong enough to cope with these obstacles and to achieve remarkable structural changes through an evolutionary growth process."[3]

But this idea of economic rationality overcoming politically generated distortions of market forces is quite off the mark. LDP leaders, whatever their rhetoric, have had no illusions about the fate of the agricultural work force. Nor have they tried to prevent its decline. On the contrary, Prime Minister Ikeda's double-the-income policy was premised on the ability of the labor market to effect a massive transfer of workers out of the primary sector and into the industrial work force.[4]

The policies pursued by Ikeda and by subsequent LDP governments were intended primarily to protect Japan's dwindling number of farmers. LDP policies have aimed at maintaining farmer income at relatively high levels; they have not sought to maintain the agricultural labor force at a particular size. The goals of LDP policies have been to buy off those remaining farmers whose relative importance in the economy was declining at a rapid rate and to ensure that the benefits of growth would not be allowed to become so distorted as to turn these stalwart supporters of the LDP against it.

To accomplish these goals, the LDP lavished an array of subsidies and other forms of financial support on Japan's small farmer population. Until near the end of the 1970s the centerpiece of this party effort was its highly visible intervention in the policy process to secure a high producers' price for rice. The government's role in pricing this staple of the Japanese diet had its origins in the wartime Staple Food Control Act of 1942. Carried over into the postwar period, it gave the government the authority to set both the price paid to farmers for the rice they produced and the price charged to consumers for the rice sold to them through government-authorized dealers.

In the early postwar years this system enabled the government to impose some order on the rice market, in a situation in which the demand for rice far exceeded the supply. But once Japan recovered from the devastation of the war and began its rapid march toward economic prosperity, the rice price control system was made to serve other ends. Support for high producer rice prices became a major ploy in the LDP strategy for rewarding its rural supporters, even though it had to be pursued in the context of rapidly declining consumer demand for rice and a Ministry of Agriculture (MAFF, formally the Ministry of Agriculture, Forestry, and Fisheries) policy of encouraging farmers to divert land to other crops.[5]

These trends notwithstanding, the LDP continued to press for higher producer rice prices and for covering with subsidies from the general accounts budget the deficit in the Food Control Special Account generated by the differential between the producers' rice price and the lower price charged consumers. As a result of this policy, the producers' rice price doubled between 1960 and 1968 and doubled again between 1970 and 1977.[6] By 1977 the deficit in the Food Control Special Account came to 33 percent of the total MAFF budget, an amount equal to half of the entire defense budget.

LDP support for higher producer rice prices has helped foster an image of the party as a party of farmers—and of farmers as being united in their political demands. But the reality of Japanese agricultural politics is more complex than this. Statistics on Japanese agriculture differentiate the farm population into three groups. There is, first of all, the group of full-time farm households, numbering a little more than half a million. (There also are said to be about the same number of people employed by government and semigovernment agencies and by agricultural cooperatives to administer the government's agricultural policies, giving rise to the quip that Japan has adopted a "one-on-one" agricultural policy.) The second group is comprised of Japanese farm households that derive the major portion of their income from farming, known as Class A part-time farm households. There are about three quarters of a million such households.

Finally, there are what are called Class B part-time farm households, where income is mainly derived from off-farm work. These Class B farmers now predominate in Japan, numbering over three million households. They are politically powerful, and they have had a profound and adverse impact on the MAFF's objective of increased efficiency through the promotion of full-time farming of larger farms and the diversion of land away from rice production.

Although Class B part-time farmers derive only a small share of their income from farming, the land they own has become an asset of growing value, making them unwilling to sell it to others who would farm it full time. The typical farm holding in Japan remains miniscule. The cultivated land area of an average farm household in 1950 was 1.0 hectares; twenty-seven years later, despite a concerted government effort at farm land consolidation that began with the passage of the Basic Agricultural Act of 1961, it was only 1.2 hectares.[7]

Because so many heads of farm households earn most of their income in off-farm occupations but hold on to their farmland, the decline in the number of farm households has lagged far behind the decline in the percentage of the labor force engaged in agriculture. Between 1960 and 1980 the number of farm households declined by 23 percent. But the farm population dropped by 38 percent, and the percentage of the labor force engaged in agriculture went down by 64.9 percent.[8]

The prevalence of farms in which the male household head holds a city job that provides most of the family income has given rise to what is referred to in Japanese as *san-chan nōgyō*,[9] the actual running of farms by women and old people. This is a fairly recent phenomenon, the cause of which is evident in figures that show the very sharp shift in the relative importance of full-time and part-time farmers in the years since the LDP came into power. In 1955 full-time farm households comprised 35 percent of the total number of farm households and Class A part-time farms comprised 37 percent. Class B part-time farm households accounted for only 28 percent of the total. The differences in the figures for 1982 are startling: full-time farm households comprised only 13 percent and Class A part-time just 16 percent of the total, while 70 percent of all farm households were Class B part-time households.[10]

The interests of Class B part-time farmers on the one hand and of full-time and Class A part-time farmers on the other diverge substantially, and their differences are mirrored in the LDP's internal organization. LDP rural-based politicians, at least until very recently, were differentiated into two groups. One group, known as the "rice faction," insisted on maintenance of the food control system, high producer rice prices, and protection of the Japanese market against foreign imports. The other, the "comprehensive agricultural policy faction," basically adopted the position identified with the mainstream of bureaucrats in the MAFF, stressing the importance of diverting land into other crops and consolidating small land holdings to make possible more efficient large farms.

In Japanese agricultural politics the rice faction has been the most adamant in its defense of farmer interests, even though its role has increasingly become one of defending the interests of Class B part-time farmers, that is, those least dependent on farming for their income. (In the 1970s the rice faction's radicalism earned for it the nickname "Betokon," a play on the name "Viet Cong" that came from *Beikon*, the abbreviation of the Diet members' Discussion Group on Rice Price Strategy, Beika Taisaku Giin Kondankai.) Class B part-time farmers are the most resistant to MAFF pressure to divert their land to other crops that do not receive hefty government price supports. The reasons are explained well by agricultural economist Egaitsu Fumio:

Both full-time and class A part-time farmers are gradually reducing their ratios of rice production in response to changes in demand. In contrast to this, class B part-time farmers are more and more inclined to rely only on production of rice. This is because distribution of rice is under governmental control; there is no marketing problem and there is no risk because prices are officially guaranteed. Thus, one of the reasons for overproduction of rice can definitely be attributed to the increasing number of class B part-time farmers.[11]

The rice faction was very powerful in the 1960s and early 1970s. But by the end of the seventies Japan faced chronic rice surpluses, an unmanageable amount of stored rice, a huge government debt, and a yawning gap in the Food Control Special Account. This secured for rice, *kome* in Japanese, a position as one of the "three K's" of Japan's fiscal problems—the other two being *kokutetsu*, the national railways, and *kenpo*, the national health insurance program. Even the most enthusiastic advocates of high rice price supports could no longer resist the pressures for a change in policy.

This policy change began in 1978 and has been pursued in the 1980s. It involved clamping a lid on increases in the producer rice price and moving with impressive speed to reduce the gap between the producers' and consumers' price of rice. The specifics of recent rice policy—the introduction of a multitiered pricing system for different qualities of rice, greater autonomy to farmers to decide whether or not to sell their rice through the government, and so on—need not concern us here. The important point is that by keeping annual increases in the producers' rice price lower than the increases in the consumers' rice price, the government has reduced the deficit per 60 kilograms of rice (*koku*, the standard unit of measurement) from ¥3,365 in 1975 to ¥341 in 1985. This is an extraordinary applying of the brakes by a party so closely identified with the interests of Japan's rice farmers. Relevant data are presented in table 2.2

This virtual freezing of the producers' rice price has actually imposed less hardship on Japanese farmers than official farm organization spokesmen like to admit. The majority of Japanese rice farmers, the Class B part-time farmers, derive on the average only 12 percent of their income from farming.[12] And they, as well as other farmers, have been the beneficiaries of MAFF subsidy programs for other

TABLE 2.2. Japanese Government Rice Pricing Policy, 1975–1985

Fiscal Year	Government Purchase Price	Increase Over Previous Year	Government Selling Price	Increase Over Previous Year	Deficit
1975	¥15,570	14.4%	¥12,205	19.0%	¥−3,365
1976	16,572	6.4	13,451	10.2	−3,121
1977	17,232	4.0	14,771	9.8	−2,461
1978	17,251	0.1	14,771	0.0	−2,480
1979	17,279	0.2	15,391	4.2	−1,888
1980	17,674	2.3	15,891	3.2	−1,783
1981	17,756	0.5	16,391	3.2	−1,365
1982	17,951	1.1	17,033	3.9	−918
1983	18,266	1.8	17,033	0.0	−1,233
1984	18,668	2.2	17,673	3.8	−955
1985	18,668	0.0	18,327	3.7	−341

SOURCE: Compiled from data in Nōrin Tōkei Kyōkai, *Nōgyō Hakusho* (various years); Nōrin Suisan Gyōsei Kenkyūkai, *Nōrin Suisan*, vol. 1 of *Gendai Gyōsei Zenshū* (Tokyo: Gyōsei, 1983); Nōrin Suisanshō Tōkei Jōhōbu, *Nōrin Suisanshō Tōkeihyō* (Tokyo: Nōrin Suisanshō, various years); and *Nihon Tōkei Nenkan* (various years).

Note: Prices and deficits are per *koku* (60 kg.) of rice.

crops and other purposes that have gone hand in hand with the narrowing of the gap between the consumers' and producers' rice prices.

Recent Japanese government rice price policy has hurt Nōkyō, Japan's organization of agricultural cooperatives, more than it has hurt the farmers Nōkyō represents. Nōkyō has had to watch its political power weaken as the focus of farmer attention has shifted away from the annual producer rice price struggle toward local efforts to obtain greater shares of the MAFF's project-specific subsidy pies.

A number of factors made it possible for the LDP to impose these low producer rice price increases. One factor was that Japan's full-time and Class A part-time farmers, as mentioned above, were by the late 1970s already diversifying out of rice. Another was that low price increases were combined with continued protection of Japan's rice farmers against competition from foreign producers. Though farmers were not getting more for the rice they produced, their dissatisfaction was tempered by knowing that the prices they did receive remained well over eight times international levels.

Even more important, however, were market forces generated by rice surpluses amidst declining consumer demand for rice in a society whose dietary habits were changing, and the government's skill in containing farmer demands by arguing that it was treating rice farmers equitably, demanding no greater sacrifice on their part than was being asked of industrial workers or others as Japan tried to adjust to an era of low growth and bring its budget deficit under control. Farmers were thrown on the defense. No longer able to demand higher government-guaranteed rice prices and other special treatment, they were forced to concentrate their energies on opposing trade liberalization and the opening of Japan's agricultural markets more fully to international competition.

The shift in agricultural policy has not done anything to deal with Japan's basic and politically intractable agricultural problem—how to transfer land valued at more than 30 million yen per hectare from the hands of Class B part-time farmers totaling more than three million households to full-time farmers numbering less than six hundred thousand. But the policy shift has had important political consequences. The annual rice price struggle has lost much of its drama. The focus of farmer demands has turned more fully to obtaining benefits from the myriad subsidy programs sponsored by the MAFF. Subsidies accounted for some 60 percent of the MAFF budget in 1980, two trillion yen that was distributed through no fewer than 474 separate programs. These programs include conventional agricultural programs such as soil and water supply improvement, as well as new programs such as the 1978 Measure for the Reorganization of the Use of Paddy Fields advocated by the comprehensive agriculture faction. But they also include programs that are related to agricultural production only indirectly, if at all.

In one village in Hokkaidō, to cite an example of the latter type, the MAFF's Agricultural Facilities Adjustment Program helped fund a potato chip factory, the Second Agricultural Structure Reform Program provided the funds for a french fried potato factory, and the Program for Promoting the Modernization of the Distribution System for Special Agricultural Products helped pay for a warehouse to store these products.[13] In 1978 the then minister of agriculture, Watanabe Michio, saw to it that the budget included ten billion yen for a new subsidy program called the Emergency Program for the Promotion of Agricultural, Forestry, and Fishing Villages. The purpose of this new MAFF program was to promote the health, welfare, and "solidarity" of the residents of these communities, its funds going toward the building of community tennis and volley ball courts, community centers, lights for community ballparks, and other facilities.[14]

The former distinction between the rice faction and the comprehensive agricultural policy faction has lost much of its earlier salience, as the following statement by a Betokon leader, Watanabe Kōzō, emphasizes:

In the past there was conflict . . . between the comprehensive agricultural policy faction which clamored for [fundamental agricultural reform] . . . and the Betokon faction which stressed maintenance of the food control law system, rice price increases and protectionism.

But now the reality is that there is overproduction of rice . . . and the nation's finances are too strained to permit rice price increases. Facing reality, even Betokon faction politicians who have a sense of responsibility have been unable to demand the impossible. . . . Now the differences between the comprehensive agriculture policy faction and the Betokon faction are quite small. The objectives are the same and the differences are between extremists and moderates over means.[15]

This evolution of agricultural policy has made the Socialist and Communist parties, sensing an opportunity to hurt the LDP in its most faithful constituency, even more protectionist and rice price–oriented than they were earlier. In terms of agricultural policy, the left has consistently attacked the LDP from the right by advocating higher producer prices for rice than the LDP has been willing to support, low consumer rice prices, and protection of domestic producers against foreign competition. That pattern has not only not changed but has become more pronounced as the opposition's frustration over its inability to capitalize on the shift in LDP agricultural policy has mounted.

Extending the Party's Reach

Japanese economic policy goals since the end of the Second World War have included not only the obvious goal of rapidly catching up with the West in per capita GNP and transforming Japan into a major industrial power. The Japanese government has been committed also to the use of tax policy and government spending programs to achieve relatively equitable income distribution.

Public finance during the high-growth years functioned to transfer resources to less developed regions and to backward industries. Rice price supports and agricultural subsidies, public works projects and subsidy programs for small businessmen, financial transfers to local governments, and other income transfer programs all contributed to reducing regional and personal inequalities in income distribution and to correcting the distortions of high growth.[16]

Both the bureaucracy and the LDP embraced this objective of fostering equity in income distribution during the developmental process. This is a major reason why the bureaucracy saw little reason to fight LDP demands for what in narrow economic terms was the irrational allocation of resources to provide subsidies for farmers and for Japan's least prosperous regions. Potential conflicts between the ruling party and the professional bureaucracy were also forestalled during the period of high growth by the fact that the economy was growing so fast that the LDP could allocate increasing amounts of money from the national budget to its subsidy programs without making hard choices about funding priorities or upsetting the Ministry of Finance's concern for maintaining the principles of fair share and of "balance."[17]

The spending programs pushed hardest by the LDP in the 1960s were mainly targeted at people in provincial Japan, reinforcing the perception of many observers that the LDP was fighting a rearguard action, delaying the political consequences of economic and social change by overrepresenting the rural electorate in the Diet and lavishing government largess upon it. It seemed beyond dispute that a rural-based party could not long survive as the predominant party in a country that was rapidly becoming one of the world's great industrial powers. By the beginning of the 1970s, however, the LDP itself had begun to come to grips with this reality and had struck out on a new course to adapt itself to the socioeconomic environment that the economic successes of the previous decade had produced.

The 1970s opened with mounting public concern over quality-of-life issues and a new awareness that rapidly rising GNP figures were not an unmixed blessing. Pollution had reached intolerable levels. *Minamata* and *Itai-itai* became known around the world as words describing new and horribly painful pollution diseases. Air pollution in Tokyo became so bad that schools had to suspend outdoor exercises for fear that the exertion would cause children to pass out. Concern also began to be expressed about how the society would handle a rapidly aging population. Problems of medical care, pensions for the elderly, and other social issues that had been put off to a later day while the country raced forward in its drive for ever-higher increases in GNP now forced themselves onto the political agenda.

Dissatisfaction with the LDP and its conservative allies in local government led to the election of numerous progressive governors (that is, candidates running with the support of the Communist or Socialist party, or both). At the height of progressive strength at the local level, many of the governors and mayors of large cities in the prefectures of the industrial belt that stretches along the Pacific Ocean from Tokyo to Kōbe were supported by progressive parties. And in the 1972 general election, the LDP won fewer seats than ever before, raising for the first time the possibility of an end to its dominant party status.

Dissatisfaction with LDP policies also found voice in the emergence of large numbers of citizen movements. These were different from the party-led nationwide mass movements of the 1950s and 1960s against the Security Treaty and against Japanese rearmament. The new citizen movements were mainly local ad hoc groupings formed to seek the redress of specific community grievances: removal of a garbage disposal site or opposition to the siting of a nuclear energy plant facility, complaints about the inadequacy of government-funded day care centers, and a host of other issues. They were not united in any nationwide organization and generally eschewed formal party ties. But while they were created to protest government—that is, LDP—policies, their emergence was more significant for what it said about the inability of the established opposition parties, the JSP in particular, to absorb and channel the new kinds of demands being produced by Japan's growing affluence. In Japan as elsewhere, citizen movements arose as a response to the inability of traditional parties to adequately aggregate demands prevalent in prosperous, postindustrial societies, that cut across class and other conventional lines of social stratification.

Many Japanese scholars saw in these movements both opportunities for the emergence of new forms of political participation and a challenge to the established party system, and these scholars were among the first to give systematic attention to the new challenges confronting political parties in postindustrial societies. The expression *datsu seitō jidai* (the "postparty age") came into popular currency in Japan in the early 1970s, referring, among other things, to the dealignment phenomenon that has become the focus of so much research in the United States and western Europe in the years since.[18]

LDP leaders, however, quickly recognized the threat to the party's hegemony posed by the rise of opposition governments in urban Japan, by the spread of new citizen movements, and by rising public demands for more and better government services as symbolized by the popularity of the concept of a civil minimum, meaning the state's obligation to insure a minimum of well-being measured not in quantitative GNP terms, but in terms of the quality of life.[19] In the 1970s these party leaders moved with impressive speed to stem and then reverse these adverse trends. No one better symbolizes this LDP policy shift or played a more central role in bringing it about than Tanaka Kakuei.

Now that he has become the symbol of all that is corrupt about Japanese politics, it is widely forgotten that Tanaka's victory over retiring Prime Minister Satō's chosen successor, Fukuda Takeo, was welcomed by the LDP and by the press. Tanaka, the "computerized bulldozer," with his blueprint for remodeling the Japanese archipelago, promised a new thrust in government policy that drew an enthusiastic public response. Within a few years, and mainly under Tanaka's leadership, the LDP sponsored legislation that replaced the previous hands-off government attitude toward industrial pollution with a package of some of the most stringent pollution control measures imposed by any country. Then in 1973, in what was typed "welfare's birthyear" (*fukushi gannen*), Tanaka introduced an upgraded social security pension system and expanded low-cost health care under the national health insurance system.

Under Tanaka's leadership the government's general accounts budget for fiscal year 1973 provided for a 25 percent increase over the previous year's budget, the largest year-to-year increase in the postwar period. Public works expenditures jumped 32 percent, social welfare was up an equally impressive 29 percent. And Tanaka celebrated welfare's birthday and the government's new enlarged spending programs by giving the electorate a two-trillion-yen tax cut. No country has moved more quickly or with more gusto to embrace so broad a range of new and expanded government-sponsored social welfare programs than did Japan in the early seventies.

Tanaka's enthusiasm for letting expenditures run far out in front of revenues could hardly have been more unambiguous. "We should . . . free ourselves," Tanaka wrote in his blueprint for remodeling Japan, "from the idea of annually balanced budgets and place more importance on balanced public finance over the long run. . . . While it seems a kindly gesture to leave no debts behind, debts are not in themselves inherently evil. . . . A fair distribution of costs among generations is necessary if we are to build a beautiful and pleasant nation to live in."[20]

But Tanaka's dream of using government spending to push the economy into another decade-long run of high growth and to spread industrialization into the far corners of the Japanese islands soon turned into a nightmare of inflation, land speculation, and ballooning government deficits. No prime minister saw his popularity plummet so far so fast. In an *Asahi Shinbun* poll taken in August 1972, one month after he came into office, Tanaka scored a popularity rating of 62 percent, the highest in the postwar period.[21] By April 1973 it had sunk to 27 percent—and this was before the October 1973 Mideast war and the subsequent oil shock, and before the revelations about Tanaka's shady business dealings that were eventually to drive him from office. By November 1973 Tanaka drew the support of only 22 percent of the public. Those who opposed him rose from 10 percent in August 1972, to 44 percent in April 1973, to 60 percent in November of that year. In his last month in office, in November 1974, Tanaka registered the highest nonsupport rating in postwar history. Only 12 percent of respondents indicated support for him, while 69 percent said they did not support him.[22]

Rampant inflation and a generally chaotic economic situation combined with Tanaka's rapidly declining popularity gave his opponents in the LDP an opportunity to slow down Tanaka's spending spree at least temporarily. In November 1973 Tanaka pushed through the Diet a supplementary budget that was one and a half times larger than the previous year's. But the finance minister, Tanaka faction

member Aichi Kiichi, died the day following Diet approval
of the budget. In his weakened political position, Tanaka
was forced to turn over the Finance Ministry portfolio to his
rival, Fukuda Takeo. Fukuda was long known as a fiscal
conservative, an advocate of balanced budgets and balanced, rather than just rapid, growth. With former MOF
bureaucrat Fukuda at its helm, the Ministry of Finance set
about applying the brakes to growth in government spending.

But Tanaka's policies had established a new floor for
government expenditures, and they had quickly generated
new expectations among the public as to the range and level
of services the government had the obligation to provide.
The result was that Finance Minister Fukuda, although he
claimed to be reintroducing fiscal responsibility, applied the
brakes to government spending only gingerly. The Ministry
of Finance pronounced the fiscal year 1974 budget a "tight"
budget, but the nominal 19.7 percent year-to-year overall
increase was tight only relative to the previous year's record
24.6 percent hike.

The 1974 budget was significant for a different reason. It was a budget that symbolized as well as anything
else the LDP's crossover from being a party of farmers in a
developing economy to being the major political voice for a
broad range of individuals and social groups living in a
modern industrial and increasingly postindustrial society.
This tight budget in fact confirmed the government's commitment to implementing the comprehensive set of social
welfare programs that had been adopted in "welfare's birthyear." For the first time the government spent more on social welfare programs than on public works. Furthermore,
social welfare–related expenditures went up 36.7 percent,
while for the first time in twenty years there was virtually
no increase in public works expenditures.

Even after Tanaka was forced out of office, the political pressures to create a welfare state continued to exercise
enormous influence on the budget process. When the Miki
administation was preparing the 1975 budget, the new min-

ister of finance, Ōhira Masayoshi, who like Fukuda came from an earlier career in the Finance Ministry, argued the MOF position that the LDP had to adopt a restrictive fiscal policy. But it proved politically impossible to do so. In the end, MOF had to settle for a face-saving requirement that budget growth be kept lower than the record 24.6 percent increase registered in 1973. It met this requirement by drafting a budget that provided for an overall increase of 24.5 percent!

Finance Minister Ōhira labeled this budget a "neutral budget," one that "placed an emphasis," as he put it, "on social welfare and education policies."[23] This "neutral" budget saw social security expenditures rise 35.8 percent and education expenses, including new subsidies to private universities, go up 34.5 percent. Public works expenditures, the LDP's favorite rural pork barrel, were kept to a 2.4 percent increase on top of the budget freeze of the previous year.

In later years the rate of increase in social welfare spending slowed as the Japanese government turned toward getting a hold on its rapidly increasing budget deficit. But despite rhetoric about the need to reconsider welfare state policies, there has been no fundamental shift away from extensive government involvement in the provision of medical care, retirement pensions, and other social welfare services.

Tanaka also led the LDP into budget areas that traditionally had been off-limits to party intervention, including allocations from the Fiscal Investment and Loan Program (FILP), Japan's so-called second budget, which has funds roughly equal to half the regular general accounts budget. An example was Tanaka's response to the growing influence of Minshō (Minshu Shōkōkai), the Communist party's front organization for small businessmen that in 1971 had reached a membership of 175,000. Anxious for a way to counter Minshōs' influence and to strengthen the LDP in the cities, Tanaka together with the Japan Chamber of Commerce in 1973 devised a program to be administered by local chambers of commerce to funnel FILP funds for low-interest, no-collateral, no-guarantor loans to small businessmen through the government-run People's Finance Corporation (Kokumin Kinyū Kōko). In 1973 this program had a budget of ¥30 billion. It continued to grow after Tanaka left the premiership. In 1974, under pressure from city-based LDP Diet members, its budget was increased to ¥120 billion, and in 1975 to ¥240 billion. In 1977 the program was extended to small retail and service industries, and its budget in 1978 was ¥510 billion. Loans were limited initially to a maximum of ¥1 million, but by the early 1980s the maximum amount that could be borrowed had been raised to ¥3.5 million.[24]

The shift that occurred in the 1970s in the LDP's priorities is also reflected in the change over time in the relative shares of the general accounts budget going to the Ministry of Agriculture and the Ministry of Health and Welfare. In 1970 Agriculture obtained 11.3 percent of general account budget expenditures, and Health and Welfare a slightly larger 13.7 percent. Five years later Health and Welfare commanded 19 percent of the budget, while Agriculture accounted for 10.2 percent of government spending. And in 1984 Health and Welfare expenditures were three times as great as government spending on agriculture, 18.3 percent of the budget going to the former while only 6.1 percent went to the Agriculture Ministry.

When Tanaka Kakuei left office, it seemed as though the frenzied pumping of government money into public works projects had come to an end: both the 1974 and 1975 budgets, as we have seen, provided for record low increases in public works spending. But this was not to be the case. Tanaka's championing of the concept of remodeling the Japanese archipelago was in political terms very much like Prime Minister Ikeda's embrace of the idea of doubling the income. In both cases, a skillful politician had understood the trends of the economy and tried to gain political advantage by adopting policies to accelerate them. Ikeda's promise to double Japanese income in ten years was actually a cautious commitment, given the rate at which the

Japanese economy was growing when he came into office. And the remodeling of the Japanese archipelago, that is, the spread of industrialization into the nation's periphery, was well under way when Tanaka assumed power. Pressures on the government, both political and economic, to continue speeding this development through public works programs grew even more powerful in the years following Tanaka's resignation.

The freeze on public works spending in 1974–75 proved to be no more than a temporary respite in the enormous investments in public works that characterized the decade of the seventies. The figures speak for themselves. Public works spending increased by 21.2 percent in 1976, 21.4 percent in 1977, 34.5 percent in 1978, and 22.5 percent in 1979. Ironically, the greatest spender on public works in the decade turned out to be not Tanaka Kakuei, but his archenemy, the fiscally conservative Fukuda Takeo.

Faced with sluggish domestic growth, a large and growing trade surplus, and pressure from the Carter administration that Japan become one of the "locomotives" to pull the world economy out of recession, Fukuda made a commitment to use the fiscal year 1978 budget to try to achieve a 7 percent growth rate. This resulted in a massive infusion of government funds into the economy through public works programs, a 34.5 percent increase over the previous year's budget that tied the record set back in 1961 for the largest annual increase in spending on public works.

But the effort failed. Despite all of this spending, the growth rate came to 5.7 percent in 1978, slightly *lower* than the 5.8 percent recorded in 1977 or the 5.9 percent growth rate registered in 1976. It is true that the growth rate would have been lower still had the government not made this infusion of funds. But the fact remains that public works spending did not bring the economy anywhere near its 7 percent growth target. Memory of the failure of its spending policies in the mid-1970s was one reason for Japanese government resistance to demands in the mid-1980s that it spend more to stimulate the domestic economy.

What Fukuda's public works spending policies did do was accelerate the spread of industrialization into provincial Japan. These policies also contributed to the growing political influence of the building and trades industry. Because of the government's emphasis on public works, the increase in secondary sector employment in provincial Japan has been particularly strong in this industry. Since 1972 there have been more males employed in construction than in agriculture; since 1980 employment in the construction industry has been greater than agricultural employment for the entire labor force.[25]

The rapid growth of the construction industry helped produce a large number of wealthy provincial businessmen who constitute something of a new political class. Tanaka, who himself made his money in this industry, best understood its heavy dependence on government spending for its continued prosperity and also its aspirations for prestige and access to power.[26] He responded to and exploited these interests more skillfully than other LDP leaders. The fact that his closest business associate, Osano Kenji, was not a leader of the mainstream business establishment but a self-made man who had amassed a fortune through his real estate and construction interests is emblematic of Tanaka's relationships with these powerful new businessmen. But however expedient it is for LDP politicians to distance themselves from Tanaka's corrupt relationships with construction and related industries, the fact remains that while Tanaka was the most aggressive in his dealings with the provincial nouveaux riches, the entire party has been caught up in the emergence of this class as an increasingly powerful political force.

Through the decade of the 1970s rapid increases in budgetary expenditures in the absence of government revenues sufficient to cover them meant the scuttling of balanced budgets in favor of an enormous reliance on public borrowings. Total general government expenditures as a percentage of GNP remained generally flat until 1973. The budget was growing in the 1960s, but the economy was growing at an even faster rate, permitting the no-hard-choices, positive-sum game referred to earlier. After 1974, however, the share of GNP accounted for by government spending increased rapidly. Total general government outlays, combining both central and local government spending, were 21.1 percent of GNP in 1971, but rose to 25.1 percent in 1975, 30.8 percent in 1978, and 34.1 percent in 1981. A country that only a decade earlier had been noted for its "cheap" government now had a government whose total general expenditures as a percentage of GNP were on a par with those of the United States.[27]

Until the late 1970s the LDP insisted on playing the positive-sum political game that it had initiated during the high economic growth years. It repeatedly thwarted Ministry of Finance demands for an overhaul of welfare programs, cuts in spending, and tax increases. In the general election campaign in the autumn of 1979, Prime Minister Ōhira, after initially lending his support to an MOF proposal for introduction of a value-added tax, was forced to beat a hasty retreat in the face of public opposition and widespread criticism from within his own party ranks.

Obviously there were many factors that contributed to the decision to pursue this kind of expansionary fiscal policy. Government money was injected into the economy in order to stimulate domestic demand, ward off unemployment, and in 1977 to respond to American demands that Japan do more to stimulate the world economy. But spending policies were driven also by mandated welfare expenditures and by the powerful political imperative of the LDP'S determination to retain public support and political power.

The Shift to Austerity

The 1970s were a critical transitional period for the LDP, during which it completed its transformation into Japan's preeminent party of the broad political center. It was a transformation spurred in part by competition between the LDP and its opposition. The LDP's determination to win had compelled it to try to preempt the political space that the centrist parties were themselves trying to occupy, championing as its own many of the policies that the opposition had been advocating. The opposition's response was to engage in a kind of politics of outbidding, demanding higher social security pension benefits, more extensive free medical care programs, and bigger tax cuts than the LDP was prepared to give.

The LDP's embrace of fiscal austerity and governmental reform as the framework for its policies in the 1980s represents the first time since 1955 that its basic domestic program has not to some degree been formulated in response to policies advocated by the political opposition. One reason for the LDP's increased popularity and new electoral strength in the 1980s was that once public opinion had shifted toward accepting the importance of deficit-cutting policies, there was no party that could outbid the LDP in its commitment to cutting down on government waste, streamlining the government administration, and pursuing an austerity policy. On the contrary, the opposition was left in the anomalous position of defending the policies the LDP had adopted earlier in the seventies and of being accused of irresponsibility for doing so.

The LDP's new austerity program was introduced in 1980 with the adoption of a "zero ceiling" formula for preparing the 1981 general accounts budget. This meant that each ministry in compiling its budget request to the Ministry of Finance would not propose spending more than it had received the previous year.[28] The zero budget growth target was not reached that year, the budget for fiscal year 1981 ending up with a total net increase of 4.3 percent. But the break with the high-spending ways of the 1970s had been made. There was no increase in public works spending, and social welfare expenditures were held to a 7.6 percent increase. Defense and official overseas development assistance, however, were exempted from the zero ceiling restraint. The 7.7 percent increase in defense expenditures was 0.1 percentage points ahead of the increase in social welfare spending. This did not herald the coming of a new age of Japanese militarism as some warned it would, but it did symbolize an important shift in government priorities.

By the fall of 1982 the brakes on government spending increases had been fully applied: the 1983 budget provided for no overall net increase whatsoever. Under Prime Minister Nakasone, subsequent budgets were prepared on a so-called minus ceiling basis, with each ministry constrained to ask for no more than a certain percentage less than it had received the previous year.[29] Again, defense spending and development aid were allowed to rise above this ceiling. As a result, net growth of the Japanese general account budget was frozen in the fiscal years 1983–1986, and the subsidy budget actually decreased in both 1985 and 1986.

These fiscal policies, which stand in such stark contrast to the expansive policies pursued by Nakasone's predecessors in the early and mid-seventies, came about neither quickly nor easily. Warnings that government deficits threatened the nation's economic health had been routine ever since the end of the Tanaka reign. Tanaka's successor as prime minister, Miki Takeo, came into office in December 1974 promising to correct social injustice but also expressing concern about mounting government costs. In his first television interview after taking office, on January 26, 1975, he made a point of saying that government was "neither a magician nor Santa Claus" and that the cost of social security programs in particular would have to be kept within a limit that taxpayers would be willing to shoulder.

Prime Minister Fukuda, who succeeded Miki, tried to slow government spending, as has been noted. The budget adopted by his cabinet for the 1977 fiscal year was called an "economic stimulus–welfare forbearance type." General budget growth was held to 17.4 percent and social welfare expenditures were only a fractionally higher 18.4 percent, marking the first time since 1971 that increases in such appropriations fell below the 20 percent level. But as we have

seen, Fukuda was forced to increase expenditures the following year in an effort to push the growth rate to 7 percent.

The Finance Ministry, wanting to tighten government
expenditures, mobilized its various advisory councils to
sound the alarm about a growing fiscal crisis. A well-pub-
licized report issued by the Ministry's Public Finance System Advisory Council in July 1975 pointed to the inevitable
increase in the burden on the state's financial resources that
would stem from a rapidly aging population, and it recommended that "increases in the level of benefits should
be stopped, the burden on the public of social security costs
should be increased, and other measures should be taken
to rationalize the system and place appropriate burdens on
the beneficiaries of social security programs."[30] Two years
later, two more of the Ministry's advisory commissions, one
concerned with the pension program and another with the
national health care system, called for a freezing of expenditures and the systems' total overhaul.

It was not only the conservative establishment that
championed the cause of fiscal reform. Progressive mayors
and governors were also feeling the pain of funding Japan's
expanded welfare programs. In 1975 Asukata Ichio, who was
then mayor of Yokohama and chairman of the National Organization of Progressive Mayors, complained that the national government's reduction of the age qualification for
free medical care for the elderly had encouraged citizens to
demand that financially troubled local governments do the
same with the programs they were sponsoring. "The competition to provide welfare services," Asukata noted, "has
become one of the causes of the chronic financial difficulties
of local government. We need to reconsider our former approaches to welfare policy and our notion that to advocate
welfare is to be progressive."[31] Similar thoughts were expressed by other anti-LDP political leaders. Kanagawa prefecture's Socialist-Communist-supported governor Nagasu
put the issue bluntly by saying that "the idea that the welfare system is improved simply by expanding the amount

of free services belongs to the past. Facing an era of low growth, we must consider new forms of welfare administration."[32]

Statements like these sparked a "reconsidering welfare debate" (*fukushi minaoshi ron*) among local progressive government leaders. But it was a debate in which national leaders of the progressive parties were for the most part silent. Unrestrained by the responsibility of government office, these leaders continued to do little else than promise to provide more government services than the LDP was willing to do. The debate on the national level between the LDP and its opposition tended to follow a ritual in which the opposition called for benefits comparable to those of western Europe and the LDP responded with demands that there be burdens comparable to those of western Europe. By the end of the decade the opposition generally, and the Socialists in particular, had lost the opportunity to offer a coherent alternative to LDP policy.

A number of factors underwrote the LDP's ability to build a national consensus in favor of austerity. Fear of renewed inflation based on the rapid increase in the size of government debt and a broad public opposition to tax increases contributed to a new public mood in favor of greater frugality in government. Even more important was the widely shared belief that excessive government spending had contributed directly to economic decline in western Europe and the United States. By the end of the 1970s the issue that concerned many Japanese was how to avoid catching "the British disease."

Comparatively equitable income distribution and the absence of intense pockets of poverty made it infinitely less painful for Japan to make these adjustments than was the case in the United States or Great Britain. A weak labor union movement and an economically unsophisticated political opposition also helped.

Also, a major catalyst in forging a public consensus on the necessity for a shift to fiscal austerity was the establishment in the fall of 1980 of a government commission on administrative reform, known in Japanese by the acronym "Rinchō" (for Rinji Gyōsei Chōsakai). Under the supervision of Nakasone Yasuhiro, who at the time was minister in charge of the Administrative Management Agency in the Suzuki cabinet, and chaired by Dokō Toshio, the octogenarian former president of Keidanren, Japan's powerful Federation of Economic Organizations, Rinchō embarked on a concerted campaign to convince the public of the need for "administrative reform without tax increases."

Bureaucratic intransigence sabotaged many of Rinchō's specific governmental reform proposals, but Rinchō's support for a budget freeze was important in consolidating a public mood that facilitated the government's shift to austerity. What began as an LDP and big-business effort to stop budget growth mushroomed into a nationwide campaign. Newspapers and television stations ran special series exposing waste in government and reporting dialogues between pundits pondering the calamity that awaited Japan should Rinchō's efforts fail. Dokō Toshio, whose frugal lifestyle, dedication to nation, and business success symbolized all the values that the government wanted to impress upon a population feared to be growing soft with affluence, became a figure of fascination to the public and a major force in building a groundswell of public enthusiasm for the government's new austerity program.

Rinchō was enormously successful in restructuring the debate over government spending—and, more generally, over the proper role of the state in society—around issues of means rather than goals. As the consensus-building process continued, voices questioning the validity of the assumptions that underwrote the Rinchō view that fiscal austerity was necessary and that a leaner, less expensive, and less intrusive government was desirable virtually disappeared from the public debate. This was the case even though an argument could be made that the budget deficit was less serious than the government presented it as being, given Japan's high savings rate, and the fact that government spending to stimulate the economy was necessary to avoid further exacerbation of trade conflicts with the United States and other countries that excessive dependence on exports for growth was certain to create. But the Rinchō assault on such thinking and the respect that an elder statesman of the business community like Dokō was able to command in Japanese society all but pushed such views beyond the bounds of relevant policy debate.

The key, however, to the LDP's ability to impose a budget freeze for several years running and to benefit from it politically lies in the evenhandedness with which the freeze was imposed. This approach is implicit in the concept of a zero or minus ceiling. Such a ceiling means that every ministry is treated the same as every other: there is an equitable distribution of sacrifice, at least in principle. The only exceptions to the ceiling are not domestic programs, but defense and aid programs that involve Japan's relations with the United States and with developing countries.

This equitable treatment approach has a particularly strong appeal in Japan, where a great deal of importance is attached to norms of evenhandedness and balance, not only in budget-making but more generally. By adhering to a policy that claimed to impose a balanced distribution of sacrifice in order to put Japan's fiscal system back on a sound basis, the LDP made it extremely difficult for pressure groups to make demands on the budget that would force noticeable cracks in the ceiling. "Pressure groups" and "interest groups" have always been somewhat pejorative terms in Japanese, used in much the same way as the expression "special interests" is now employed in English. The zero/minus ceiling approach effectively constrained these special interests from obtaining special treatment.

On the other hand, the emphasis on equal treatment was also a powerful constraint on policy. Since budget cuts were rationalized almost entirely in the name of evenhandedness, interest groups were able to impose what amounted to a virtual veto over government policies that would favor one group as against another. Thus the effectiveness of the approach in putting a stop to the growth in gross government spending was balanced by the difficulties it posed for efforts to restructure budgeting priorities in anything other than a slow, incremental manner.

The dynamics of this sytem produced a situation in which resistance to a more expansionary fiscal policy emanated not only from a Ministry of Finance concerned about reducing the national debt, but from a ruling party worried about the potentially adverse political consequences of spending more. LDP politicians publicly called for special treatment for farmers, or for small businessmen hurt by yen appreciation, or for programs to improve housing conditions. But party leaders were well aware that breaking the dike of a no-growth budget would spark an intense competition for resources among LDP-linked interest groups that was potentially more troublesome for the party politically than the continued imposition of an evenhanded freeze. Foreign demands that Japan increase government spending to stimulate the domestic economy were premised on the ability of the government to allocate funds in a manner that would maximize their economic impact. But Japanese political realities virtually guaranteed that any new increments in spending would be fought over by LDP politicians demanding equal treatment for their supporters, and would end up as spending on public works projects, parceled out in a manner that would be fairly equitable vis-à-vis LDP Diet members but would not necessarily be the most effective in economic terms.

The deeply rooted image of the Japanese policy process as being dominated by a kind of bureaucratic rationality does not mesh well with this reality. Japan's fiscal consolidation policies of the 1980s do not reflect only the power of the Ministry of Finance. These policies were also the product of the political pressures generated by a broad-based predominant party that endeavors to avoid alienating any of the important elements of the social coalition that keeps it in power. Although this approach entails a cost in the sense that it imposes a degree of inflexibility in determining budgeting priorities, it has been enormously successful in securing public support for the government's effort to reduce the national debt and in strengthening the LDP at the polls.

3.

THE LIBERAL DEMOCRATIC PARTY: THE ORGANIZATION OF POLITICAL POWER

The evolution of Japanese politics since 1955 has involved changes not only in the dynamics of the party system and in the policy priorities of the ruling party. There has also been an important evolution in LDP organization. The stability of LDP rule has enabled the party to establish clear rules to regulate many of its activities, and it has brought about important changes in the characteristics of Japan's political leadership and in the role the party's leaders play in making public policy. The party is no longer adequately described simply as a coalition of factions. It has evolved a complex organizational life of its own, one in which factions themselves have developed organizational structures considerably different from what they were in the party's early years.

Throughout the LDP's history, factions have provided the primary political community for Japan's political elite, providing a setting of intimacy and common purpose. When the party was first formed, factions were very much the personal entourages of powerful political leaders. The first generation of LDP faction bosses put their factions together man by man, as it were. Factional organization was marked by an inner core of men intensely loyal to the faction leader and by strong *oyabun-kobun* (patron-client) relationships in which the faction leader provided political funds and access to government and party posts in return for his faction members' support, and most importantly, for their votes in the party presidential election.[1] The old party factions, moreover, were linked to the conservative parties of the pre-1955 merger and the prewar period. Personal loyalties were reinforced by attachments to these pre-LDP groupings and by the camaraderie among men who had fought many political battles together in the turbulent postwar years.

The patron-client aspects of the relationships between faction bosses and their followers in the early years of LDP rule have become much less evident in factional organization in the 1980s. Factions have evolved into less leader-dominated, more collegial structures; their members often refer to them as their *mura*, their village, a term that itself reflects this collegial quality.

One important reason for this shift is the generational change in factional leadership that has occurred. All faction leaders today have inherited their factions, and there are few LDP politicians left who are cut out of the mold of the old-line political bosses who dominated the party's factional politics in earlier years. The faction that was built by former Prime Minister Ikeda Hayato has had five generations of leaders, having passed from the hands of Ikeda through those of Maeo Shigesaburō, Ōhira Masayoshi, and Suzuki Zenkō to its current leader, Miyazawa Kiichi. The faction that was led originally by Kishi Nobusuke is now in its third leadership generation, having formally passed from Fukuda Takeo to Kishi's son-in-law and Fukuda's heir apparent, Abe Shintarō, in 1986. Similarly, the faction led by Satō Eisaku was taken over by Tanaka Kakuei and then by Takeshita Noboru. Both Nakasone Yasuhiro and Kōmoto Toshio are second-generation faction leaders. Nakasone took over leadership of most of the faction that had been led by one of the LDP's powerful founding members, Kōno Ichirō. Kōmoto succeeded to the leadership of a faction that was long under control of the last politically active member of the LDP's original group of faction leaders, Miki Takeo.

With each passing generation, the ties that bind the faction leader to the faction's members have become less intense. Tanaka Kakuei was exceptional in this regard, since the ties between him and his followers were very much in the old *oyabun-kobun* mode. But after he left the center of the political stage, the Tanaka faction came to reflect the same general pattern. Over time, as the number of members in each faction increased, the number of factions in the party was reduced by half or more. In the late 1980s there were only four major factions—Takeshita, Nakasone, Miyazawa, Abe—and one minor one, led by Kōmoto. There was also a small group of Tanaka's followers led by Nikaidō Susumu that refused to join the Takeshita faction. In the 1960s there were as many as ten factions fighting over the distribution of party and governmental posts.

Ōno Bamboku, one of the LDP's early and powerful faction bosses, was once quoted as saying that "forty is just the right number for a faction. Less than that is a problem but more than that is a problem too." Ōno was quoted by journalist Watanabe Tsuneo in his classic book *Habatsu* (Factions), the first systematic analysis of factional organization in the LDP. In prefacing Ōno's remark, Watanabe wrote:

There is a kind of natural law controlling the size of factions. . . . If a faction has more than fifty members [in the lower house], it faces competition between its own members in the same electoral district. . . . Political funds needed to take care of faction members and the problems of getting members into leadership positions are other reasons why it is difficult to maintain such factions. . . . When I asked Ōno what he meant [by the remark quoted above] he also referred to these three points: competition within the same electoral district, money, and [party and government] positions.[2]

Since the mid-seventies, however, this "natural law" has failed to operate, despite the fact that the electoral system remains the same and that politicians continue to compete for political funds and for party and government positions. Following the 1986 general election, the Tanaka faction had 140 members and the other three large factions each had between 84 and 89 members. The small faction headed by Kōmoto had only 34 members, a number not far below what used to be considered optimal size but one that now raised questions about the faction's continued existence.[3]

One of the popular explanations of this increase in faction size is that it was provoked by Tanaka Kakuei's determination to build his faction's power so as to be able to retain his influence despite his indictment in the Lockheed corruption scandal. Once Tanaka set out to control the party by creating a mammoth faction, this argument goes, other factions were forced to follow suit. This competition resulted in the disappearance of the party's smallest factions and created a new situation in which a few factions came to dominate the party landscape.

Tanaka's determination to make his faction as large as possible was no doubt a factor in provoking the increase in size and decrease in number of LDP factions. But his role in bringing about what is a basic structural change in factional organization should not be exaggerated. Tanaka does not represent a new style of political leadership in Japan. Rather, he was the last of an old school of political bosses whose power derived from their ability to provide patronage to a large circle of followers. Notwithstanding colorful stories about the power of the "shadow Shogun," as Tanaka was called in the last years before he suffered a stroke in 1985, the most impressive and meaningful characteristic of the Tanaka faction's increase in size was that the faction grew as Tanaka's personal power declined, and it continued to increase in numbers even after he was incapacitated and his ability to influence others in the faction was gravely compromised. What this suggests is that there were new systemic pressures at work in the LDP in the mid-1970s that, more than Tanaka's personal influence, brought about this consolidation of LDP Diet members into a few very large factions.

One of the most important of these factors was a change in patterns of political funding. The costs of election campaigning and of maintaining the day-to-day operations of a Diet member's political office have always been very high in Japan, making the ability to raise a huge amount of political money an essential condition for political success. In the first two decades of LDP rule, large proportions of these funds were raised by faction leaders and dispensed to the party's backbenchers through the factional machinery.

But a 1976 revision of the law regulating political funds that is discussed in chapter 5 made it nearly impossible for faction leaders to continue to monopolize funding channels as they had previously, and it created new, if unintended, incentives for individual politicians to raise a large part of their political funds on their own. At the same time, the revised law reinforced other factors that were reducing the relative importance of political contributions from the business establishment—the *zaikai*—and of the channeling of these funds to the LDP's politicians through faction leaders. Provincial businessmen rose in importance as sources of political funds as the importance of the *zaikai* declined. And individual Diet members, rather than their faction leaders, were the ones who had close relationships with these local businessmen. These changes in political funding removed one of the major constraints on faction membership.

The growth in faction size also has something to do with the generational change in leadership noted above. Factions have been able to grow larger in part because there are so many fewer old-line political bosses around. Small factions led by people like Funada Naka, Shiina Etsusaburō, or Kawashima Shōjirō, which did not have the resources to attract many new candidates, nonetheless were able to survive as long as their original leaders were active because of the loyalty of their followers, which had its roots in relationships formed before the 1955 merger of the conservative parties. But once these leaders passed from the scene, their factions soon disappeared.

New candidates are not always drawn to a particular faction because of personal ties with its leader. A Diet hopeful often shops around for factional support, looking for a faction that has no candidate in his district and that has the wherewithal to help him with his campaign and support him as he works his way up the party ranks. Increasingly this has come to mean joining a large, well-organized faction. Cabinet ministers and other well-known members of that faction will lend their support with campaign appearances and with introductions or words of encouragement to possible funding sources. And once in the Diet, the new faction member will be part of a "village" that is at the center of the political action. There are virtually no incentives to opt for membership in a small faction or to remain unaffiliated with the party's factional groupings.

The most important factor in determining factional membership is the factional affiliation of LDP Diet members already elected from the district in which the new candidate plans to run. Given the intraparty competition fostered by the electoral system, incumbent LDP Diet members invariably view the entry of new candidates as a threat to their reelection and use their faction's influence to try to block them from gaining the party's support. Thus potential candidates seek the support of factions that do not have incumbents in their districts. Factions in turn seek candidates in districts where they are unrepresented. The result is that there are very few districts that have two Diet members from the same faction; in April 1986 there were only six.[4] Even following the 1986 election, when the LDP increased its representation by over fifty seats, there were only nine districts with two LDP members from the same faction.[5]

The evolution of the LDP's organization has brought about not only a consolidation of factions into a few large groupings, but has affected their role in the political system as well. The central function of factions continues to be to mediate the recruitment of the LDP's leadership, but the dynamics of that mediation have changed. The stability of LDP rule over several decades, to cite one important example of these changes, has led to the adoption of strict seniority rules to manage the recruitment of cabinet ministers and holders of high party office. LDP Diet members, as is discussed in more detail later in this chapter, gain initial entry into the cabinet almost entirely on the basis of the number of times they have been elected to the Diet. Factional affiliation is important in deciding what cabinet portfolio a particular Diet member receives, but it is of secondary importance in determining when he is appointed. Moreover, the number of cabinet posts any particular faction gets varies in direct proportion to its size relative to the other factions, a system of proportional representation that has itself further spurred the consolidation of factions into ever-larger groupings.

There also emerged in the mid-1970s a pattern of power-sharing of the party's major posts among the four largest factions. There are four senior positions in the LDP— president (who is concurrently prime minister), secretary-general, chairman of the executive board, and chairman of the policy affairs research council (the PARC). By custom the positions of chairman of the executive board and of the PARC have almost always gone to Diet members who are not in the prime minister's faction. But until 1974, when Miki became prime minister, the LDP secretary-general had usually come from the same faction as the prime minister.

Miki, however, politically too weak to control this key position, was forced to give it to Nakasone Yasuhiro. Miki's successor as prime minister, Fukuda Takeo, was also un-

able to control this key party post; he had to let it go to his
rival, Ōhira Masayoshi. In 1978 Prime Minister Ōhira tried
to reinstate the old system by appointing a member of his
own faction, Suzuki Zenkō, as secretary-general. But he ran
into fierce opposition and was forced to back down, saving
face by appointing another member of his faction to the post
until at the time of his first cabinet reshuffle he replaced
him with a member of the Nakasone faction. Neither of
Ōhira's successors, Prime Minister Suzuki nor Prime Minister Nakasone, challenged this system. Thus, since 1974,
the four major factions have shared control over the party's
four major posts.

   These patterns of power-sharing of the party's top
posts and proportional factional representation in the cabinet contributed to virtually eliminating the erstwhile distinction between mainstream and antimainstream factions
that was so central to the factional politics of the 1950s and
1960s. In those years the mainstream factions, those that
comprised the party's ruling coalition, tended to dominate
the cabinet and the party's senior posts, while the antimainstream factions looked for opportunities to enter the
coalition or to topple it and replace it with one of their own.
But all factions are now in the ruling coalition; they share
the major party posts and are represented in the cabinet in
proportion to their relative strength. A great deal of factional maneuvering goes on over the party presidency and
over particular cabinet and party offices. But there obviously are fewer possibilities for coalition arrangements in
a party of four very large factions than in one of ten factions
of varying sizes, and there are greater incentives to encompass all factions in the ruling coalition in order to maximize
its stability.

   Some observers believe that the evolution of the LDP
since the early 1970s has also brought about a diminution
in the role factions play in the party's decision-making processes. Satō and Matsuzaki, for example, suggest that "the
main decision-making unit in the LDP shifted from factions
to the policy affairs research council's division and com-

missions and then further to the groups of middle-ranking Dietmen known as *zoku* who are knowledgeable about particular areas of government administration."[6] But there is no convincing evidence that factions ever comprised the main decision-making unit in the party. From the beginning the role of LDP factions was to decide who the party's leaders would be, not what their policies should be. The role of the PARC did expand, and the *zoku* phenomenon, which is discussed below, did become more pervasive, but this was not caused by—nor did it produce—a contraction in the role of factions.

To the contrary, factions have become somewhat more policy-relevant as they have become more collegial in structure and as individual politicians have become more active in policymaking. Factions as such do not take positions on policy issues, nor do they exhibit any ideological coherence. But some factions have developed disproportionate influence in certain policy areas. The Tanaka faction virtually monopolized Construction Ministry–related posts in the party and government throughout the 1970s. The Fukuda faction has controlled the education division (*bunkyō bukai*) in PARC more often than any other faction.[7] Members of the Nakasone faction have taken a particular interest in telecommunications. Most importantly, factions provide a collegial setting in which Diet members look to each other for assistance and favors in policy-related matters as well as in political funding and other activities. But these factional roles have evolved in a context of growing party involvement overall in the policy process. An expanding party role in decision making, in other words, has permeated all party institutions.

The LDP Ladder of Success

The almost complete routinization of the system for promoting LDP's Diet members up to the point of initial entry into the cabinet is one of the most striking features of recent LDP organization. The system is comparable to the way large Japanese corporations promote their managerial labor force. Up to a point—section chief in a company, first entry into the cabinet in the LDP—promotion is determined almost exclusively by seniority. What posts at any particular rank a young businessman or an LDP Dietman obtains on his way up the organization may hinge on his perceived abilities and his relations with others higher in the hierarchy, but for roughly the first fifteen years of his career he can expect to move up the rungs of the promotional ladder in an almost entirely predictable manner.

A major difference between large business organizations and the LDP, however, is that in business firms, seniority in terms of years served parallels seniority in terms of age, since white-collar workers typically are recruited right out of college and stay with one firm for their entire careers. But there is no age-graded seniority in the LDP. Promotion depends on the number of times elected, not on age and not on the number of years passed since first being elected. Thus a politician who loses an election but makes a comeback in a later one usually falls behind others who were elected for the first time with him but were not later defeated.

During their first three terms in office, LDP politicians are mainly appointed to positions that provide training for more responsible positions later on in their careers. One of the most important of these early positions is appointment, usually in the second or third term, as a parliamentary vice minister. This position carries with it few responsibilities, but it enables the politician to learn about a number of policy issues in some depth and to develop relationships with bureaucrats and with the interest groups that form the ministry's public clientele. During his first three terms in office, the LDP politician will usually also serve as vice chairman and then as chairman of a division (*bukai*) in the party's policy affairs research council and as a director (*riji*) of a Diet standing committee.

Promotion to fairly important posts in the party and

in the Diet comes in the fourth and fifth term. The LDP politician at this stage will be given experience as one of the party's vice secretaries-general or as a vice chairman of the executive council or of PARC, and as chairman of one of the Diet's standing committees.

Most LDP politicians are recruited into the cabinet during their sixth term in office. This means that an LDP Diet member appointed to the cabinet after being elected in 1983 to his sixth consecutive term in office has served in the Diet anywhere from fourteen years, if he was appointed to the cabinet in 1983, to sixteen years, if he was appointed in December 1985, in the last cabinet reshuffle prior to the 1986 election.

Since there are more LDP politicians with the requisite seniority for appointment to the cabinet then there are cabinet posts, there is a fairly rapid turnover in cabinet appointments to give everyone who qualifies the opportunity to serve. Between July 1972 and October 1986 there were seventeen major cabinet reshuffles. According to one calculation, the average term of a cabinet minister is 278 days.[8]

Satō and Matsuzaki correctly point to this promotion system as an important example of the "institutionalization" of the LDP. It is not, however, an entirely new phenomenon. "There are very few Diet members with cabinet experience," Watanabe Tsuneo observed in 1964, "who have been elected fewer than five times. The cases of cabinet entry of someone with few[er] election victories are limited to powerful people from the prewar political and bureaucratic worlds and powerful people from the business establishment. . . ."[9] As these prewar figures disappeared from the scene, the exceptions to the rule dwindled into insignificance and the system of promotion through seniority was consolidated.

Seniority, however, only carries a Diet member to his first cabinet appointment. It does not guarantee reappointment to the cabinet or appointment to the highest party posts. Only 40 percent of LDP Diet members who have served in the cabinet once are ever appointed to it again.[10] The other

60 percent comprise the core of the so-called policy tribes or *zoku,* often concentrating their policy-related activities on the ministry they served as parliamentary vice minister early in their careers.

This routinization of patterns of leadership recruitment and the LDP's monopoly of governmental power has brought about important changes in the characteristics of politicians recruited into the LDP's Diet contingent. Until the late 1960s, LDP leadership was characterized by a combination of what might be typed streetwise professional politicians and policywise former bureaucrats. Former high-ranking civil servants and politicians whose entire careers had been spent in elective public office were the two dominant groups in the party. There was a considerable degree of tension between them: the *tōjin,* the political professionals, felt that many of the bureaucrat-politicians still behaved in accord with the prewar saying "bureaucrats exalted, people despised"; the ex-bureaucrats, for their part, were derisive of the *tōjin's* lack of understanding, or even interest, in the critical and complex issues of domestic and foreign policy.

But it was a winning combination. The professional politicians gave the party a strong populist appeal, at least in rural areas where it derived most of its support. And the former bureaucrats linked the party to a powerful bureaucratic establishment, facilitating the policymaking process and avoiding debilitating struggles between a party determined to show that it was in charge and bureaucratic institutions that were long used to being dominant.

In these initial years of LDP dominance, the ex-bureaucrats in the party were the more powerful. The fact that many of them rose to high political positions shortly after leaving senior posts in the bureaucracy meant that they often represented bureaucratic interests, reinforcing rather than countering bureaucratic influence in the policy process. Former bureaucrats held the prime ministership continuously from March 1957 to July 1972.[11] Although they represented about 30 percent of the LDP's Diet members, they typically comprised upwards of 50 percent of cabinet members.[12] In the early years of LDP rule, bureaucratic influence was not only strong but seemed to be increasing. Writing in 1962, Scalapino and Masumi concluded that "the bureaucratization of the conservative party, as in the late Meiji and Taishō eras, once again has been taking place. This time, however, it could begin from a relatively high base line."[13]

But the bureaucratization of the LDP never took place. The number of former bureaucrats elected to the Diet has remained about the same for thirty years. In 1958, 26 percent of LDP Diet members were men with previous careers in the bureaucracy;[14] in 1983 the figure was 24 percent.[15] There have been fluctuations from one election to the next, but the long-term trend has proved remarkably consistent: the higher civil service regularly provides about one-fourth of LDP Diet members.[16]

These figures conceal an important change, however, in the kinds of bureaucrats that have become politicians. In the initial years of LDP rule, Diet members who had formerly been bureaucrats were mostly men who had risen to the highest posts in their ministries: division chief (kyoku-chō) and administrative vice minister (jikan), the highest appointive office in the Japanese bureaucracy. But since the early 1970s the trend has been toward the political recruitment of junior and middle-ranking bureaucrats, those who leave the bureaucracy to run for the Diet before going any higher than section chief (kachō). In the five elections between 1958 and 1969, there were thirty-nine former bureaucrats elected to the lower house for the first time. Twenty-five of them had served as division chief or vice minister, only fourteen as section chief or below. Between 1972 and 1983 there were also five lower house elections and exactly the same number of former bureaucrats elected for the first time. But of this later group of thirty-nine, only twelve had served as division chief or vice minister, whereas twenty-seven had left with the rank of section chief or below.[17] Most of the ex-bureaucrats now recruited by the LDP are men in their thirties and early forties who have opted for a career in politics instead of a career in government administration. They do not bring with them the prestige, contacts, influence, or the experience that high-ranking bureaucrats brought to the LDP in its early years. And they do not rise to high positions in the LDP much more quickly than Diet members from other career backgrounds.

The consolidation of promotion patterns in the LDP, whereby initial appointment to the cabinet is almost entirely determined by the number of times elected regardless of career background, has greatly reduced the advantages ex-bureaucrats enjoyed in earlier years. The data provided by Satō and Matsuzaki underscore this point. As of March 1986, of 109 LDP Diet members who had been elected five times or less, only 5 had been recruited into the cabinet. Of the 130 who had been elected seven times or more, only 4 had not yet been appointed to the cabinet.[18] Between 1972 and May 1986, Diet members who were appointed to the cabinet for the first time had been elected an average of 6.28 times. For those who had come from previous careers in the bureaucracy the average was 5.47, and for bureaucrats who had not risen higher than the section chief level it was 6.0.[19]

That is to say that former high-ranking civil servants on the average entered the cabinet for the first time one election ahead of other LDP members and that former lower-ranking civil servants have a marginal advantage at best over other LDP Diet members. Since 1955, lower house elections have been held an average of every 2.8 years. Thus, even LDP Diet members who have reached the highest bureaucratic positions have had to wait, as a general rule, an average of fourteen years before being appointed to the cabinet. There have been very few exceptions to this rule for more than twenty-five years. In 1979 Prime Minister Ōhira appointed Gotōda Masaharu, a former director general of the National Police Agency, as minister of home affairs during Gotōda's second term in the lower house. This is the only case since 1960, when Shiina Etsusaburō was made MITI

minister in his third term in office, that a former bureaucrat
has entered the cabinet before being elected to at least his
fourth term in the lower house.[20]

Of the six men who have been prime minister since
Satō Eisaku retired in July 1972, only two, Fukuda and Ōhira,
had careers as high-ranking civil servants prior to entering
the Diet.[21] And they served as prime minister a total of three
and a half years. Moreover, of the three "new leaders"—
Abe Shintarō, Miyazawa Kiichi, and Takeshita Noboru—only
Miyazawa comes from the bureaucracy, where he served in
the Ministry of Finance. Takeshita was previously a prefectural assemblyman and Abe a reporter for the *Mainichi Shinbun*. Among the fifty-five Diet members who as of January
1986 had been appointed at least twice to the cabinet and/
or the three top party posts (secretary-general, chairman of
the executive board and chairman of the policy affairs research council), nineteen were former bureaucrats. From 1972
to 1983 the policy affairs research council had nine chairman. All were nonbureaucrats.[22]

This evolution of the LDP's system of internal promotion has considerably weakened the importance of career
background as a relevant variable in explaining either the
distribution of power within the LDP or the party's relationship to the career bureaucracy and to the decision-making process. Career backgrounds in the LDP today are significant for what they indicate about access routes to the
Diet for the politically ambitious. They are no longer as important as they once were for explaining how the politically
successful exercise their power.

Local politicians, for example, continue to provide a
major pool from which LDP Diet candidates are recruited,
but they are no longer just "streetwise"; many of them are
actively involved in the policy process. These professional
politicians account for about a third of LDP Diet members.
They are professional politicians in a very literal sense. Although many are nominally advisors or are connected in
other ways to business firms, the overwhelming majority of
them make politics their full-time career.

Local elective assemblies provide a well-trodden path to parliament in many countries. But in Japan the fact that many Diet members come from backgrounds in local elective politics reflects important features of LDP organization. These include the absence of effective party organization at the local level and the importance of networks of extensive personal relationships in mobilizing electoral support. Local politicians in command of their own personal political machines have obvious advantages in such a system.

These features are not unique to the LDP. Local politicians are a major presence in all of Japan's political parties. One-third of JSP candidates elected in 1983 had prior experience as elected members of local governing bodies. Although the JSP has come to depend increasingly on labor leaders for its candidates (about two-thirds come to it by way of the union movement), successful labor union–based candidates have been drawn mainly from those who have won elections on the local level before running for the Diet.

Fully half of the Kōmeitō's successful candidates in the 1980 election (seventeen out of thirty-four) and 39 percent in 1983 came to the Diet after experience in local politics. In the case of the DSP, fifteen of its thirty-nine successful candidates in 1983 were formerly local politicians. Even in the Communist party, which unlike other Japanese parties has a strong local party organization, eight of its twenty-seven successful candidates in the 1983 election had previously served in local elective office. Overall, one out of every three Diet members elected to the lower house in 1983 came to that position after local elective political experience.[23]

In recent years, however, another access route to the Diet has become particularly well traveled, to the point that it now channels the single largest group of new LDP Diet members. This is the so-called second-generation phenomenon, the increasing recruitment of candidates who are the sons of Diet members. In the 1983 election, 112 successful candidates were sons or sons-in-law of present or former Diet members, accounting for 43 percent of all successful

LDP candidates elected that year. In 1986 the number was 115, some 38 percent of the 304 candidates elected.[24]

Entry of large numbers of second-generation politicians into the Diet in recent years is one of the most notable changes in the backgrounds of LDP Diet members over the thirty years of LDP rule.[25] Family ties have long been a factor in providing a route into the Diet, and they have not been irrelevant to the political careers of a fair number of politicians in the United States and elsewhere. But they became an especially predominant feature of LDP recruitment patterns in the 1970s and 1980s, when many Diet members who had filled the political leadership vacuum created by the Occupation purge of wartime politicians retired from active political life or died.

The success of these second-generation politicians in getting recruited by the LDP and in winning election to the Diet reflects in part the highly personalized nature of Japanese political organization on the local level. The son of a retiring politician or of an incumbent who has died in office is usually uniquely situated to appeal to bonds of sentiment and loyalty built up over the years between his father and his father's supporters. These bonds and the other advantages that come with an inherited campaign organization and name recognition have produced a much higher success ratio for new second-generation candidates than for other new candidates. In the 1972 election, seventeen of twenty-five new second-generation candidates won. This is a success rate of 64 percent, compared to an average success rate for all new candidates of 24.5 percent.[26] In the 1986 election, 52 percent of new second-generation candidates won, compared to a 13 percent average success rate for all new lower house candidates.[27]

An analysis of second-generation LDP Diet members elected in 1986 indicates a considerable diversity in career background. Twenty-two had worked as secretaries to their fathers and twenty came from careers in the national bureaucracy. Only eight, however, had ever served in elective office prior to being elected to the Diet. The single largest category, thirty-one members, is comprised of "salary-men"—white-collar employees in large corporations who resigned before reaching senior positions in the company.[28]

The second-generation phenomenon has closed off opportunities for other ambitious politicians to get into the Diet, but it has brought greater diversity in career back-grounds and life experience to the LDP's Diet member con-tingent and has played a role in giving the party a more modern look. Japan's emergence as a world economic power has forced even the LDP's most parochial Diet members to become more aware of international affairs, and the party as a whole has slowly been becoming more "internation-alist," a popular word in present day Japan. But this is es-pecially true for second-generation politicians, particularly salarymen who have worked for banks, trading companies, and other corporations involved in international business and have spent time working abroad. Many of these poli-ticians convey a more cosmopolitan image than an earlier generation of LDP politicians or the present generation of largely union-based opposition party politicians. And they appeal to a young and urban electorate partly for that rea-son.

The most dramatic example of this popularity was provided by the LDP members who created the New Lib-eral Club. The NLC's support came almost entirely from metropolitan districts and their adjacent "bedtowns." The party was widely regarded as a more modern party than the rural-based LDP. Yet its best known leaders—Kōno Yōhei, Nishioka Takeo, Yamaguchi Toshio—are all second-generation politicians.

Some analyses of Diet member career backgrounds show a high and increasing number of former secretaries of Diet members. But a large number of these are second-gen-eration people. The LDP continues to draw some of its can-didates from among Dietmen secretaries, newspaper re-porters, and people in other walks of life. But these have been sources of political talent in Japan for a long time. Their continued presence reveals little else than the fact that the

LDP's Diet contingent reflects more diverse career backgrounds than that of other parties even though access to
the Diet has been narrowed as a result of the prevalence of
second-generation politicians.[29]

Instability at the Top

The system for recruiting the LDP's leadership that evolved
in the 1970s presents an apparent paradox: despite the routinization of recruitment patterns for initial entry into the
cabinet and the emergence of a stable system of factional
power-sharing of major party posts, the 1970s saw the
emergence of unprecedented instability at the top level of
the party's leadership. Over the fifteen years from 1957, when
Kishi became prime minister, to the end of the Satō administration in 1972, Japan had only three prime ministers—
Kishi, Ikeda, and Satō. During the next ten years, from the
advent of the Tanaka administration in 1972 to the coming
into office of Prime Minister Nakasone in November 1982,
there were six prime ministers—Tanaka, Miki, Fukuda,
Ōhira, Suzuki, and Nakasone.

Not only did the party presidency after 1972 turn over
every two years until Nakasone was elected to a second two-
year term in 1984, but in no case did the incumbent leave
office willingly. Prime Minister Tanaka was forced to resign
in scandal; Prime Minister Miki was pushed out of office by
other party leaders furious with him for permitting Tanaka's arrest and indictment. On the eve of a Tokyo economic
summit meeting of the leaders of the advanced industrialized countries that he was to chair, Miki's successor, Fukuda Takeo, found himself out of office as a result of the
successful efforts of the Tanaka faction to manipulate a new
presidential primary system to get Tanaka's ally, Ōhira
Masayoshi, the prime ministership. And in 1980 Ōhira died
in the midst of an election campaign that had been called
because his opponents in the LDP had brought down the
government by absenting themselves from the Diet during

a vote on a motion of nonconfidence sponsored by the opposition parties. After that election, the party chose Suzuki Zenkō as prime minister, a man whose major qualification for the position was that his lack of preparation for it made it certain he would reign as a temporary caretaker while other faction leaders tried to get their bearings and plan their strategy. This instability only came to an end, or an interlude, when Nakasone Yasuhiro became prime minister in 1982.

How can this shift from stability to instability in the party's top leadership be explained? In part it was a consequence of the political stability of the previous period, most particularly the long eight-year reign of Satō Eisaku. A senior bureaucrat in the Ministry of Transportation before being recruited into politics by Prime Minister Yoshida, Satō was a noncharismatic leader, but one who was enormously skilled in managing factional alliances. Carefully parceling out cabinet and party posts and other patronage, he was able to defuse every challenge to his power, becoming known as *jinji no Satō*, "Satō the personnel manager."

But the one personnel change that Satō proved unable to manage was his own succession. Satō had wanted Fukuda Takeo, the leader of the faction that had previously belonged to Satō's elder brother, Kishi, to succeed him.[30] But during his long years in office, Satō left the day-to-day operations of his faction largely to Tanaka Kakuei, a professional politician who was not only skilled in the art of factional politics, but who projected an image of dynamism and energy that neither Satō nor Fukuda possessed.

Tanaka's decision to challenge Fukuda for the party presidency forced Satō to remain officially neutral since he could not compel his faction members not to support Tanaka. Tanaka won the contest only to be forced out of office two years later after a popular monthly magazine published a devastating account of his business dealings.[31] Had Tanaka not become prime minister in 1972, the party's history would have been written differently. At the least Miki Takeo would not have become prime minister, and a former prime minister would not have been indicted in the Lockheed scandal.

But to place too much emphasis on the impact of Tanaka Kakuei on the LDP's politics in the 1970s is to ignore other factors that were more important in provoking this leadership instability. The end of the Satō period coincided with the coming into full bloom of the second phase of LDP dominance, with its bare LDP majority in the Diet and the emergence of a multiparty system. Increased competition from the political opposition and a real concern that the LDP might lose its Diet majority made the ruling party infinitely more sensitive to shifts in the popularity of its leader among the general public than had ever before been the case.

One need not denigrate the importance of personal linkages between voters and LDP politicians in influencing voting behavior in order to recognize that in a period when the LDP commanded a narrow majority, and in the context of an electoral system in which a minor swing in the vote can spell the difference between victory and defeat for any one candidate, the possibility that the prime minister's popularity might affect the electoral choice of, say, even 4 or 5 percent of voters came to assume extraordinary importance to LDP politicians worried about their ability to survive the next election. Recruitment of Diet members into the cabinet could be routinized because the process was confined to the party itself. But recruitment of the prime minister became increasingly contentious as LDP members became convinced that his popularity could affect the party's performance at the polls.

The party's instinct for survival that produced the rapid turnovers in leadership in the 1970s was not entirely unprecedented. The conviction that the continuation in office of Prime Minister Kishi after the Diet's passage of the revised Security Treaty in 1960 would be a major liability for the party resulted in his departure and the advent of an administration that downplayed foreign affairs while it tried to concentrate the public mind on making the country get rich quick. But in the 1970s the pressures to shore up the party's popularity were more persistent, and the belief that the prime minister's personal popularity was an important factor in the party's electoral performance became deeper and more widespread among the LDP's Diet members. Indirectly, public opinion had penetrated the proverbial smoke-filled back room of LDP politics. It was instrumental in convincing LDP leaders to force Tanaka to resign and to agree to have Miki succeed him. And it was an especially important factor in the party's decision to make a major organizational innovation in 1977, when a new system for choosing the party's president was adopted.

Prior to 1977, the LDP's president was formally chosen by a congress composed of the party's Diet members and representatives from each of the LDP's prefectural chapters.[32] The actual selection process, however, took place in back room bargaining between LDP faction leaders. The system, which was widely known to involve the changing of hands of large sums of money, had long been the object of public criticism, and the party from its earliest years had promised to eliminate "money politics" and to purge itself of what it often referred to as the pernicious influence of factionalism.

Just before leaving office at the end of 1976, Prime Minister Miki, who had a long-established reputation as an advocate of party reform, proposed the introduction of a primary among the party's rank and file as a way to reduce the power of factions and the role of money in choosing the party's president. According to his proposal, any Diet member with the support of ten other Diet members would be eligible to run in the primary. The party's Diet members would choose as their party's president one of the two candidates who came out with the most votes. But Miki did not have the power to overcome the strong opposition his proposal drew within the party, and he left office without its being acted upon.

Miki's successor as prime minister, Fukuda Takeo, quickly picked up the idea of a party primary. Fukuda had also been a longtime critic of the LDP's money politics, his

criticism becoming all the more acute after he lost out to
Tanaka Kakuei, the party's most skillful practitioner of the
art, in the fight to succeed Prime Minister Satō. Within four
months of Fukuda's taking office, the party adopted a new
two-phased presidential election system.

The new arrangement stipulated that when Prime
Minister Fukuda's term expired in November 1978, there
would be a primary in which any LDP Diet member who
had the support of twenty other Diet members could run.
There would be a nearly month-long campaign. A week after the voting, the party's Diet members would convene to
choose as their party president one of the two candidates
who garnered the most votes. Little did Prime Minister Fukuda know that he would be the first casualty of this new
system.

Although the system was intended ostensibly to
weaken factional control over the selection of the party
president, its introduction encouraged factions to move beyond the coteries of the Diet members that comprised them,
to extend their activities into the electorate itself. The new
system set off an intense competition among faction members to register as many of their personal supporters as possible in the party and thereby ensure a high voter turnout
for their leaders.

From a membership of 455,000 in December 1977, the
LDP's rank and file swelled to a million and a half members
one year later, and to over three million members at the end
of 1979. Abuses of the system quickly became legend, with
politicians not only registering their own supporters as party
members, but paying their dues and filling out their mail
ballots in the primary for them. Scores of fictitious voters
were also put on the party rolls. It is entirely possible that
the cost of the new reformed system approached, if it did
not surpass, that of the old maligned one.

The ultimate irony for Fukuda was that the factions
that were most skillful in exploiting the new system were
those of Ōhira and former Prime Minister Tanaka. These

two factions virtually controlled the party organization. Ōhira himself was the party's secretary-general, and Tanaka faction member Takeshita Noboru, an acknowledged master of campaigning and political organization, held the important position of chairman of the party's organizational bureau. Since the Tanaka faction did not have a candidate of its own to run, it threw its support behind Ōhira. Fukuda was so badly trounced in the primary that he gave up the formality of the Diet members' vote and withdrew, turning over the party presidency and the prime ministership to Ōhira.

Although enthusiasm for this system quickly evaporated after its first use, it was not possible to scuttle completely an arrangement that had been sold to the public in the name of party modernization. Instead, the party amended the rules to make it increasingly difficult for a primary to be held. Under rules in effect since 1981, candidacy in the primary requires the support of fifty Diet members (rather than the ten in Miki's proposal or twenty in the system used in 1978). There also must be at least four candidates in order for a primary to be held. And the top three winners in the primary (not two as previously) would then become candidates for president in an election among the party's Diet members. By limiting candidates to those who could muster fifty supporters, it was thought that only the major faction leaders would be able to run. And by requiring four candidates, the new rules seemed to insure that a primary would be avoided if two factions would agree not to compete with each other.

The test of this new revised system came in 1982 when Suzuki Zenkō resigned as prime minister. It seemed almost certain that no primary would be held. The Tanaka and Ōhira factions had thrown their support to Nakasone Yasuhiro. Only Abe Shintarō, the heir apparent of the Fukuda faction, and Kōmoto Toshio, who had taken over the leadership of the Miki faction, appeared to have enough backers to secure the necessary fifty-Diet-member endorsements. Since the rules required at least four candidates for a primary and there were only three—Nakasone, Kōmoto, and Abe—it seemed that there would be no primary and that Nakasone would win in a Diet member vote.

But Fukuda, still smarting from his defeat at the hands of Tanaka and Ōhira in 1978, decided to "lend" enough of his faction members to make it possible for another candidate to enter the race. Thus, Nakagawa Ichirō, a rising star on the party's right wing who had formed a small faction of his own, obtained enough signatures to enter the race. A primary was held after all.[33]

The result was an expensive campaign by four candidates in a party that now had an official membership of three million people. Once again the vote was structured closely along factional lines. Nakasone, with the backing of the Tanaka and Suzuki (formerly Ōhira) factions as well as his own, won easily. Kōmoto came in a distant second. Nakasone was then formally elected president in a vote among the party's Diet members. Two years later, in 1984, Nakasone won a second term in office. This time there were no other candidates and no primary. And in 1986 the party decided to extend his term for one additional year. The issue of whether or how to give the party's rank and file an opportunity to vote on this matter never even came up for discussion.

Quite obviously the primary system has not had the impact it was intended to have. It did not open to the public the process of selecting the party president. It did not weaken factions, and it did not lessen the importance of money in deciding who is to lead the party. The reform had a number of important unintended effects, however. It encouraged factions to extend their reach further into the electorate than ever before. It also reinforced other trends that were encouraging factions to increase their memberships. The fifty-member endorsement rule disadvantaged leaders of small factions. And because so much of the primary vote is mobilized by Diet members for their faction leaders, the more faction members a candidate had supporting him, the more votes he could expect to obtain in the primary itself.

However, the most impressive example of public opinion having some influence on the party presidency is provided by Prime Minister Nakasone, the first of the six prime ministers who have come to office since 1972 to remain for more than two years. Nakasone became prime minister in 1982 only because he had the support of the Tanaka faction. Initially he was one of the party's weakest presidents, dependent on the Tanaka faction's support for his survival. But Nakasone became the first LDP leader to convert personal popularity with the electorate and an image of prime ministerial competence into political power within the LDP. He had never been popular with other political leaders in his own party, and it is highly unlikely that he would have been elected to a second term in 1984 or had his term extended in 1986 for an additional year were it not for his popularity among the general public and the enormous electoral success he enjoyed in the summer 1986 general elections.

Nakasone also used his time in office to convert prime ministerial power into party power in a very concrete way. As prime minister, he was able to attract to his faction many new Diet candidates and Diet members who had been unaffiliated or were in the very small factional groups that disappeared in the early 1980s. His faction numbered fifty-two members in 1981, a year before his appointment as prime minister, and was the fourth largest in the party (behind Tanaka, Suzuki, and Fukuda). After the 1986 general election, the Nakasone faction had eighty-seven members, ranking it second only to the Tanaka faction in terms of lower house members and just slightly behind the Miyazawa faction in total numbers.

If the choice of the prime minister—or at least the LDP's decision as to how long to allow the person who becomes prime minister to occupy that office—is responsive to public opinion, it not only follows that a popular prime minister like Nakasone can stay in office despite his relative factional weakness, but that unpopular prime ministers can be driven out of office regardless of their factional strength.

Nakasone's ability to win two and a half terms doesn't necessarily herald a new period of leadership stability. Quite to the contrary, if Nakasone's popularity had much to do with his "presidential" and take-charge leadership style, there may be a return to rapid turnover among his successors, all of whom are cut out of a more traditional Japanese mold.

Policymaking and the LDP

The longer the LDP has been in power, the greater has become its involvement in policymaking. This reality is now widely noted and commented upon by Japanese and foreign observers of the Japanese political scene, and various reasons are being offered for why this should be the case. Indeed it has become so much the fashion to emphasize the LDP's recently expanded policy role that there is some danger of forgetting that the LDP has always played important roles in government decision making and that the bureaucracy continues to be an extraordinarily powerful player in the policy process.

The LDP has played the central role for years in setting the framework for the formulation of policy, articulating national goals and policy priorities and helping build a national consensus behind them. This is a function that the Japanese bureaucracy, with its deep-seated sectionalism and conflicting ministerial interests, has not been able to perform when the issue has involved broad national goals that cut across ministerial jurisdictions.

The LDP has also found itself having to play a central role in making decisions on a wide range of critical or crisis issues to overcome the bureaucracy's innate inclination toward caution and procrastination. The most obvious examples have concerned major issues of foreign policy: Hatoyama's decision to normalize relations with the Soviet Union in 1956; Kishi's decision to renegotiate and then push through the Diet a revision of the U.S.-Japan Security Treaty in 1960; Tanaka's decision to normalize relations quickly with the People's Republic of China in 1972, to name just a few. These were all decisions emanating from the political, not the bureaucratic, leadership.

Since the early 1970s, as trade issues became increasingly heated political issues in Japan's relations with the United States and other countries, the LDP has found itself increasingly involved in a wide range of economic policy decisions, from forging compromises on issues involving specific sectors such as textiles, steel, and automobiles, to formulating "packages" to liberalize the Japanese economy. And since the mid-seventies, when the national consensus on the priority of GNP growth unraveled and growth itself slowed, the LDP has been an important participant in policymaking over a wide range of domestic policy issues as well, ranging from tax policy to environmental protection legislation.

In the years prior to the first oil shock of 1973, however, involvement in policymaking for all but a handful of the most senior LDP politicians, who for the most part were former high-ranking bureaucrats before entering the political world, was mainly confined to activities aimed at securing benefits of a direct, pork-barreling kind for their constituents. Because the economy was growing so rapidly, LDP politicians were able to obtain these benefits by relying on small shares of an ever-expanding budget pie. They focused their attention on "revival negotiations," a highly publicized set of negotiations between party leaders and the Ministry of Finance in which the LDP invariably was successful in reviving some programs that the MOF had cut. In the end, however, this bargaining resulted in a total budget expenditure that was kept within the limits set by MOF in its initial budget draft.[34]

LDP politicians were also adept at directing the flow of government expenditures for agriculture and for highway and bridge construction to their constituencies. The *sensei* in the Diet, the honorific title with which Diet members are addressed, behaved as their districts' most senior *local* politicians, largely unconcerned with issues that could not be translated directly into votes or political money. They were not involved in formulating policy to any great extent, or even, for that matter—with notable exceptions such as Tanaka Kakuei—in determining how much money would go to particular prefectures. But they were often at the center of decisions as to where within the prefecture certain funds should go, or what companies should obtain government construction contracts.[35]

Even in this early period of LDP rule, however, the flow of influence and power between the bureaucracy and the LDP was not as simple or one-way as is commonly assumed. This is true even for matters of industrial policy where bureaucratic power was particularly strong. Clearly the bureaucracy, the Ministry of International Trade and Industry (MITI) in particular, played a central role in formulating government policy. But there had to be a considerable amount of anticipatory reaction underlying bureaucratic behavior. The bureaucracy had nothing to gain by alienating the LDP. The postwar constitution gave to the Diet, and thus to the LDP which controlled it, the ultimate power to force the bureaucracy to do as it wished. Bureaucrats were keenly aware of this basic change from the prewar period in the formal rules of the game; they understood LDP policy objectives, and they knew that by incorporating party interests into their policy proposals they could retain a considerable degree of autonomy. Accordingly, the bureaucracy was responsive to LDP needs without necessarily having to be ordered to be.

The LDP, for its part, also had much to gain from avoiding direct confrontation with the bureaucracy. It had little policy expertise of its own, except for that of former high-ranking bureaucrats themselves, and it was keenly aware that Japan's bureaucrats, with their reputation for competence and their confidence in their own abilities intact, were fully capable of sabotaging LDP policies that they were determined to oppose.

But overt LDP intervention in the policy process has increased over time, and that quantitative increase has brought about a qualitative change in the party's role. The LDP not only continues to be a major actor in making critical decisions relating to foreign policy; it has also become a major force in the formulation of a wide range of other government policies that in earlier years were largely treated as issues best left in the hands of bureaucrats.

The LDP has not only become more deeply involved than before in all aspects of the budget process, but it has come to intervene much more directly and aggressively in many policy questions that are not budget-related or are tied only indirectly to budgeting decisions. Such involvement has concerned issues as varied and as exotic, in terms of the LDP's historical experience in decision making, as legislation to protect intellectual properties or to regulate a newly privatized telecommunications industry. In December 1984 seventy-two members of the LDP formed a Diet Members League for the Promotion of an International Market in connection with Ministry of Finance plans to create an offshore banking facility. In an earlier phase of LDP dominance, few Diet members except for some alumni of the MOF would have understood what the issue meant, much less have seen a need to get involved in it. But in the mid-1980s, financial liberalization and internationalization were intensely political issues. In this particular case, LDP involvement appears to have been sparked mainly by the desire of local banks to secure opportunities through the offshore banking facility to get involved in international financial transactions, an area that had heretofore been dominated by the major city banks.[36]

A number of factors have contributed to this expanded LDP involvement in public policy decision making. The end of budget growth is surely one of the most important. It has forced the LDP to go to the budget bone, as it were, rather than simply live off the fat.

A general decline in bureaucratic authority is another. The bureaucracy was particularly powerful in the 1950s and 1960s, when the national consensus on the desirability of rapid GNP growth over and above all else was so overwhelming that many issues that in other countries were intensely political were treated in Japan largely as matters of administrative decision. The Japanese continue to place a high value on economic growth, but the willingness to give absolute priority to policies aimed at raising the GNP has come to be qualified by a concern about pollution, urban crowding, and other social costs of rapid growth, and by a greater interest in quality-of-life issues, including such things as medical care, retirement pensions, and parks and recreational facilities. Questions of how the country should grow and for what purposes, in other words, have become highly politicized issues demanding a political response that the bureaucracy is incapable of providing.

Bureaucratic power has also been weakened by the liberalization of the Japanese economy. This has removed or lessened many formal levers of bureaucratic authority and, inasmuch as liberalization involves issues of tremendous political sensitivity both domestically and in Japan's relations with her trading partners, it has forced the LDP to involve itself in a whole range of complex economic decisions.

Bureaucratic institutions, however, remain powerful and to a considerable degree autonomous actors in decision making, in part because the only political appointees in Japanese ministries are the minister and parliamentary vice minister, and because political leaders get involved only rarely in making personnel decisions within the bureaucracy. This clearly insulates the bureaucracy from political pressures in a way that is unimaginable in a country like the United States. At the same time, however, close relations between high-ranking bureaucrats and Diet members are essential in order to facilitate the policy process. At one level these linkages are manifested in a Japanese version of what are sometimes referred to in the United States as iron triangles of politicians, bureaucrats, and interest groups allied in the pursuit of certain policy goals in competition with other iron triangles. But it is also manifested in a powerful bias in favor of compromise among the top bureaucratic and political decision makers.

The pattern of decision making that has evolved in Japan combines heated competition between individual LDP Diet members for the government's scarce resources with an acceptance by them of the need to contain their competition within the macrobudgeting framework and the priorities established by the party's leadership and the bureaucratic elite. The result is a kind of contained competition in which backbenchers and the party's policy "tribes," the *zoku*, compete for opportunities to service their constituents within boundaries set by the country's top political and bureaucratic leadership.

These characteristics of the party-bureaucracy relationship render beside the point much of the debate between those who argue bureaucratic dominance or LDP dominance. The bureaucracy is not strong enough to ignore the party in power, nor is the dominant party so powerful that it can force-feed the bureaucracy its policy preferences. Important characteristics of the Japanese system, which have become more pronounced over the years of LDP dominance, have been the propensities of both party and bureaucracy to accept the legitimacy of the other's playing a central role in decision making and to develop close party-bureaucratic linkages.

An increased role for LDP Diet members in decision making has coincided with the quite striking disaggregation, or fragmentation, of interest group activities that has been part and parcel of a growing pluralism in Japanese society. Large umbrella-like organizations, whether the business community's Keidanren or the farmers' Nōkyō, have been losing influence relative to more interest-specific groups or to ad hoc groupings within the larger organizations. The disaggregation of farmer demands and the relative weakening of Nōkyō have been noted in a previous chapter. The offshore banking facility issue points to an important fragmenting of interest articulation by the banking community. The major city banks, trust banks, and small local banks each have distinctly different interests which they seek to protect and maximize through the political system. Keidanren has not incorporated the new rich provincial businessmen—the real estate dealers and building trades entrepreneurs who have come to exercise enormous political influence. And while Keidanren continues to represent big-business interests overall, more important to the exercise of political influence are industrial sector groupings and powerful individual corporations, many of which have "our *sensei*" in the LDP.

The ability of LDP members to infiltrate the decision-making system as much as they have derives in part from the fact that many politicians who have been in the Diet for twenty or thirty years have developed both policy expertise in certain areas and close personal relationships with bureaucrats and relevant interest groups. This increase in policy expertise among the longtime Diet members who do not come from a bureaucratic background is an important factor in accounting for the decreased salience of the former bureaucrat/nonbureaucrat division in the party.

The increase in policy expertise among LDP Diet members, however, is not fully accounted for by the long years many of them have been in office. The LDP has always had its policy experts, although they tended to be dominated by former high-ranking Ministry of Finance officials on the one hand and representatives of agricultural interests on the other. And there still are LDP politicians whose interest in policy issues never rises above the most obvious pork barrel opportunities.

There is no simple correlation between length of time served in the Diet and interest in policy issues (though there is of course an enormous difference in influence depending on how senior a member is). Interest in policy issues that transcend constituency boundaries seems particularly high among new LDP Diet members. This cannot be explained by length of service, but is rather the manifestation of a more basic change in Japan's political leadership culture. Because of the LDP's increased role in governmental decision making, policy expertise has acquired a new importance in demonstrating leadership potential. And, in addition to all else,

LDP politicians are more interested and involved in policy issues in part because they believe that this is how politicians in a virtually permanently ensconced ruling party in a democratic society should behave.

The increased intervention of LDP Diet members in the policy process has drawn considerable attention to the party's policy affairs research council. On paper, the PARC is an elaborate organization with a multitude of divisions (*bukai*), commissions, special committees, project teams, and so on.[37] The most important are the divisions and the commissions. In 1987 there were thirty-two commissions and seventeen divisions. Commissions are usually headed by senior people in the party and are supposed to deal with broad, basic policy questions rather than with specific pieces of legislation. Some commissions, most notably the commission on the tax system, have secured strategic positions in the government's overall decision-making structure.[38]

Bukai, the divisions of the PARC, correspond to ministries and Diet standing committees. If there is anything comparable to the American congressional committee in the Japanese decision-making system, it is the division and not the Diet's committees. The division provides the setting in which LDP politicians can have an impact on the formulation of legislation; by the time a bill gets to the Diet, that work is done.

But to compare the divisions to congressional committees is to exaggerate their importance. Unlike congressional committees, divisions have no staff of experts to help them formulate new policies; their major source of expertise is the bureaucracy itself. Moreover, since Japan has a parliamentary system rather than the American system of a separation of legislative and executive powers, almost all legislation is written by the government (i.e., the bureaucracy) in the form of cabinet bills. Nor are divisions organized in a way that would permit many of their members to play a meaningful role in making decisions. They are extremely large. Small ones have forty members or so; large ones number well over a hundred members.

The divisions and the commissions perform at least three important functions. First, they are important in educating Diet members about policy issues. This is particularly true for the division. Occasionally an LDP politician on the way to a division meeting will remark that he is going off to "study" a particular issue. This is not false modesty. Division meetings offer relatively inexperienced politicians a chance to be briefed on important issues. If the politician is serious and ambitious, he may then seek further contact with the young bureaucrats who participate in these meetings and begin to develop a network of relationships.

A second function of the divisions is to help Diet members convince their constituents that they are doing something significant on behalf of their interests. Once a politician becomes a division chairman, he is generally regarded as a person of real influence. For the party's young backbenchers, what one learns at the division at least provides grist for speeches back home and an opportunity to claim involvement in policymaking.

A third function is to provide strategic institutional positions, through division and commission chairmanships and vice chairmanships, from which LDP politicians are able to enter the decision-making system. Legislation must be approved by the divisions, and the support of the relevant commission is essential to forming the consensus necessary to initiate a new policy thrust. Thus a leadership role in the PARC's committees has become a major avenue for the exercise of *zoku* power.

Zoku is a term that has become popular since the 1970s to describe Diet members who have a considerable amount of expertise and practical experience about a particular area of government policy and enough seniority in the party to have influence on a continuing basis with the ministry responsible for that policy area. The term means "tribe," and it is used to refer both to individuals and to groups of similar individuals. Usually excluded from the *zoku* category are junior Diet members, who may have an interest in a particular area of policy but not enough seniority to have much influence, and the party's most senior leaders, whose leadership extends across the full spectrum of policy issues.

There are definitional problems because *zoku* are not organizations like factions, and there are no generally accepted rules for determining when people become *zoku* or when they "graduate" from this status. The problem of defining *zoku* is compounded by the fact that the concept itself has undergone significant change over the decade or so that it has been in general use. Initially *zoku* were defined in terms of the ministries over which they exercised their influence. The "big three" *zoku* groups were in construction (*kensetsu zoku*), agriculture (*nōrin zoku*), and commerce (*shōkō zoku*). There were also education *zoku* (*bunkyō zoku*), transportation *zoku* (*un'yu zoku*), defense *zoku* (*bōei zoku*), and so on. These terms are still used, but *zoku* have become increasingly specialized, concentrating their activities not only on a specific ministry but on a narrow issue area within that ministry's purview. Thus there are politicians who are known as tobacco *zoku* and others who are air transportation *zoku* (*kōkū zoku*) or telecommunications *zoku* (*tsūshin zoku*). Former Prime Minister Suzuki, even though he is part of a group that is generally regarded as being above *zoku* status, is still the party's preeminent fisheries *zoku* (*suisan zoku*). And at least one LDP Diet member has the reputation of being a powerful sewage *zoku* (*gesui zoku*).

Whatever the definitional problems, however, the term *zoku* points to important features of the LDP and of the Japanese government's decision-making processes, namely, the increasing number of LDP Diet members who are involved in policy decisions, and the tendency for them to concentrate their intervention in particular ministries where they command some expertise and good personal connections.

Zoku align with bureaucrats and interest groups, in a kind of Japanese version of the iron triangle mentioned earlier, to secure government resources for their policy objectives. But the iron triangle analogy should not be carried too far. *Zoku* also play an autonomous role vis-à-vis the two other corners of the triangle, trying to find areas of compromise between what interest groups want and what the government is prepared to give. *Zoku*, after all, have to maintain their relationships for many years if they are going to continue to be effective. If they promise more to interest groups than they can deliver, they quickly lose their credibility with these organizations; and if they force the bureaucracy to do more than the bureaucrats believe is reasonable, they may enjoy a one-shot victory but they undermine the personal bureaucratic relationships that are essential to their long-run effectiveness. Also, in the Japanese pattern of contained competition, PARC leaders play an important role in forging compromises between competing bureaucrat-*zoku* alliances. It is because of this mediating role that the LDP's *seimu chōsakai*, the PARC, is sometimes jocularly referred to in Japanese as the party's *seimu chōseikai*, "the group that adjusts policy differences."

Over thirty years the LDP has been transformed from a "coalition of factions" to a much more complex, differentiated institution which has clear rules regulating the recruitment of leaders and which plays varied and important roles in making public policy. It has also developed a relationship with the bureaucracy that has become increasingly close. One consequence of this is that the political opposition has been deprived of the opportunity to exploit bureaucratic-LDP differences and has been largely unable to utilize the bureaucracy's expertise. Thus the evolution of the LDP and the development of its relationships with the bureaucracy have contributed to a situation in which the JSP and other opposition parties are at a virtual loss for ways to mount an effective challenge to LDP dominance.

4.

THE JAPAN SOCIALIST PARTY: PERPETUAL OPPOSITION

Amidst all of the changes that have occurred in Japanese politics over the past thirty years, one of the most profound has been the decline of the Japan Socialist party. In the early years of LDP rule, the JSP was a powerful and seemingly growing party. It had the support of a large number of the young, well-educated urban electorate as well as of organized blue-collar workers, precisely those constituencies whose numbers were being rapidly increased by Japan's rush toward industrialization.

Seen as the party of the future by many of the politically ambitious, it was able to draw on a relatively large pool of talent for its Diet candidates. Union leaders accounted for less than 30 percent of JSP candidates elected in the first postmerger lower house election in 1958. Local professional politicians, lawyers, journalists, and a number of high-ranking national government bureaucrats who saw the JSP as a vehicle to national political power also populated its Diet member contingent.[1]

Two decades later, however, political recruitment in

the JSP was channeled almost entirely through that part of the union movement organized into the Sōhyō union federation. As the JSP's popularity declined and the possibility of its coming to power receded, aspirants for political power gravitated more and more to the LDP, while the Socialists turned increasingly to Sōhyō unions to provide candidates who could appeal to union loyalties for votes and rely on union organization for financial support and organizational backbone.

Increasing dependence on unions in the Sōhyō federation helped accelerate the JSP's decline in popularity among voters in urban Japan. Sōhyō unions are strongest in the public sector: among teachers, railway workers, postal office workers, and local government employees in particular. These unions can provide fairly powerful campaign machines in the relatively small constituencies of semiurban and rural Japan where their members enjoy extensive community ties and, in the case of public school teachers in particular, are part of the local social elite; they can support candidates there better than they can among the more anonymous, less easily mobilized voters of Japan's large urban and metropolitan election districts. By relying so heavily on Sōhyō, the JSP by the 1970s was no longer a predominantly urban party. In the 1976 lower house election, for example, it won 60 percent of its seats in semiurban and rural districts. Only 26 percent of its lower house members were elected in urban districts and just 14 percent in metropolitan ones. In Tokyo the JSP's share of the popular vote in 1976 was only 17.2 percent, compared to 27.1 percent a decade earlier.

The JSP's importance in influencing the agenda of politics radically declined as public interest in the issues that formed the heart of its initial appeal waned. JSP popularity derived almost entirely from its opposition to constitutional revision, to any turning away from the democratizing reforms that had been introduced during the early postwar years when Japan was under American Occupation, and from its opposition to rearmament and to the U.S.-Japan Security Treaty.

But over time, as the constitution remained un-amended and as democratic reforms came to be accepted as commonplace in Japanese life, the urgency of the JSP plea for defense of the "Peace constitution" faded. Furthermore, concern that military alliance with the United States might involve Japan in wars of American making were allayed by a growing sense that alliance with the United States was a positive factor in providing for Japanese security and that it did so in a way that enabled Japan to avoid major rear-mament; this concern was also lessened by U.S. rapproche-ment with China. The latter came as an enormous blow to the large pro-Peking wing of the JSP, which had long main-tained that the Security Treaty made it impossible for Japan to have normal relations with the Chinese and threatened to involve Japan in war between the United States and China.

The JSP's support of socialism had always been a muted element in the party's public appeal; it would have been more appropriately labeled the "Japan Peace party." But as public interest in the party's positions on the con-stitution and rearmament sagged, the JSP's internal argu-ments over socialist ideology not only became more intense but became a more prominent part of the party's public face. Predictions of the inevitable collapse of the capitalist world order and the crisis awaiting the Japanese economy sounded increasingly quaint and irrelevant to a society enjoying the fruits of rapid economic growth. Ideological conflict within the party intensified as public support declined, each de-velopment reinforcing the other.

This decline in the fortunes of the Japan Socialist party was hardly anticipated in the late 1950s. The JSP obtained 32.9 percent of the vote in the 1958 lower house election, a slightly higher percentage than the 31.9 percent the larger and much longer established Social Democratic party of West Germany had won in the previous year's Bundestag elec-tion. In both Germany and Japan these centers of political party opposition seemed poised to break through the "one-third barrier" in parliamentary seats, an expression that was of popular currency in both countries at the time.

An American student of the history of the Japanese socialist movement, George Totten, reflected the common view, and the optimism of Japanese progressives in the late fifties, when he wrote in the opening pages of his book on the prewar socialist movement in Japan that "a movement can come back to life again and rise from its own ashes. . . . This time the feeling is that [the Socialists] will inevitably reach power, a goal that has sometimes seemed close at hand only to recede frustratingly into the future again."[2]

The somewhat curious thought that something might "recede" into the future rather than into the past captured the mood of the time. Power had so far eluded the JSP's grasp, but history appeared to be on its side. It rode atop a number of popular mass movements: against nuclear weapons, constitutional revision, a teacher rating system, and the Security Treaty, the last being a movement that was to climax in the massive antitreaty protests of 1960. And, though considerably smaller than the LDP, the JSP drew its support from a more diverse constituency.

Figure 4.1 compares the support structure of the LDP and of the JSP in 1955. In that year, according to *Asahi Shinbun* survey data, fully 68 percent of LDP supporters came from the traditional sector of farmers and owners of small businesses. Only 13 percent of the party's supporters were white-collar workers, and another 15 percent were blue-collar workers.

The JSP, by contrast, drew its support much more widely across occupational groups. Blue-collar workers provided a third of the JSP's support. Another quarter came from white-collar workers. Farmers, reflecting the popularity of a number of JSP Dietmen who had been active in the tenant farmer movement before the war, contributed another quarter of JSP support, while owners of small businesses and merchants accounted for 13 percent. In the mid-1950s, in other words, the JSP had the qualities of a small "catch-all" party, with a reach that was wider than the LDP's and that was deepest among those groups—blue-collar workers and white-collar salarymen in large industry—whose numbers were being increased by the growth of the Japanese economy.

The view that time would help the Socialists and hurt the conservatives was not simply a manifestation of Socialist wishful thinking; it was shared by many conservative politicians as well. As late as 1963 one of the LDP's then popular leaders, Ishida Hirohide, argued in a famous article in the journal *Chūō Kōron* that current trends, by spreading higher education among the masses and forcing wide-reaching changes in the occupational structure, would un-

FIGURE 4.1. Distribution of LDP and JSP Support by Occupational Category, 1955

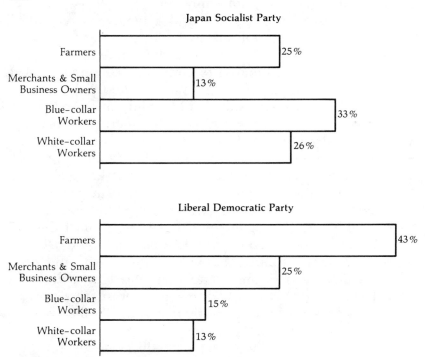

SOURCE: From data in Asahi Shinbunsha Yoron Chōsashitsu, *Nihonjin No Seiji Ishiki.*

dercut the LDP's traditional bases of support and bring the Socialists to power within the decade.[3]

Ishida's prediction was entirely on the mark insofar as LDP electoral support was concerned. He predicted that if an election were held in 1968, the LDP would get 46.6 percent of the vote and the Socialists slightly more than the LDP. In the actual election held a year later, the LDP won 47.6 percent. But Ishida and others failed to anticipate how ineffective would be the Socialists' response to the economic and social changes being produced by double-digit growth, large-scale internal migration, and other effects of Japan's economic miracle. JSP popular support shrank from 32.9 percent in the 1958 election to 21.4 percent in 1969. Even adding the vote for the Democratic Socialist party, the total Socialist vote came to only 29.1 percent in the year when Ishida foresaw the possibility of the head of the Socialist party moving into the prime minister's residence.

After decades of decline and a tenacious refusal to adapt its policy prescriptions to Japan's changed circumstances, the JSP in 1986 adopted a new statement of purpose, one that was intended to convince the public that it had put old-fashioned Marxism and outdated policy issues behind it.[4] Its chairman, Ishibashi Masashi, declared that he now presided over a "New JSP." But the party had become so bereft of attractive leadership and of new ideas, and so weakened by a decade and more of bitter, debilitating ideological and factional strife, that the announced arrival of the New JSP did little either to lift the spirits of a profoundly demoralized party or to spark a revival of public enthusiasm for it. The New JSP slogan could not hide the fact that by the early 1980s the Socialist party had become the most conservative of Japan's parties, unable to break with old policies or articulate new ones, and dominated by politicians who, lacking any hope of capturing governmental power, set their sights on little more than getting themselves reelected.

If the LDP's ability to retain political power through three decades of massive social changes is a story of adaptability deriving from the determination to win, the JSP's decline and loss of its erstwhile position as the dominant force in the opposition camp is a story of inability to adapt to change. There are many reasons for the JSP's inability to adapt to its changing environment, but their roots are to be found both in the structure of the postwar LDP-dominated political system and in the prewar history of the Japanese socialist movement.

The Enervating Impact of Permanent Opposition

The JSP's status as Japan's permanent opposition has had a cumulative, enervating impact on the party. It has also had a devastatingly corrupting influence. As JSP leaders have seen the chances of their party coming to power slip through their fingers, their efforts have become increasingly centered on securing a role for themselves and benefits for their supporters within a system of one-party dominance. This has led to an ever-widening gap between the party's rhetoric and its actual behavior, or to use Japanese terms, between the party's *tatemae,* its stated principles and ostensible policies, and its *honne,* its real intentions.

On the surface, the JSP has been an antisystem party, committed not only to expelling the LDP from power, but to fundamentally reorganizing Japan's political and economic system. But in practice the JSP has used its contacts with the LDP leadership to secure benefits for its supporters, operating as a lobby for public sector unions and its other supporting constituencies. The LDP, in turn, has tried to satisfy some of the JSP's demands as a way to avoid forcing it to act more in accordance with the antisystem stance embedded in its rhetoric.

But this relationship with the LDP, because it violates so basically the JSP's *tatemae,* is maintained by under-the-table deals rather than by overt compromise. For the LDP, giving the JSP small payoffs is a small price to pay for Socialist restraint in obstructing the legislative process. These payoffs need not necessarily be financial, or corrupt in a legal sense. They often involve things like working out the timing of a Socialist walkout from the Diet in protest of some LDP proposal, or agreeing not to ram through one bill in exchange for Socialist agreement to let others come up for a vote.

This relationship, and long years in opposition, have enabled several JSP Diet members to develop considerable lobbying skills that depend in effect on covert access to those who have political power. There are Socialist *zoku* just as there are *zoku* in the LDP. It is a fairly common practice for Socialist Dietmen to get themselves reappointed to the same Diet committee session after session. This gives them some access to bureaucratic expertise that is otherwise not widely available to them, and it enables them to develop their own expertise and personal relationships with relevant bureaucrats, interest groups, and LDP leaders. Thus, a longtime JSP member of the Budget Committee can boast in private conversation of his close ties with bankers and with senior Ministry of Finance bureaucrats with whom he has dealt since they were young section chiefs. And the party's agriculture *zoku* can help a supplicant for government assistance get a hearing with someone in the Agricultural Ministry, much as an LDP politician can.

Japanese bureaucrats are prohibited by law from joining political parties, which imposes upon them a formal position of political neutrality that means that in effect they serve the party or parties that control the cabinet and are in charge of the government. As a result the JSP has not been able to develop its own major independent channels of access to bureaucratic expertise and influence. To a considerable extent Socialists must depend on the goodwill of the LDP to make their lobbying efforts pay off. To be in such a position of dependence on the ruling party, while maintaining a stance of adamant and uncompromising opposition to it, is fundamentally and unavoidably corrupting.

Permanent opposition status has also spawned an enormous amount of cynicism among those in the party who hold elective office and who have come to believe that they are elected in spite of the party, not because of it. This has made the party mainly an arena for power struggles, the bitterness of which is only exacerbated by the fact that party power is the only power for which these politicians ever expect to compete.

With no hope of coming to power, there is little motivation for taking an active part in the party's policy formation process or its organizational building efforts. The Socialist party's parallel organization to the LDP's policy affairs research council, the policy affairs council (Seisaku Shingikai), is largely under the control of party headquarter bureaucrats and a few activist Diet members. To the extent that Dietman get deeply involved in the policy process, they do so through the Diet committees on which they sit. The party organization is left almost entirely in the hands of left-wing party activists.

Over time, this has become increasingly the case as JSP Diet members have accepted the permanence of their party's opposition status and focused their attention on nurturing their own local personal support organizations. By the early 1970s many of them did not bother to get their local constituency associations to choose them as voting delegates to the party congress. Diet members were brought back into playing an active role in the party congress only by the near success in the mid-1970s of the attempt by the party's Marxist-Leninist fraction, the Shakaishugi Kyōkai (Socialist Association), to use its voting power in the party congress to control selection of the party's leadership.

Permanent opposition, in other words, has encouraged a large degree of irresponsibility among the JSP's leadership. Knowledge that it will never have to act on the policy proposals it puts forth has encouraged the party to take extreme positions and has created almost no incentives for it to try to construct new and realistic ones. With an absence of perceived incentives for the party to change, permanent opposition has in Japan generated its own self-reinforcing mechanism.

But the particular patterns of organization, rhetoric, and behavior that have characterized the Japan Socialist party, as well as its failure to mount an effective challenge to LDP hegemony, are not solely the result of the cumulative, enervating impact of permanent opposition status. They also have roots in the proletarian movement of the prewar period and in the timing of the emergence of socialism as the major ideology embraced by Japan's opposition parties.

The JSP's Historical Legacy

Both the LDP and the JSP have clear links to parties that existed in prewar Japan, the LDP with the Seiyūkai and other prewar conservative parties, and the JSP with the noncommunist proletarian parties (*musan seitō*) that became active upon the adoption of universal manhood suffrage in 1925. But the conservatives, many of whom had been leaders in the prewar parties, did not let their prewar factional rivalries or their desire to amend the Occupation-imposed constitution to restore some of the elements of the prewar constitutional order deflect their attention from the primary tasks of winning elections and running the government.

The Socialists, however, remained preoccupied with the factional and ideological disputes that had raged in the prewar period. Many Socialist leaders were singularly unable to discard their self-image as leaders of a movement dedicated to Japan's revolutionary transformation. Their inability to do so was due in part to the fact that they did not play a major role in bringing about postwar democratic reforms. The American Occupation forced upon Japan the kinds of political reforms that in other countries were the result of years of domestic political struggle. Neither could they claim to have played a heroic role in opposing militarism in the prewar or wartime period. There was no organized Resistance in wartime Japan, and many of the leaders of the socialist movement were enthusiastic supporters of state socialism.

Deprived of the opportunity to play a major role in bringing about democratization, and coming out of a recent history of collaboration with the wartime government, Socialist leaders continued to be preoccupied to an extraordinary degree with the need to pursue political "struggles" and to give voice to the party's revolutionary traditions. Total opposition was the stance most consistent with what the Socialists wished their self-image to be.

The reluctance of party leaders to part with the ideological traditions of the prewar period is also linked to the early history of the Japanese socialist movement. Although the total number of people involved in the movement was exceedingly small, there quickly developed any number of splits along ideological and personal lines. A postcard published by the Heiminsha in celebration of its first anniversary in 1905 is indicative of the potpourri of ideas that were vying for support among Japan's socialist intellectuals at the time.[5] The card carried sketches of Marx, Engels, Lasalle, Bebel, Tolstoy, and Kropotkin.[6] In doing so it reflected, in particular, the strong influence on these early Japanese socialists not just of German Marxism but of Russian anarchism as well.

Preoccupation with the theology of socialist thought was perhaps unavoidable, inasmuch as socialist activists in these early years of the twentieth century were almost all intellectuals who had virtually no contact with the workers whose interests they were claiming to represent and no large organized labor movement with which to interact. Japan, of course, was not unique in having intellectuals occupy important positions in leftist parties.[7] But in Japan they exercised a virtual monopoly within the early socialist parties. These intellectual leaders had little contact either with workers or with those few union organizers who were trying to create a union movement.

Writing in the 1950s and looking back on the early socialist movement, Yamakawa Hitoshi, one of the founding fathers of the Communist party and later the leading figure in the Rōnōha, which became a major stream within the noncommunist left, noted that he and others active in the socialist movement would make speeches in which they would begin with the phrase "we workers." But "looking back on it, none were workers." A Socialist party was formed in 1906 (and quickly disbanded by the government), but it had almost no working class people in it. "It was mainly made up of middle class youth who did not have to worry about losing their means of livelihood even if the police came to get them two or three times."[8] If he could live over again, Yamakawa wrote in his autobiography, he would act differently, concentrating his energies on building a labor movement and trying to deal with the daily problems of ordinary workers. As it was, the socialists "raised their socialist red flags too early and were treated as outcasts by the government and ordinary citizens alike."[9]

Although it was pitifully small, this early socialist movement did have an impact on the postwar Japan Socialist party. For one thing, it left a legacy of a deeply pacifist and reformist Christian socialism. Five of the six founders of the first socialist party in Japan, the 1902 Social Democratic party (Shakai Minshutō), were Christians. One of them, Abe Isoo, at the age of eighty was one of the three elder statesmen of the socialist movement who issued the call for the formation of the JSP in the weeks following the end of the Second World War.[10] The emphasis on social reform and pacifism that characterized Christian socialism in the early part of the century were carried over into the postwar JSP by several leaders on the right and center who were themselves part of this tradition, including the JSP's only prime minister, Katayama.

The other legacy of the early socialist movement was its contribution to the Socialist party's preoccupation with ideology. Much of the activity of the intellectual study groups that comprised the movement in these early years involved translating socialist texts from European languages and then using these translated texts as weapons to engage in ideological duels with other socialists. Even in 1980 the Socialist party chairman, Asukata Ichio, complained about the penchant for party leaders to engage in a "translation debate" (*hon'yaku ronsō*) largely irrelevant to the Japanese situation. But Asukata was himself a major participant in this translation debate, championing the ideas of French *autogestion* and Yugoslav worker self-management.[11]

But the galvanizing event for the modern socialist movement in Japan was the Russian Revolution. The pre–World War I socialist movement in Japan had been subjected to increasingly severe government suppression, symbolized by the Red Flag incident of 1909,[12] and culminating in the Great Treason incident of 1911.[13] Thus there was virtually no socialist movement in existence in Japan when news of the Russian Revolution reached Japanese shores. This timing is of crucial importance for explaining the postwar JSP's preoccupation with Marxist doctrine, its so-called complex vis-à-vis the communists, its readiness to give rhetorical support to the Leninist concepts of proletarian dictatorship and democratic centralism, and for the particularly pernicious overtones that accompany the word "revisionism" (*kairyōshugi*) in the Japanese socialist lexicon. This timing resulted in a situation in which a major wing of the social democratic left arose out of a schism within the Communist party and over arguments about the correct interpretation of Marxism and Leninism.

In western Europe, the Russian Revolution and the subsequent issuance of Lenin's twenty-one demands (which most importantly called on European socialist parties to accept the authority of the Comintern and to adopt the "Communist Party" as their official name)[14] resulted in the creation of Communist parties out of already existing and in many cases extremely large and powerful socialist parties. In Japan the situation was strikingly, and fatefully, different. Japan's first Communist party, formed in 1922, did not result from a split in an already established socialist movement, but preceded the creation of noncommunist socialist parties.

This is of more than mere historical interest. The ability of French socialism, for example, to survive a succession

of catastrophic defeats and disappointments owes something to the fact that there was a strong socialist tradition
prior to and independent of the Russian Revolution, "one
which had already absorbed and transformed Marx," as
George Lichtheim has written, "before encountering the
challenge of Lenin."[15] But in Japan, as Satō Noboru aptly
put it, "Our country's intellectuals were baptized into socialism at a time when Marxism held an unchallengeable
position of dominance in the international socialist movement, a period when Marxism held a monopoly in the market place of socialist ideas."[16]

   As news of the October Revolution in Russia reached
western Europe, it was widely believed that the new Soviet
regime was a large-scale exercise in syndicalism and that
Marx as practiced by Lenin forged the link between the party
and the syndicalist movement. In Japan the initial interpretation of the revolution as a victory for syndicalism was even
more extreme, since Japanese socialists had almost no exposure to Lenin's writing and much more limited channels
of communication with Russia than their European coun-
terparts. At the same time they had considerable knowledge of Russian anarchism.

   Yamakawa Hitoshi writes that when news of the Russian Revolution first reached Japan he had no idea who Lenin
was. Referred to by Japanese newspaper reports as the
"syndicalist Lenin" or the "Blanquist Lenin," it was only
when a colleague brought back from the United States a
book written by an American on the writings of Lenin and
Trotsky that Yamakawa and other "communist" leaders in
Japan began to learn what Lenin's ideas were.[17] When the
Comintern called for a Japanese delegate to attend a meeting of Far Eastern socialists in Peking, it seemed appropriate that Ōsugi Sakae, Japan's leading anarchist thinker,
should be the one to go. But Ōsugi quickly concluded that
there was no way to unite anarchism and bolshevism. Unlike many others who had been anarchists and changed to
support of communism when the nature of the Revolution

became clear, Ōsugi stuck to his anarchist views, a choice for which he was later to pay with his life.[18]

It should be noted that although it had only a brief history in Japan, anarcho-syndicalism left a considerable impact on the left, particularly in reinforcing an ambivalence about the primacy to be attached to electoral politics, which is one of the most salient features of the JSP. The strength of the syndicalist tradition, in fact, probably has much to do with the similarities one can observe in the orientations of the Japanese and Italian socialist parties.

Many socialists and left-wing labor leaders both before and after the Second World War could not bring themselves to reject completely "direct action" (*chokusetsu kōdō*) extraparliamentary struggles in favor of reformist parliamentarianism. Yamakawa Hitoshi never could shake his lack of enthusiasm for parliamentary action. In his famous 1922 treatise "A Change of Direction for the Proletariat" that marked his break with the Communist party, Yamakawa stressed the isolation of the proletarian movement from the masses and argued that it had to become more practical. But he warned against reformism and putting faith in parliamentarianism and advised that the proletariat should abstain from voting should universal suffrage become a reality.[19]

In contrast to the LDP, which set winning elections as a goal superseding all others, the JSP's ambivalence about its primary goals was manifested from the very beginning of the party's existence and remains evident today. The organizational plan adopted by the party's youth bureau in May 1946, for example, stated:

The organizational unit of the Socialist party at present is the local section. In participating in this unit, workers, farmers, and others abandon their class position and participate as propertyless individuals. . . . This organizational structure may be advantageous for elections but it shows a tendency to separate the party and the masses. . . . On this point, we must recognize that the Communist party is one step ahead of us. . . . We must change our party's course 180 degrees to turn away from government power and toward expanding our roots ever deeper in the masses, the factories, the schools.[20]

This resistance to putting primary emphasis on winning elections echoed the attitudes of the prewar noncommunist proletarian parties. The Japan Labor-Farmer Party (Nihon Rōnōtō) founded by Asō Hisashi in 1926, for example, adopted a statement at its first congress in 1927 that "our party is going to contest [the general election] based on a policy which sees the general election as a good battleground for mobilizing the masses and for exposing the policies of the established political parties. It is definitely not our party's goal to make winning elections our priority concern."[21]

Antipathy toward an unqualified acceptance of the primacy of electoral politics has proven extremely durable. The first action plan of the reunified Socialist party in 1955, for example, called on the party to abolish its "parliamentary centeredness" and to expand its activities among the masses. "We must manage the party," the document declared, "so as not to fall into a pattern of parliamentary centeredness and the primacy of elections."[22]

Shakaishugi E No Michi (The Road to Socialism), a document that was adopted by the JSP in 1964 as an official supplement to its platform, again highlighted the party's ambivalence toward electoral politics. Victory at the polls was recognized as a party objective, but the left wing's insistence on the primacy of extraparliamentary action received the greater emphasis:

Mere involvement in electoral struggles will not only create problems for increasing the party's strength in the Diet but, even if a majority were obtained, it would not be able to establish a stable government. The only road to peaceful revolution is the coalescing of democratic forces in the institutions of society (factories, bureaucracy, media, local government, the military), the emergence of a major political and economic crisis, and the victory of the JSP at the polls.[23]

JSP ambivalence about the primacy of elections does not mean that the party's politicians seriously treat other goals as more important than winning elections. This may be true for parties such as the Communist party, which views elections as but one part of a larger strategy of organization building and political activity. Socialist ambivalence about strategy and goals means that candidates struggle to win elections while the party organization, and the general party ethos, undercut those efforts in the name of a more noble revolutionary struggle.

The resistance of party activists to giving priority to winning elections and the readiness of the party leadership to give support to the rhetoric of direct action are constant sources of complaint from JSP politicians elected to local office. In one typical plea, the national conference of JSP local assemblymen deplored the tendency "in the party's [left wing] to underplay the importance of elections. Victory in elections needs to be established as a goal as important as the antiwar movement and the labor movement."[24]

The Ascendance of the Rōnōha

Another and related consequence of the timing of the emergence of the socialist movement in Japan was the disproportionate influence within the postwar Socialist party exercised by the advocates of Rōnōha Marxism. The Rōnōha (labor-farmer faction) took its name from a journal, Rōnō, founded in 1927 by Yamakawa and others as a vehicle for carrying on an ideological debate with the JCP. The JCP position was represented by the Kōzaha, a name that came from a series of monographs entitled the Nihon Shihonshugi Hattatsushi Kōza (Lectures on the Development of Japanese Capitalism). The Rōnōha never became a political party, nor was it ever a coherent faction within any political party in the prewar period. It was only in the postwar JSP and in the 1970s in particular that the Rōnōha, organized into the Shakaishugi Kyōkai (Socialist Association) and led by Sakisaka Itsurō, a disciple of Yamakawa Hitoshi and one of the early members of the Rōnōha in the 1920s, sought to gain control of the party congress and over the party leadership.

The prewar Rōnōha did not have a completely unified theoretical view, its leaders quickly falling into the nit-picking arguments that consumed the energy of Japanese Marxist intellectuals. But this group, which called its magazine a "journal of orthodox Marxism-Leninism,"[25] differed from the Communists in three important ways insofar as its prescription for political action was concerned. First, it argued that the Meiji Restoration had led to the complete victory of the bourgeoisie and that there was a need, therefore, for a one-stage socialist revolution. This position had the political effect of putting the Rōnōha on the right of the JCP, because it made it possible to argue for revolution without arguing for the overthrow of the emperor system. The Communists argued that the emperor system was the continuance of absolutism and demanded its overthrow as the first stage in a two-stage revolution leading to socialism. By challenging the emperor system, the JCP was forced to operate illegally. The Rōnōha, on the other hand, though it proclaimed allegiance to Marxist-Leninist ideas, was able to operate for a decade as part of the legal left by avoiding an attack on the imperial system.

Second, the Rōnōha called for the creation of a legal united front party that would draw together all anticapitalist groups—the masses of workers and peasants, as well as the lowest stratum of the middle class. Yamakawa drew the phrase "united front" (kyōdō sensen) from the thesis on the United Labor Front adopted by the fourth congress of the Comintern in 1922. But in contrast to the Comintern, which used the term to refer to a united struggle under communist leadership of communist and socialist parties, Yamakawa used it to refer to a single party that would not have a maximum program like the Communist party but rather would be dedicated to protecting the livelihood of the unpropertied masses in the face of the political control of a reactionary bourgeoisie. According to Yamakawa, since the Japanese working class was far from ripe for revolution, there was a necessity for a united front party that would protect the everyday interests of the masses and in so doing raise the masses' level of consciousness.

For Yamakawa such a party was to secure minimal objectives for the working class in a situation of overwhelming bourgeois power; it was not the instrument for overthrowing that power. Thus, Yamakawa's call for a united front party was a call to reject the vanguard approach of the Communist party. But Yamakawa, while rejecting at least for the time being the need to organize a vanguard party, nevertheless remained committed to the idea that there would be a concrete revolutionary transformation to socialism, the definition of which became the third characteristic distinguishing the Rōnōha from the JCP.

The Rōnōha stressed the need for a peaceful revolution, and in so doing gave vent to a romanticized, chiliastic view of Marxism that went far beyond comparable tendencies among European Marxists. Its view was essentially that history would do the work of bringing the revolution about; that the inevitable internal contradictions of capitalism would swell the numbers of the working masses and their antagonism to their bourgeois rulers; that, when the moment was ripe, the masses would rise in all their fury to capture state power. The job of the united front party, it would seem, was mainly to educate the masses and reduce as much as possible their misery as this inevitable historical process unfolded.

The Leninist element in Rōnōha thinking came into play in the process of consolidating the peaceful revolution. Both Yamakawa and even more so his disciple Sakisaka anticipated that the bourgeoisie would launch a massive effort to overthrow the socialist revolution and that the working class would have to respond by establishing a dictatorship of the proletariat and would then have to use all of the resources at the state's command—the militia, the police, the press, educational institutions, and so on—to defend the revolution. Accordingly, the Rōnōha—particularly as represented by the Shakaishugi Kyōkai and Sakisaka—were more ambiguous about the use of violence than their advocacy of "peaceful" revolution suggests. Nonetheless, in terms of their political behavior rather than their theoretical musings, the salient fact was that the Rōnōha and the self-styled Marxist-Leninists who were influential in the postwar JSP rejected the use of violence in the long political process leading up to Japan's eventual revolutionary transformation.

The influence of the Rōnōha on the prewar proletarian parties and on the postwar JSP was much greater than might be gleaned from the number of its official members. The Rōnōha provided the only coherent alternative to the Communist party that could at one and the same time justify legal political action through the united front party and remain committed to revolution and to a Marxist-Leninist orthodoxy. More than any other group or stream of Marxist thought in twentieth-century Japan, the Rōnōha is responsible for that peculiar blend of reformism and radicalism, of romantic Marxism, militant Leninism, and social democratic parliamentarianism that has characterized and befuddled the Japan Socialist party.

In June 1951 Yamakawa Hitoshi and a number of other people identified with Rōnōha Marxism formed the Shakaishugi Kyōkai and a new journal to propagate their ideas titled *Shakaishugi* (Socialism). The Kyōkai embraced a large part of the anti-JCP Marxist left.[26] It quickly became active as a kind of supplier of theoretical arguments for JSP politicians opposed to the reformism of the JSP right and the doctrine of violent revolution then being espoused by the JCP.

In 1953 the Kyōkai leadership had the opportunity for the first time to give expression to Rōnōha ideology in a major party platform. The JSP had split in 1951 into a Right JSP and Left JSP, as noted in an earlier chapter. The latter decided to draft a new basic program and turned to Sakisaka Itsurō to write it. The result, as Sakisaka cheerfully noted, was that "the ideas of the Rōnōha which have since before the war consistently pursued the correct application of Marxism-Leninism to Japan have for the first time become manifested in a party platform."[27]

Sakisaka took over leadership of the Kyōkai upon Yamakawa Hitoshi's death in 1958 and quickly achieved new prominence by the major role he played in the Miike coal strike of 1959.[28] Though a total failure in securing anything the strikers had fought for, the "Miike struggle" holds a position of special importance for the JSP left. The Kyōkai in particular considers it to be more significant than the 1960 *anpo* anti-Security Treaty demonstration in the history of leftist struggles against Japan's monopoly capitalism. Miike was viewed as a model of militant opposition to the rationalization policies of Japan's "monopoly capitalists." Sakisaka, who was from Fukuoka prefecture where the strike took place, spent two years at Miike "arming" the union protesters with Marxist-Leninist ideology. Although it ended in defeat, the strike greatly increased the Kyōkai's strength and Sakisaka's dominance over it.

Sakisaka was much more committed to bringing about a "unity of theory and practice" than his more theoretically inclined mentor Yamakawa had been, and he lost little time in moving the Kyōkai into a politically activist role. At its Third National Conference in August 1961, the Kyōkai called for the unification of Marxist theory and practice and urged its members to be active in the JSP and in building the JSP-affiliated youth organization, Shaseidō. The following year the Kyōkai adopted an action plan for the first time, and in 1963 it established a central executive committee and a system of local activists that made it look more and more like a political party in its own right.

Importantly, the development of the Kyōkai as a coherent organization to give political expression to the ideas of traditional Rōnōha Marxism came about at a time when pressures were building within the JSP and in socialist parties in western Europe to bring their basic programs into line with the new realities of international politics and economic growth. In West Germany this process of redefinition led to the adoption in 1958 of the Bad Godesberg program. In Italy, where the Socialist party (PSI) came closest to the JSP of all European socialist parties in its ideological out-look, policy positions, and tactics, there were also momen-tous changes. After Soviet suppression of the 1956 Hun-garian uprising, PSI chairman Nenni returned the Stalin Peace Price awarded to him in 1951; at the party congress a year later, he stressed his party's full acceptance of democratic parliamentarianism and the existence of a multiparty sys-tem; and in January 1962 the PSI withdrew its objections to Italian membership in NATO. The following year it entered the government for the first time since 1947 with Nenni as deputy prime minister.

But in the Japan Socialist party these pressures for change resulted in a complicated struggle in which factional interests and ideological convictions became hopelessly en-tangled. As a result, the party lost the opportunity to fash-ion a program more relevant to the public issues that were emerging as Japan entered a period of unprecedented afflu-ence. Former allies on the party left became bitter enemies, one group demanding fidelity to the party's traditional ide-ology as represented by Rōnōha Marxism, the other, now identified as being on the party right, calling for change in the name of structural reform. No other single event is as critical in explaining the JSP's decline into a permanent and increasingly weak opposition force than the party's han-dling of this issue of structural reform.

The Rise and Fall of Structural Reform

Structural reform reached Japanese shores around 1957. Its advocates in the JSP particularly liked to point to its genesis in the thinking of Italian Communist party chairman To-gliatti, since this gave it a kind of leftist seal of approval and made it possible for them to argue that they were of-fering a radical alternative, not right-wing revisionism. The basic doctrine of structural reform was quite simple: namely, that over time and by increasing its influence over government, the working class acting through its elected representatives would be able to bring about a change in government structures that would not mean merely the amelioration of the worst excesses of the capitalist system but the actual transformation of that system into socialism.

The theoretical debate over structural reform was protracted but uninspired, and it quickly degenerated into a shouting match between factions struggling for power in the JSP. In keeping with the party's translation debate habits, the *kōkakuha*, as the structural reform group was known, cited Togliatti and the Italian Communists to defend their position while their opponents quoted critics of the Italians such as the French Communist Roger Garaudy.[29] Sakisaka led the ideological attack against the structural reform heresy, arguing that it was nothing other than Bernsteinian revisionism. "Socialists are socialists," Sakisaka insisted, "because of the existence of basic contradictions in capitalism; if capitalism could regulate those contradictions by itself, socialism would lose its reason for existing."[30]

Structural reform became a heated issue in the Communist party as well as in the JSP. Opposition to it by the JCP mainstream led several people to leave the party in the late 1950s. A number of them came over to the JSP to join the group of structural reformers that had emerged there. The JCP's final rejection of structural reform in 1961 resulted in a serious party split and the defection of seven members or candidate members of the party's central committee.

Interest in structural reform in the JSP initially was confined to a small number of intellectuals in the party secretariat and had no particular proponent among the party's elected politicians. But Eda Saburō, an ambitious politician in the left-wing faction of Suzuki Mosaburō, saw structural reform as a vehicle for staking his own claim for leadership and quickly embraced the new doctrine as his own.

In March 1960, after Nishio Suehiro led his supporters out of the JSP to form the Democratic Socialist party, the JSP became engulfed in a bitter struggle for the party chairmanship. The fight was between Kawakami Jōtarō, whose large faction now, with the departure of Nishio, alone represented the non-Marxist, reformist wing of the party, and Asanuma Inejirō, an erstwhile leading lieutenant in the Kawakami faction who was the incumbent secretary-general and who now sought the support of the party's left wing in his attempt to defeat his former faction boss for the party's top post.[31] The party's left-wing factions split, with the faction led by Wada Hiroo supporting Kawakami while the large Suzuki faction threw its support to Asanuma, who narrowly beat out Kawakami.

With all of the publicity being given to the Kawakami-Asanuma fight, little attention was paid to the choice of Eda Saburō as the party's new secretary-general. Eda was a relatively little-known member of the upper house with a background in the farmer union movement and intellectual ties to the Rōnōha group that went back to his membership in one of the prewar proletarian parties, the National Masses party (Zenkoku Taishūtō). His major party posts prior to being selected as secretary-general were as manager of the party's newspaper and chairman of the party's organizational bureau. He made himself popular with party activists in the latter capacity because he instituted reforms that gave them a larger voice in the party congress than they had ever before enjoyed. This particular reform was eventually to come back to haunt Eda, inasmuch as it enabled the Kyōkai, which devoted its energies to building its support among party activists, to take virtual control of the party congress in the mid-1970s and drive Eda out of the party.

In 1960, six months after being elected party chairman and on the eve of a party congress, Asanuma was assassinated. The shocked congress delegates met and then quickly adjourned, doing little more than adopting Secretary-General Eda's report on the party's "new line," which was based on the structural reform theory. At the next party congress, in March 1961, Eda formed an alliance with the Kawakami and Wada factions which resulted in Kawakami becoming chairman and Eda being reappointed secretary-general.

Eda had initially been put forward for the secretary-general position by the Suzuki faction in the belief that he would represent the interests of a faction that Sasaki Kōzō, Suzuki's chosen successor as faction leader, would control. Needless to say, Sasaki was furious at the success of Eda's power play and undertook a counterattack which was conducted largely in the guise of an attack on the theory of structural reform. By the end of 1961, "the structural reform debate was no more simply an issue of party policy," as Shimizu Shinzo has written, "but was transformed into a weapon in a new factional struggle over posts and leadership of the party."[32] At a party congress held in January 1962, Eda tried to deflect the ideological attack by agreeing to a resolution that declared that structural reform was only an important "tactic" in the party's activities and not the party "strategy" for realizing a peaceful revolution. He also agreed to the establishment of a Socialist Theory Committee that was given the task of formulating a new statement of the party's basic line.

During the period between the party congresses held in January and November 1962, Eda announced his Eda Vision, calling for a standard of living comparable to that of the United States, government-sponsored welfare services as advanced as those in the Soviet Union, a system of parliamentary democracy as developed as in Great Britain, and Japan's "Peace constitution." This completed the transformation of structural reform from a theory debated by intellectuals into a political slogan by which Eda hoped to ride to power in the JSP. Structural reform became the rallying cry for a JSP "new look," and Eda, with his shock of white hair and his personal magnetism, became a popular national figure, the first politician in Japanese history to obtain wide popularity through the appealing image he was able to project through television.

Determined to fight off the Eda challenge, Sasaki attacked structural reform and Eda's support of it, accusing him of unprincipled behavior for putting forth a revisionist theory and for creating "misunderstandings among many socialist countries and mak[ing] particularly difficult relations with China" by stressing the importance of maintaining good relations with the United States.[33] Sasaki also attacked Eda's inclination to appeal to the public rather than to the party's rank and file: "The task of the Chairman is not to stir up popularity through television appearances but rather to create an esprit de corps [in the party] . . . and unify party action. Popularity should be the popularity created by the entire organization, not by one individual if it is to propel the party forward."[34]

This criticism of Eda as being self-centered and "un-Japanese" in his leadership style was to be echoed years later in the opinions some LDP leaders expressed about Prime Minister Nakasone. But popularity among the public at least indirectly helped Nakasone stay in power in a party that was concerned about obtaining as much public support as possible; it did not help Eda improve his power position in a party that was prisoner of a rhetoric that demanded "respect [for] the traditions of the fighting party."[35]

The intense factional fighting over the issue of structural reform culminated in the final scrapping of that doctrine by the JSP in 1964. There were two party congresses that year, the first in February and the second in December. At the February congress, the Sasaki faction, seeing that it could not yet get control of the party, removed its candidates from competition for all party posts and moved into a position of being an "inner party opposition," a tactic with a history nearly as long as the party itself.[36] Sasaki turned his attention to repairing his faction's relations with activists on the local level and to building momentum for defeating the right (which now consisted of the Kawakami faction, which had long functioned at the party center; Eda, who was an erstwhile member of the left wing Suzuki-Sasaki faction; and Wada, who prior to Nishio's defection had taken a position on Suzuki's left).

At the December 1964 congress, the Sasaki faction won

majority control of the party's executive council. Kawakami, however, remained as titular head, and Narita Tomomi, who had been a candidate of the structural reform group when he was chosen to replace Eda as secretary-general in November 1962, was retained in that post.[37] This congress also adopted a report of the Socialist Theory Committee that had been established two years earlier which concluded that "structural reform is an excuse for conciliation and retreat in party action, a form of revisionism in the context of economic growth, and is not to be adopted by the party as a party strategy."

Thus was the attempt at ideological redefinition shattered on the battlefield of factional conflict. The congress adopted as an official supplement to the party platform a document prepared by the Socialist Theory Committee. Titled *Shakaishugi E No Michi* (The Road to Socialism), and referred to simply as the *michi* by its supporters, it began by lauding the Soviet system and omitting from its concept of the socialist world any of the countries in western Europe with social democratic governments.[38]

The *michi* tried to find a middle ground between advocacy of a dictatorship of the proletariat and a commitment to pluralistic democracy, though the final formulation came very close to an endorsement of this basic Leninist concept:

It is natural that the proletariat must exercise a form of class rule when it grasps state power in place of the bourgeoisie. . . . But the so-called dictatorship of the proletariat of the Sovet Union or China which experienced violent revolution in all likelihood will be unnecessary in the case of Japan because of its historical and social conditions; it is likely to take the form of something closer to the ideal of socialist democracy.[39]

According to Katsumata Seiichi, who was chairman of the committee that drafted the *michi*, the document did not refer specifically to the dictatorship of the proletariat because it might create misunderstanding: "In the event that the Japanese working class seized state power, there would naturally be class rule by the proletariat. But since the relationship between socialist democracy and proletarian dictatorship invites misunderstanding, the phraseology should be changed." But Katsumata concluded that the difference between the construction of socialism in Japan and in the Soviet Union or China "is not a difference regarding the essence of the dictatorship of the proletariat but a difference in the form and manner of carrying out that function."[40]

The *michi*, as mentioned earlier, vented the traditional ambivalence about parliamentarianism that had long characterized the party. But it also discussed various transitional forms of government that might be created along the road to the socialist revolution, leaving enough stops on the way to satisfy every shade of opinion in the party. On balance, however, it restated the left wing's traditional ideological positions. For the next two decades the Kyōkai successfully rebuffed all efforts to replace it with a less dogmatic statement of the party's philosophy and goals.

The new mainstream coalition was consolidated at a party congress held in May 1965. Kawakami Jōtarō, who resigned as party chairman in March because of illness, was replaced by Sasaki Kōzō, while Narita Tomomi was retained as secretary-general. Narita, having seen the balance of power swing in favor of Sasaki, had quickly moved to consolidate his own power base by allying himself with Sasaki.[41] From then on, Eda became more and more of an outsider in his own party, pushing his Eda Vision and "new socialism" in the 1960s, and the *sha-kō-min* line—i.e., a centrist coalition between the Eda wing of the JSP, the Kōmeitō, and the DSP—in the seventies, until he finally left the party on March 26, 1977 to form the Social Citizens League (Shakai Shimin Rengō).

An important reason for Eda's defeat was the decision by the centrist Katsumata faction, and by individuals like Narita Tomomi who were not members of that faction but were likewise regarded as being in the party center, to throw their support to Sasaki. This development reflected a pattern long evident in the JSP, one in which power has gravitated toward a center that is opportunistic and inclined to form alliances with the left because of leftist strength among activists in the party congress and a tradition of leftist posturing at the national level.

To cite an important example of this pattern, after the 1947 election in which the JSP won 143 Diet seats and emerged as Japan's single largest party, the party's right and left wings were divided over the issue of whether the JSP should lead a coalition government. The right, led by Nishio Suehiro, argued that the JSP should join a coalition led by a conservative prime minister, taking as many cabinet portfolios as possible and setting conditions in terms of specific policy objectives for its participation. The left, led by Suzuki Mosaburō and Katō Kanjū, adamantly opposed participation unless the JSP got the prime ministership. The centrist factions, which held the balance of power, sided with the left. Nishio's comments, written in the 1960s, are worth citing:

At the time, the gentlemen of the centrist factions were always opportunistic, fully committed neither to realism nor theory but going along nonchalantly with the trends of the time and obfuscating the real nature of the issues. It is clear from the subsequent history of the JSP that this has always been a cause of confusion about the party's course.[42]

In the early 1970s a member of the Sasaki faction remarked about the then party chairman Narita, another centrist who had moved steadily to the left in order to retain power, that he was "like an English language typewriter. The more you hit it, the further to the left it goes."[43]

A pattern of organization in which power gravitates toward a center that is fence-sitting and opportunistic is not unique to the Japanese Socialists. Guenther Roth, in his brilliant study of the Social Democratic party in Imperial Germany, put the formula exactly right when he wrote that within a few years of the adoption of the Erfurt Program in 1891,

a permanent right and left wing developed, which made the top leadership "centrist"; this meant that it continued its attempt to

strike a balance between radical rhetoric and moderate practices.
. . . Radicalism in the ranks and the parliamentary goals of the
party forced a conflicting pattern upon the leadership which pre-
scribed, on the one hand, a specific radical rhetoric at the party
convention and, on the other, moderate demands and a more
diffuse rhetoric in parliament and during election campaigns.[44]

The same point is reflected in the formula allegedly coined
by Fujimaki Shinpei, a former official in the JSP headquarters, that "the JSP goes left at the convention and right at
the election," and in another expression popular in Socialist
circles, *chūō saha de jimoto uha*, "left at the [party] center,
right in the constituency."[45]

After the German Social Democratic party (SPD)
adopted the Bad Godesberg Program in 1958, Willy Brandt
commented that it was "a program that represents German
Social democracy in a party that has the courage and the
strength to appear what it is."[46] But the JSP was not able
to screw up its courage for a sharp break with its own past.
For one thing, it lacked the self-confidence of the SPD, the
conviction that a more modern program would substantially
improve the party's electoral appeal.

For all of its ideological posturing, the JSP is remarkably cynical about the electorate's interest in party principles. For many JSP politicians, ideological statements primarily serve the purpose of keeping party militants happy.
They are grist for party congresses, not for public elections.
For JSP Dietmen whose electoral strength is rooted in local
personal bases of support and in the organizational backing
proffered by labor unions, the party's ideology and program are seen as largely irrelevant to their vote-getting ability. There was little reason, therefore, to believe that structural reform would make a difference, except to the factional
struggle for power within the party itself.

Furthermore, in contrast to West Germany where the
organized labor movement threw its support behind the Bad
Godesberg Program, structural reform, and any effort to pull
the JSP into a more realistic stance, was vigorously opposed
by Sōhyō. For Ōta Kaoru and other Sōhyō leaders at the

time, structural reform implied support for an emphasis on improving working conditions and downplaying political struggle, a position that had been embraced by the unions in the DSP-supporting Dōmei federation. It was Eda's misfortune that his thrust for structural reform came at a time when Sōhyō was still under the control of a leadership strongly attached to militant Marxist rhetoric.

Nearly twenty years later Ōta, whose attack against structural reform and the individuals associated with it was merciless, took a considerably less strident view:

In Japan as well [as in Italy], after "*anpo* and Miike" the [feeling] that one could not just go on with Marxist-Leninist dogma resulted in the structural reform debate. I am in principle in agreement with structural reform. The labor movement itself is like a structural reform movement in itself. . . . But, unlike in Italy, unions [in Japan] are not independent of capital. Accordingly the JSP, which depends on the unions, is not independent either. In that kind of noncombative situation, yelling about structural reform rather is a minus for socialism.[47]

Also twenty years after the structural reform debate, Sasaki Kōzō was to write a book titled *Shakaishugitekiteki Seiken* (Socialist-like Government), the *teki* in this case being a modifier used somewhat as "-like" is used in English, suggesting a kind of watering down of the noun it is modifying, particularly when, as in this case, it is used twice. According to Sasaki, the only way to approach socialism was to promote socialist-like policies, attaching as many *teki* as necessary to "socialist" to make it acceptable to the electorate: "There is no other way to achieve full socialism except to obtain governmental power as quickly as possible, gradually implement socialist policies, and remove each *teki* one by one."[48]

The rejection of structural reform, when contrasted with the SPD's embrace of the Bad Godesberg Program, points up a more fundamental feature of the JSP in terms of the weight of the historical baggage it brought into postwar Japanese politics. The SPD's confidence that a new pro-

gram could bring it to power was spurred not only by a
belief that people cared about what it said it stood for, but
by the self-perception that it was destined to be a party of
power. The SPD, after all, had been the most powerful political party in pre-Nazi Germany and ran the government
during the Weimar era. Its definition of a new program was
part of a general thrust to recover that leadership role.

But the JSP had only one experience in government,
and that was the disastrous experience of the Occupation-
period Katayama and Ashida coalition cabinets. The party
emerged from a deeply rooted tradition of total opposition
to the ruling forces, a tradition that owes a debt not only
to the experience of the proletarian parties of the 1930s, but
probably to the origins of the party movement in nine-
teenth-century Japan in a stance of total opposition to the
ruling cliques as well.[49] Despite the fact that the JSP drew
as much support in Japan in the mid-1950s as the SPD did
in Germany, there were few Socialist leaders who actually
believed that structural reform could be a vehicle to take
them to state power. They set their sights much lower than
that, focusing their attention on securing power in the party,
not in the polity, thereby making structural reform little more
than a tool in an intraparty power struggle.

The Kyōkai's Advance and Retreat

The defeat of structural reform and Sasaki's victory in the
factional struggle with Eda Saburō left the Shakaishugi Kyōkai
as the only coherent voice of leftist ideology in the JSP, enabling it to embark on a period of growth that by the mid-
seventies confronted the party with a major internal crisis.
In 1968 the Kyōkai adopted a controversial Thesis in which
it defined itself as "a group of Marxist-Leninists" and set
the organization's basic task as being "the establishment of
a socialist society through the strengthening of the class
character of the Socialist party."

The Kyōkai Thesis also made clear the tasks of a JSP government:

The revolutionary socialist government will revise the constitution. . . . The revolutionary socialist government will immediately have to grasp control over or abolish organs of state power such as the administration, the courts, education, and the military. . . . The revolutionary socialist government is a dictatorship of the proletariat. Whether . . . only one or several political parties will be allowed depends, as Lenin said, on the country's internal and external historical conditions. . . . But the existence of political parties that represent the interests of monopoly capital will not be permitted.[50]

The Thesis was unstinting in its support of Soviet leadership of the socialist world. It is ironic that while the Rōnōha was created in 1927 partly in opposition to Comintern demands that the Communist party accept Moscow's leadership, the Kyōkai under Sakisaka became the most faithful follower of the Soviet line of all political groups in Japan. The Kyōkai supported Soviet positions on virtually every issue, published translations of Soviet journals, and was widely rumored to be receiving Soviet financial support.

The Kyōkai first drew a considerable amount of public attention in November 1970 when its members physically protected the party congress held that month against efforts by "new left" groups to invade the meeting hall. At the next congress, in 1972, the Kyōkai secured party support for the faction of the party's youth organization, Shaseidō, that supported Sakisaka, one of the three major factions into which Shaseidō had earlier split.[51] This effectively purged Shaseidō of new left radicals. The following year the JSP, which had some years earlier suspended financial support for the youth organization, resumed aid to what was now a Kyōkai-dominated organization.[52]

By working through Shaseidō and through other party-affiliated organizations such as the Rōdō Daigaku (the "la-

bor college," which organizes study sessions for party
members in the labor movement) and by getting its supporters into positions of dominant influence on the party
newspaper, by the time of the party's 38th congress in 1974
the Kyōkai had the support of close to a majority of delegates to the party congress, even though it had only three
Dietmen who publicly acknowledged their membership in
the organization.

The Kyōkai grew powerful because of the comfortable assumption of JSP leaders that party ideologues would
not challenge party factions for political control. The traditional pattern of left-wing rhetoric and right-wing behavior
had become so regularized among the party's Dietmen that
they remained indifferent to the Kyōkai's efforts to organize
the party rank and file until they confronted a situation in
the mid-seventies in which the Kyōkai appeared to be on
the verge of upsetting the party's traditional power relationships. Not only was the Kyōkai using its power at the
party congress to influence leadership selection and the party
program, but it also had begun to use its power at the local
level to take over local JSP organizations and control constituency nomination of Diet candidates.

It was one thing for the Kyōkai to try to make better
Marxists out of the party's activists. It was quite another to
challenge the party's unwritten rules that, as in the LDP,
called for the automatic renomination of incumbents and the
concentration of party power in the hands of its Diet members. The Sasaki faction, which had been happy to enlist
the support of the Kyōkai to camouflage its power struggle
with Eda Saburō as an ideological attack on structural reform, now turned its attack against this group seeking "unconditional central control and strict discipline." The December 1974 issue of the faction's magazine, Shinrō, declared
that the party could only be weakened by Sakisaka's "theory of expulsion" and that the Kyōkai was violating the basic premise of the united front party, which called for ideological pluralism and unity in action.[53]

The fight between the Kyōkai and anti-Kyōkai forces came to a head in 1977 when an anti-Kyōkai alliance emerged between erstwhile rivals Sasaki Kōzō and Eda Saburō and a small group of Diet members known as the Atarashii Nagare No Kai (the New Current Group). This last group, led by a popular former TV newscaster, Den Hideo, claimed to be admirers of Francois Mitterand and the *autogestion* theories of the French Socialist party. Cloaking power struggles in the garb of ideological conflict was not entirely thrown to the winds. The Sasaki faction, which had long been close to Peking, attacked the Kyōkai's loyalty to the Soviet Union and its allegiance to the Soviet line. But such concerns, which were the focus of many newspaper accounts of the Sasaki-Kyōkai conflict, were entirely secondary to Sasaki's determination to maintain, and the Kyōkai's effort to overturn, a system in which party power was in the hands of the leaders of factions of Diet members.

The party held three party congresses in 1977. At the first one, in February, the Kyōkai forces were able to get the congress to reelect Ishibashi Masashi of the centrist Katsumata faction as party secretary-general, over efforts by the Sasaki, Eda, and Atarashii Nagare No Kai groups (the new right) to replace him with a member of the Sasaki faction. The Kyōkai was also successful in defeating all five anti-Kyōkai candidates for positions on the party's central executive board.

Following this congress, Eda Saburō, despondent about the chances to bring change to the JSP, announced his resignation from the party and his intention to form his own political party. But less than two months after making this announcement Eda suddenly died, leaving his new party, the Social Citizens League (Shakai Shimin Rengō), without any well-known leader. Six months later Den Hideo and two other leaders of the Atarashii Nagare No Kai quit the JSP. They later joined with Eda's supporters to form the Social Democratic League (SDL, Shakai Minshu Rengō).

Another congress, convened in September after the

party's poor showing in the summer upper house election, was held amidst enormous tension and conflict. The chairman of the party, Narita Tomomi, and his secretary-general Ishibashi, both of whom had seen the party through nearly a decade of decline and growing turmoil, resigned. Narita recommended that the party choose the popular mayor of Yokohama, Asukata Ichio, as his successor. Asukata, however, refused to be a candidate, and Narita and Ishibashi were kept on in their posts until new leaders could be chosen.

The crisis was ultimately resolved at a party congress in December 1977, when Asukata finally agreed to become chairman on condition that the chairman's powers be strengthened, the Kyōkai abandon its Thesis and desist from its efforts to purge the party of members who did not share its Marxist-Leninist views, and that the chairman henceforth be elected by the party rank and file. Asukata apparently hoped that a direct election system would energize the JSP in the way the presidential primary in the LDP seemed to be breathing new life into that party. It was not the primary, however, that energized the LDP, but, as we have seen, the energy of the LDP that gave life to the primary. Nothing seemed to be able to breathe such life into the JSP.

Once confronted by the party's Dietmen, the Kyōkai had little choice but to give up its effort to transform the JSP into a party unified in its commitment to Rōnōha Marxism. A party split would have left it with virtually no representation in the Diet and no support among Sōhyō's top leadership. The Kyōkai's objective had been to capture the party. When that failed, Sakisaka accepted Asukata's conditions and retreated, expressing confidence that eventually capitalism would meet its doom and the socialist revolution triumph.

The JSP's Continuing Decline

The one seemingly bright spot in this otherwise dark time in Socialist history was Asukata's decision to accept the party chairmanship. Asukata's reputation for dynamic leadership as mayor of Yokohama generated expectations that he would provide a similar kind of leadership for the JSP. But his five-year stewardship of the party was deeply disappointing. Like other leaders before him, he set his sights on establishing party peace by skillfully balancing right and left. He quickly fell into a pattern of leadership that saw the arena for political action by this permanent opposition as being bounded by the party itself. He also continued the JSP's time-honored leadership style of combining militant rhetoric (for example, calling on the party to unify the working masses, "all of whom are victims of monopoly capitalism")[54] with moderate behavior. Before becoming mayor of Yokohama, Asukata had been a member of the Diet and was affiliated with the extreme left-wing Peace Comrades (Heiwa Dōshikai) group. Now as party chairman, he was able once again to indulge in revolutionary rhetoric and demonstrate his credentials as a socialist baptized in Rōnōha Marxism.[55]

He also focused a great deal of his and the party organization's energies on a futile effort to create a party of one million members. This effort was met with a decidedly lukewarm response by party militants who did not want to see the "fighting spirit" of the party diluted, by local union leaders who resented the apparent effort to weaken their stranglehold on the rudimentary party organization that existed, and by voters who could see little benefit in this anachronistic effort to make a mass membership party out of the JSP.

Although the Kyōkai was forced to retreat because of the combined opposition of the Sasaki and Eda factions, one important consequence of the struggle was that it accelerated the disintegration of factional organization in the JSP. In the 1950s and 1960s the JSP was organized into factions much in the same way as was the LDP. The difference between the two parties was that Socialist party factions claimed to represent particular ideological positions which they used as weapons in power struggles, while LDP factions as such took no ideological stances.

LDP factions, as we have noted, have grown in size and become more complex organizations over the years that the LDP has held governmental power. JSP factions, by contrast, have grown weaker as the party's popularity has declined. By the end of the 1970s they were all essentially leaderless. Eda had left the party in 1977, Sasaki was defeated in the 1976 election and subsequently retired from politics, and Katsumata, though still in formal control of his faction, was no longer an active leader. Furthermore, the fight with the Kyōkai had forced the Sasaki faction to take a tactical position on the party right, thereby obfuscating ideological differences without ever resolving them. And the turmoil surrounding the Kyōkai in 1977 resulted in the chairmanship of the party going to someone who had no faction of his own and who at the time was not even a member of the Diet. Asukata subsequently was elected to the lower house from a district in Tokyo, but he never tried to build a factional organization or to build a strong party organization on any other basis. Instead he pursued the futile quest for a party of one million members. The result was a party that lacked organizational coherence.

When Asukata resigned in 1983, the only person to declare his candidacy to succeed him was Ishibashi Masashi of the the Katsumata faction, the party secretary-general from 1970 to 1977 who had been forced out of office with Narita. As the new party chairman, Ishibashi now proclaimed his stewardship over a post-Marxist New JSP. But he found it extraordinarily difficult to articulate policies that would give substance to this political slogan.

As a result of the July 1986 general elections, Socialist representation in the lower house fell to eighty-five seats, the lowest number since the disastrous election of 1949 that followed the collapse of the Katayama and Ashida cabinets. Shortly thereafter Ishibashi resigned as party chairman and was replaced by Doi Takako, a seven-time Diet member and the first woman to be made head of the Socialist party, or any other party, in Japan. She had no power base in the party, however, and her activities during her first year in office gave no indication that she would inspire either the party or the electorate to reverse the Socialists' relentless decline.

Although years of one-party dominance have stimulated ever-greater intervention by the LDP in the government's decision-making processes, the Socialist party has settled into permanent opposition status during these same years, becoming further and further removed from the public policy issues of primary concern to the electorate. Its emphasis on mass movements and extraparliamentary political action has met with increasing public indifference. Its lack of policy expertise, particularly on economic matters, has made it largely irrelevant to the public policy debate. Its defense of the interests of the public sector unions that have given it sustenance have become increasingly unpopular. And the tenacity with which it has clung to issues that had brought it public support in an earlier phase of postwar politics has greatly reduced its ability to influence the government on those matters that have subsequently come to the top of the public policy agenda.

The combination of the cumulative impact of permanent opposition party status and the particular historical conditions that have influenced the JSP's behavior have left it groping for a role in a society whose development it cannot explain and whose problems have become more and more divorced from the issues it had made the mainstay of its public appeal. "Behind the revolutionary verbiage of tradition," to borrow what one French observer said about the French Socialist party of the 1950s, "it has become profoundly conservative and opposed to change."[56] It is not impossible that the JSP will tap new sources of public support much as the French Socialist party did under Francois Mitterand's leadership. But the chances of that happening are slim given the changes that have transpired in public attitudes about parties and politics and the evolution of the Japanese party system.

5.

CAMPAIGNING, FINANCING, AND THE MODERN PARTY

The dominant form of party organization in Japan, as applicable in basic respects to the JSP as to the LDP, is characterized by factional groupings, control by Diet members over the party's policymaking processes, and the absence of meaningful party organization at the local level. The critical role of forging linkages between parties and voters is performed by individual Diet members and their own personal support organizations, the *kōenkai*.[1]

The Kōmeitō and Communist parties are the only significant exceptions to this dominant organizational form. The JCP has made its elected politicians subordinate to the party and has imposed a degree of discipline on its members that is as untypical of Japanese parties as it is usual for Communist ones. The Kōmeitō has so far avoided overt factionalism among its Diet members, and it too is more highly disciplined and has a more committed following—in this case the membership of the religious organization Sōka Gakkai—than is usual for Japanese parties. But these two small parties are clearly exceptions to the rule. Moreover, as the Kōmeitō has grown larger, it has adopted more and more the characteristics of the more conventional Japanese party, particularly in terms of Diet member control.[2]

Nevertheless, the model of modern party organization that is widely embraced in Japan and implicit in the structure of laws regulating political activity could hardly be at greater variance with this dominant organizational form. The model calls for highly articulated, mass membership party organizations, ones in which the party enjoys a mass following that provides the bulk of its income, a structure that reaches down to the grass roots, and clear principles and policy goals.

In his classic study of political parties, Maurice Duverger years ago coined the phrase "contagion from the left" to characterize the impact mass membership working class parties had on the organization of bourgeois parties. Duverger's point was that working class parties, relying out of necessity on their memberships for their financial and organizational strength, ended up creating a party structure so powerful that other parties were forced to emulate it.[3] Others have contested Duverger's theory, arguing that the major impetus to the creation of mass membership parties was not a contagion from the left but rather the adoption of universal manhood suffrage. In Britain, for example, where the expansion of the suffrage predated the emergence of a workers' party, the Conservative and Liberal parties had already developed membership systems before the Labour party was born.[4]

But whatever the limitations of Duverger's contagion from the left theory in explaining the development of mass membership parties, there is no doubt that a profound contagion from the West influenced Japanese attitudes about what constitutes modern political parties. These attitudes are not only embraced by the political elite, conservative and progressive alike, but pervade Japanese views more generally.

The following statement is taken from an *Asahi Shinbun* book on political parties. The figures it cites are now out of date, but the point of view it presents is representative of Japanese views of what constitute modern political parties:

One of the peculiarities of our country's political parties in comparison with other countries is the weakness of political party organization itself. The LDP has some 300,000 members and the JSP less than 50,000. Even leaving aside the British Labour Party with its membership of 6,350,000, Japanese parties are strikingly weak compared to the Italian Communist Party with over 1,600,000 members, or the 700,000 Socialist Party of West Germany. Even so, at election time the LDP gets 22 million votes and the JSP 12 million. What is the secret?[5]

Implicit here is the assumption that there is only one modern, legitimate form of party organization, that is, the party that enrolls large numbers of its supporters as party members. The Italian Communists, the West German Social Democrats, and the Labour party of Britain are treated as though they provide a uniform type of party structure against which Japanese parties, conservative and socialist, are to be measured. No mention is made of American parties, which are at least as "peculiar" as Japanese ones. And the secret of why the LDP and JSP should be able to get so many votes when so few of their supporters are enrolled as party members is then revealed to be the backward and premodern features of Japanese political organization and behavior.

A perception of the European mass membership party as representing the modern form of political organization has been so strong in Japan that the establishment of mass membership, highly articulated party organizations has been promoted as a goal synonymous with party modernization itself. This has been the case even though it has little support in Japanese political traditions, and in spite of the fact that it is becoming an increasingly obsolete model for party organization even in the countries that gave birth to it.[6]

Nevertheless, neither in academic writings, nor in the mass media, nor in the world of real politics has there been much questioning of the relevance of this organizational form.

On the contrary, political commentary in Japan, at least until very recently, typically has taken the country's political parties to task for continually failing to achieve it. And Japanese party leaders have felt compelled to make gestures in the direction of creating more modern political parties— gestures which, if they have not brought them any closer to an essentially prewar European mass membership party model, have nonetheless affected the ways in which parties function.

The interplay between the public commitment to moving the party system more in the direction of European-style mass membership parties, and the continuing strength of deeply entrenched indigenous patterns of party organization which have little in common with this model of the modern party, imparts a special quality to Japanese party organization. This interplay was particularly evident in the mid-1970s when the LDP, rocked by revelations of payoffs by the Lockheed Corporation to former Prime Minister Tanaka and other LDP politicians, and pressed by Tanaka's reform-minded successor, Miki Takeo, to deal with the problems of "structural corruption," reluctantly agreed to support a major reform of laws regulating political funding and election campaigning.

The Postwar Pattern of Corruption

Political corruption scandals have been no stranger to postwar Japanese politics. The earliest erupted in 1948 when executives of the Shōwa Denkō company, then Japan's largest fertilizer producer, were accused of giving bribes to senior government officials in order to secure a low-interest loan from the government-run Reconstruction Finance Corporation. In all, sixty-four people were arrested in the Shōwa Denkō scandal (*Shōden jiken*), including an incumbent cabinet minister (the head of the Economic Stabilization Board), former Prime Minister Ashida and his Vice Premier (and JSP leader) Nishio, nine members or former members of the

Diet, and ten senior government bureaucrats (including later Prime Minister Fukuda). Forty-three people eventually were indicted, including Ashida and Nishio.[7]

The 1950s produced its own spectacular corruption scandal involving shipping companies that were giving bribes and kickbacks to government officials and LDP leaders in return for government contracts and subsidies. One of the central political figures implicated in this shipbuilding scandal (*zōsen gigoku*) was the LDP's then secretary-general, Satō Eisaku. A warrant for Satō's arrest was drawn up, but on the day it was to be issued, April 21, 1954, Prime Minister Yoshida had his minister of justice order the chief public prosecutor not to arrest Satō. The justice minister cited as his prerogative to take such action a provision, Article 14 of the Public Prosecutors' Agency Law, that gives the minister the right to exercise administrative authority (*shikiken hatsudō*) over the public prosecutor.

Satō was indicted later in the year, however, on charges of violating the Public Funds Regulation Law. But the case was dropped in 1956 as part of the general amnesty that was proclaimed to celebrate Japan's admission into the United Nations.[8] A decade later, while Satō was prime minister, a number of incidents involving corruption among LDP Diet members arose. They were known collectively as the black mist scandals and led to the "black mist dissolution" of the Diet in January 1967.

These and other scandals resulted in a considerable amount of hand-wringing by LDP leaders and solemn promises of more virtuous behavior in the future. They also made political ethics a popular political cause for the opposition parties and a major campaign issue in virtually every postwar Diet election. But they resulted in very little in the way of tangible political reforms. Occasional minor changes were made in laws governing election campaigning and political funding. But the LDP parried demands for far-reaching reforms by insisting that they should be part of a general overhaul of the election system, including the adoption of a single-member districting system.

The corruption scandals that arose in the mid-1970s around Tanaka Kakuei changed this pattern, however. Tanaka was forced out of office in December 1974 amidst charges of extensive corruption involving real estate and construction interests. Party leaders were deeply divided over the question of who should succeed him and were worried that a failure to do something to deal with the corruption issue would hurt the party at the polls and might precipitate a major party split.

Unable to agree among themselves on a successor and afraid that an open factional fight would tear the party apart, the LDP's faction leaders agreed to put the decision in the hands of Shiina Etsusaburō, one of the party's elder statesmen and its vice president at the time. This became known as the Shiina Arbitration.[9]

The party grudgingly accepted Shiina's unexpected recommendation that Miki Takeo be made party president to help the LDP survive "the greatest crisis in its history."[10] Miki had always been outside the mainstream of LDP politics, associated with neither the Democrats nor the Liberals in the pre-LDP days but with the small Japan Cooperative party (Nihon Kyōdōtō). A wily politician, he had managed to stay near the center of political power even though he led one of the LDP's smallest factions and was also somewhat distrusted by mainstream politicians because of his liberal views, his incessant criticism of factionalism and calls for party modernization, and his background as an independent-minded professional politician.[11]

But in 1974 these characteristics were welcomed as strengths by a party under attack for its structural corruption. Whatever their misgivings about his qualifications to be prime minister, and however much they disliked allowing the leader of one of the party's smallest factions to attain the party's highest post, LDP leaders hoped that Miki's long-term advocacy of political reform would help the party convince the public that it was serious about doing something to change its ways and would blunt the adverse impact of the Lockheed scandal.

It also seems quite certain that Shiina and others believed that Miki, because of his weak power base in the party, could be controlled by the party's bosses. They became painfully aware that they were mistaken in this judgment when in July 1976 Miki did nothing to stop the arrest of former Prime Minister Tanaka for alledgedly accepting a 500-million-yen bribe from the Lockheed Corporation.

The Lockheed scandal, with its involvement of a major foreign corporation and the sordid relationships it exposed between LDP politicians, businessmen, and Kodama Yoshio, a shadowy right-wing political fixer, rocked Japan's political world as had no previous scandal. It provoked an unrestrained media attack on Tanaka and on the LDP, and it created a chaotic situation within the LDP as Shiina and other party leaders, furious with Miki for not stopping Tanaka's arrest by invoking the same power that had been used during the shipbuilding scandal to protect Satō, now pressed forward their "down with Miki" (*Miki oroshi*) campaign.[12] He was finally driven from office four months after Tanaka's indictment, in the immediate aftermath of the party's poor performance in the December 1976 general election.

But Miki was not forced out before he had gotten two major reform bills through the Diet. One was a revision of the Public Offices Election Law, the law that regulates in great detail election campaigning practices. The other was a revision of the law regulating political contributions and spending. Together these bills provided for the most extensive revision of the basic laws governing election campaigning and political financing since the American Occupation.

Whether they would have been adopted had someone else been prime minister is unclear. Clearly Miki felt more strongly about the need for reform than did most other LDP leaders, and he skillfully manipulated public criticism of LDP "money politics" to press his proposals on a reluctant party. But the actual contents of the reforms that were presented to the Diet were written by Home Ministry bureaucrats and were built on reform proposals that had been made by a succession of government commissions over the previous fifteen years.[13] Although they made possible some new forms of campaign activity, they reflected long-held and deeply rooted Japanese attitudes about the imperatives of modern party politics.

The central purposes of the revisions of both laws were to encourage a shift from candidate-centered to party-centered election campaigns, and to redirect the flow of political funds so that they would go more to parties and less to factional organizations, and come more from individuals and less from a relatively small number of corporations, labor unions, and other major interest groups. As a result, the focus of election campaigns was to shift away from individual candidates and therefore away from appeals to voters based on personal connections and the reputations of the candidates, to center instead on party policies and principles.

The reforms did generate important changes in the patterns of political funding and in campaign practices, as we shall see. But they did not bring about the kind of fundamental change that was ostensibly their objective. Japanese politicians rose to the challenge posed by these reforms by searching out every conceivable loophole in the law that might allow them to avoid having to change their time-tried ways of doing things. In the process, the new reforms offered eloquent testimony to the difficulty of engineering political change in a society that has strong and resilient political institutions and long-established traditions. They also drove deeper the wedge separating form and substance in Japanese political life, widening the gap between actual political practices and the kind of party organization and behavior called for by formal legal rules. And they demonstrated not only that the consequences of reform cannot be entirely anticipated, but that they often exacerbate the problems they are intended to correct, or create others that are worse.

Revising the Election Law

The Japanese election law is premised on the notion that a distinction can be drawn between political activities (*seiji katsudō*) and election campaigning (*senkyo undō*). Election campaigning, according to the theory embraced by the election law, involves activities that are intended to secure votes for a particular candidate in a specific election; they are subject to extensive legal regulation. Political activities, on the other hand, seek to spread public understanding of the party's principles and policies and to increase the party's influence among the electorate. They are not activities designed to obtain votes for particular candidates in particular elections and thus do not constitute election campaigning.

Prior to 1952 the legal fiction was maintained that parties were free to engage in political activities during the campaign period as long as those activities were not directed to obtaining votes for the party's candidates. Since winning votes for its candidates was the primary purpose of party activity, this simply created an enormous gap between the law's formal regulations and actual behavior.

Revisions of the law in 1952 and 1954 then tried the opposite tack by imposing a blanket prohibition on all party activity during the campaign period. This meant that political parties were legally permitted to participate in election campaigns only as third parties (*daisansha*), subject to the same severe restrictions that, as noted later in this chapter, were applicable to other third parties, namely, the voters. To the extent that the law was effective, it drove political parties out of the campaign process.

In 1962 the law was revised in a way that, according to the Home Ministry, "changed by 180 degrees the previous principle restricting all political activity during the election campaign period and made it possible for political parties to engage in election campaigning during the election period as part of their political activities."[14] In other words, political parties were now not only allowed once again to engage in political activities during the campaign period, but for the first time were permitted to do so for the purpose of securing votes for their candidates.

But the distinction between individual candidate campaign activities and party political activities was not forsaken. Parties were permitted to engage in certain activities to secure votes for their candidates, but they were still legally prohibited from doing anything to obtain votes for any particular candidate. Specifically, the 180-degree turn consisted of a change in the law that permitted political parties to convene no more than four meetings (literally, recommendation speech meetings, *suisen enzetsukai*) for each of their candidates and allowed parties to display posters announcing these meetings (limited to no more than 500 posters for each meeting). But, symbolic of the effort to shift the voters' attention from candidates to party policies and principles, the law expressly forbade parties from mentioning the names of any of its candidates on these posters.[15]

The 1975 revision of the election law greatly expanded the scope of permissable political party campaign activities. In terms of the revised law, qualified parties are those that run at least twenty-five candidates in the lower house or ten candidates in the upper house. These parties may display posters, for example, calling on the electorate to vote for the party. There are limits on numbers.[16] And, following the practice established in 1962, parties are prohibited from mentioning the names of any of their candidates on these posters.

Political parties may now also distribute unlimited numbers of handbills. But here too conditions are attached. Parties may not use more than three types of handbills and they must register them with the Home Minister. Handbills may be handed out to people on the street or sent through the mails or distributed in other ways. But they cannot be taken to people's homes, since this would provide a way around the law's prohibition of house-to-house canvassing. Nor can they simply be "scattered" indiscriminately. The

Home Ministry, obviously expecting the worst, warned that "dropping them from a small airplane over an apartment house complex" would violate the law.[17]

The law continues to permit the practice introduced by the 1962 revision whereby parties may convene public meetings during the campaign period. The rules have been relaxed so that they now restrict the number of meetings to four times the total number of party candidates while setting no limits on the number of meetings that can be held in any particular election district. Candidates may be mentioned by name and endorsed in the speeches made by party leaders. The candidates themselves may appear and make speeches. The only caveat is that the meetings must be formally convened by the national party organization and not by the candidates themselves, and party leaders other than the candidate must participate to demonstrate that the primary purpose of the meeting is to publicize the party's policies and not the party's candidates.

The other major area of new and unrestricted party campaign activity involves advertising in print and electronic media. The Japanese government exercises tight control over use of the mass media for political advertising. Candidates are not allowed to buy time on television or radio or space in newspapers or magazines. Instead, the government pays for a number of political advertisements that are made available to every candidate. These include five newspaper ads of specified length which may appear in any newspaper the candidate chooses. They also include four television and two radio appearances. In principle, each candidate is permitted two appearances on NHK, the national public Japan Broadcasting Company, and two on any private channel he wishes. He is also permitted one radio broadcast on NHK radio and one on a private station. Each television and radio appearance is limited to five and a half minutes.

This is the extent of permissible use of the media for campaign advertising by lower house candidates. Unlike many other campaign rules, this one is virtually impossible to evade. Moreover, newspapers and the broadcast media are constrained both by law and by their own industry codes of conduct from giving unfair advantage to any candidate. The law prohibits, for example, the publication of opinion poll data showing the relative strengths of candidates (though it does not prohibit articles based on these polls, nor polls that are limited only to measuring the popularity of political parties). Television stations are scrupulous in avoiding giving exposure to one candidate that is not given to another. Thus a news story on a local television station about the day's campaign invariably avoids using footage that shows the face or the name of one candidate if it does not give equal exposure to the others. What television viewers usually get to see of their candidates on their TV screens are their backs.

But since 1975, in addition to this limited free advertising permitted candidates, political parties have been permitted to advertise in newspapers, magazines, and on radio and television. There are no restrictions on the amount of space or time a party may buy. The law also gives every qualified political party the opportunity to run four newspaper advertisements at government expense. But there is one important prohibition that applies to all party political advertising: it is against the law to mention the candidacy of any individuals. Advertisements can be used only to publicize the party's policies. Party leaders and other Diet members can appear in these advertisements, but only in the context of their party roles; it is illegal to discuss their own candidacy in the election.

Most of Japan's parties have taken advantage of this new freedom to advertise and have produced both short spot commercials and longer documentaries to be used on television during the campaign. This new activity has helped spur the growth of political advertising as a significant business in Japan in the past decade. All of the large advertising agencies have political advertising sections, and several small companies have successfully established themselves as election campaign consulting organizations. They not only help parties prepare advertisements but work with individual candidates, particularly those running in urban and metropolitan districts, and especially members of the LDP, in preparing constituency opinion surveys, writing campaign speeches, and designing campaign posters.

Nowhere else where comparable technologies are available have the print and electronic media had as minimal an impact on election campaign styles as in Japan. Whether this situation would change if individual candidates were given the opportunity to use the media more freely in their campaign activities is an open question. To the extent that electoral support is built on personal ties and powerful local personal political machines, media advertising could be expected to have a more limited impact than it has had in other societies.

But Prime Minister Nakasone has shown enormous skill in utilizing the electronic media to build his personal support—and, as noted in an earlier chapter, to use this popular support to strengthen his position in the party—and there are any number of younger LDP politicians who would make good use of the media if given the freedom to buy time for political advertising. But there is no evidence that either Home Ministry bureaucrats determined to continue a policy of restricting individual candidate campaigns, or incumbent Diet members afraid to make any changes in the rules of the game that might adversely affect their own reelection changes, will permit basic changes away from the existing pattern of highly restrictive use of the media for political campaigning.

Candidate Campaigns and Popular Participation

The belief that modern politics require party-centered rather than candidate-centered election campaigns in which voters vote for policies and principles rather than for particular individuals made it inevitable that the granting of new campaign freedoms to political parties would be tied to continued restrictions on campaign activities permitted to individual candidates. Thus the extensive restrictions and prohibitions on campaign activities by individuals running for the lower house that have characterized Japan almost uninterruptedly since the introduction of universal manhood suffrage in 1925 continue to prevail. These include among other things the prohibition against pre-election campaigning,[18] house-to-house canvassing, the use of more than one campaign car or of more than one campaign office, and the blanket prohibition against distributing any written materials except those expressly permitted under the law. The latter are limited to 35,000 postcards, and handbills numbering from 60,000 to 100,000, depending on the size of the district. The government also prints an election brochure for each election district that contains a statement by each candidate and is delivered to every household. The distribution of other printed materials by candidates is legally prohibited.

The law prohibits not only the distribution but the display of written materials except for items expressly permitted by law. The latter are mainly posters displayed on official government poster boards and a certain number of additional posters advertising the time and place of a candidate's planned speech. Prohibited is the display or distribution of written materials on behalf of a candidate's campaign, including "newspapers, name cards, greeting cards, posters, signs, paper lanterns, placards, postcards, telegrams, slides, movies, neon signs, advertising balloons, and characters written on walls or fences or in the sand on the road," to quote a senior official's book on the revised law.[19]

Prior to the introduction of universal manhood suffrage in 1925, there were no restrictions on campaign activities except for a prohibition of campaigning in the polling places themselves. In 1925 a prohibition on canvassing and limitations on the distribution of campaign literature were introduced. And in 1934 additional restrictions and more severe penalties for violating them were adopted. A revision of the election laws immediately after the war eliminated most of these restrictions,[20] but they were reintroduced in 1947 and in following years.

The government's motivations for introducing restrictions on campaign practices in 1925 were more in accord with the spirit of the Peace Preservation Law that was adopted that year to strengthen government control over political activity than with the democratic implications of universal manhood suffrage. Restrictions were increased in the 1930s as the government became more repressive. They were designed particularly to make campaigning by proletarian parties more difficult.

But the restrictions themselves were largely modeled after the British Corrupt and Illegal Practices Prevention Act of 1883 and reflected at least in part a desire to eradicate corrupt election practices. Concern about eliminating political corruption was a major reason for the reintroduction of many of these restrictions in the early postwar period, and it has been cited as justification for retaining them to the present day.

Although deregulation in other areas of Japanese life has become a major thrust of recent government policy and has been forced on often reluctant bureaucrats, there is no strong constituency advocating the deregulation of election campaigning. Home Ministry bureaucrats for their part have been loath to give up their longstanding formal and informal regulatory power over the campaign process. As one of them noted:

Some people point to the extreme brevity of the official campaign period and the severe restrictions on such basic forms of expression as speech and printed materials in arguing for a relaxation of [the restrictions on] election campaigning. But, after all, these rules were not created in a day. They are the accumulation of long years of electoral experience and they reflect a consideration of a number of features of Japanese elections. As a result, they have persisted to the present day without basic revision.[21]

Home Ministry bureaucrats have rationalized the retention of extensive restrictions on campaign activity also by claiming that the electorate is politically too immature to be granted greater freedoms. This throwback to prewar bureaucratic paternalistic attitudes is not as openly propounded today as it was before the introduction of democratic political reforms in the postwar period. But it is evident, for example, in the Home Ministry's official explanation of why the ban on house-to-house canvassing, first introduced in 1934, needs to be retained:

Campaigning at a voter's house or at some other place out of public sight where individual voters are asked directly for their vote makes for a hotbed of bribery, appeals to special interests, and other crimes against free and fair elections. Of course, this kind of evil practice would be removed if the level of the electorate's political consciousness is raised and if it becomes general for people to vote on the basis only of their own will. But the present reality has not reached that stage. Therefore, it is necessary to eliminate opportunities for that kind of unfairness as much as possible.[22]

Bureaucratic resistance to dismantling the elaborate structure of government rules and regulations over the campaign process has not been challenged by the LDP, since it also sees advantages in retaining the present system. Extensive campaign restrictions operate mainly to disadvantage new candidates relative to incumbents. The latter have countless ways to reach constituents, and they benefit from restrictions that make it difficult for new candidates to increase their name recognition and build strong campaign organizations. This, combined with the inclination for incumbents to favor retention of a system with which they are familiar and within which they already have been successful, and to resist changes that entail unknown risks, create powerful pressures against reform.

The advantages incumbents gain from the extensive legal campaign restrictions and prohibitions largely account for the absence of opposition party enthusiasm for fundamental campaign reform. Opposition parties generally have not pressed for a relaxation of campaign restrictions also out of fear that greater deregulation of campaign practices would redound more to the benefit of LDP candidates, with their larger financial resources, than to themselves.

But over time, interest in deregulating candidate campaign activities has waned especially because there has been a virtual institutionalization of patterns of evasion and circumvention of many of the law's restrictions. Since the law declares illegal a far greater range of activities than the public regards as illegitimate, there has emerged a kind of unspoken agreement among the parties and government authorities not to look too closely at some of the practices that are formally prohibited under the law.

The major loophole that makes it possible for politicians to engage in more campaign activity than the law would seem to permit is the distinction mentioned earlier between political activity and election campaigning. As long as a politician avoids mentioning that he is running for office in a specific election and does not directly ask voters to vote for him, he can claim that his activities are political activities and not election campaigning. This has given rise to a long noncampaign period prior to the fifteen-day or so official campaign. This has had the perverse effect of encouraging candidates to campaign vigorously (and spend a great deal of money doing so) whenever rumors arise of a possible dissolution of the lower house, so that they can get their campaigning during the noncampaign concluded before the official campaign period, with its myriad restrictions, begins.

A poster or a newsletter announcing, for example, that an LDP Diet member will be giving a speech "to report on the situation in the Diet," as long as it takes place prior to the official campaign period, can be claimed to be a legitimate part of his political activities. In the days and weeks leading up to the official campaign period such political activity increases at a frenetic pace, only to come to a sudden halt when campaigning officially begins.

Even within the official campaign period, some practices that are formally banned do in fact take place. The most important is the practice of house-to-house canvassing. Despite the legal prohibition against canvassing, this particular practice—in its inimitable Japanese form—has grown steadily in importance. Until fairly recently it was a campaign technique employed mainly by opposition parties, which could mobilize campaigners from the unions or, in the case of the Kōmeitō, from the Sōka Gakkai. It was of more secondary importance for LDP candidates, who were not able to recruit as many campaign workers as were union-based opposition party candidates, and who saw reliance on local elites to gather the vote through their networks of personal relationships as the most effective campaign strategy.

But today canvassing has become an important element in LDP campaigns as well, a development that in large part reflects a weakening of the politicians' confidence in the ability of local elites to mobilize sufficient support. No longer certain that victory can be delivered by their traditional campaign machines, LDP candidates, particularly in more urban constituencies where the influence of local elites on voters is especially limited, have become enthusiastic advocates of canvassing. The expression *rōra sakusen* ("roller strategy") is now as commonly heard in LDP campaign strategy meetings as *jinkai senjutsu* ("human wave tactics") has been for many years among the opposition parties. Many LDP politicians now believe that the only way to secure victory at the polls is to have their campaigners move through their districts like streamrollers (thus the "roller" of "roller strategy"), knocking on every door and asking for support. Though a violation of the ban on canvassing, the roller strategy and human wave tactics are widespread. The police do not aggressively look for violators and limit themselves to issuing warnings to those caught at it.

The result of this system of legal restraints and the institutionalization of modes for circumventing them has been to turn the election law into a kind of obstacle course through and around which candidates move in their search for votes, rather than an accepted and respected framework within which campaigns are conducted. The government has been aggressive in pursuing cases of bribery and other offenses that violate the criminal code as well as the election law and has been willing to permit politicians to engage in campaign activities with much more freedom than a strict enforcement of the law would allow. Nonetheless, formal restrictions force candidates to cloak their campaign activities in one guise or another. And these restrictions leave with the government the latent power to intervene more forcefully in the campaign process.

The election law's restrictions and the politicians' success in circumventing many of them have also exacted a considerable price in terms of discouraging popular participation in campaigning. Volunteers are rare in Japanese campaigns—for the parties of the left as well as of the right. The young people working in a campaign headquarters or accompanying the candidate on his campaign trips through his district are almost invariably hired on a part-time basis or are seconded from the labor unions. Candidates who have tried to develop campaigns based on volunteer help have been few and far between. The few who have been successful have received enormous media attention precisely for this reason.

For the average citizen there is considerable uneasiness associated with the campaign process because of uncertainty as to which activities are legal and which are not. Moreover, a long legal history of treating voters as third parties in the campaign process has helped generate a rather broad public acceptance of the notion that the average citizen should be an outsider to the campaign process, an audience for and a target of campaigns rather than an active participant in them. Therefore, unless one is actively mobilized for participation, the inclination in Japan is to stay out of campaigning, and stay out of trouble. As a consequence, despite a comparatively high level of popular participation in social organizations generally, the Japanese exhibit a low level of involvement in election campaigns and in political party activities.

The Financial Costs of Political Life

The 1975 revision of the election law increased government financing of candidate campaign activities. The government covers within specified limits the cost of candidate campaign posters, the printing and mailing of campaign postcards and handbills, the renting of halls for speeches, the cost of running the campaign car, and, as mentioned earlier, the costs of radio, television, and newspaper advertisements.

But increased public financing of election campaigns has done nothing to reduce the costs of campaigning. Election campaigning in Japan remains extraordinarily expensive even though candidates are restricted under the law in the amount they may spend on their campaigns. This amount, which was increased in 1975, varies according to the number of voters and the number of lower house seats in any particular district. In the 1986 lower house election, the range of permissible campaign spending went from ¥13,624,000 in Nagano 3 to ¥19,560,000 in Hokkaidō 1, roughly between $90,000 and $130,000 at an exchange rate of 150 yen to the dollar.

It is an open secret, however, that the reports that candidates are required to file with the Home Ministry detailing their campaign expenditures account for only a small part of total expenses. It is not unusual for even a long-established incumbent with a strong political base to spend a million dollars or more on his campaign; new candidates often spend considerably more than that. And rare is the LDP candidate who can finance a campaign with less than half a million dollars.

It is not unusual anymore for an American congressional candidate to spend comparable sums. But in the United States, increased campaign costs have been propelled mainly by the expenses involved in television advertising. In Japan, candidates spend nothing on media advertising.

Reliable figures on the cost of election campaigns in Japan are difficult to come by not only because they are larger than what politicians declare in their reports to the government, but also because most expenditures are made in the period of the noncampaign before the fifteen-day official campaign, and thus are difficult to separate from the day-to-day costs involved in being a Diet member. These normal costs themselves are considerable. With government support for only two secretaries and a small office and an allowance for postage, telephone, and transportation, every Diet member has to raise a large amount of money for his everyday nonelection-related expenses. Discussions with a number of LDP members suggest that these expenses range anywhere from five to ten million yen per month on average (that is, between roughly $30,000 and $60,000 a month).[23] In an election year, these expenses generally double or triple.

Why do election campaigns and normal Diet member political activities cost as much as they do? The answer is not that money is used to buy votes. Vote buying is insignificant in Japan, and there is virtually no fraud in vote counting. The fundamental reason for the high cost of campaigning in Japan is that every LDP politician must build and maintain his own political machine. He can rely neither on party organization, which hardly exists on the local level, nor on party loyalties among the electorate which, to the extent that they do exist, are effectively neutralized by an electoral system that forces candidates from the same party to compete with one another. Maintaining one's own political machine means helping prefectural and local assemblymen with their election campaigns, employing one large staff in the district to look after one's support organization, and another large staff in Tokyo to handle constituent requests and to raise money to make all other activities possible.

Politicians also spend a great deal of money on their election campaigns because it is less risky to spend than not to spend. Herbert Alexander, a specialist on American political financing, has made the point that at least half of campaign expenditure in the United States is wasted, but that nobody knows which half.[24] Quite the same can be said about campaign expenditures in Japan. Furthermore, voters' distaste for the corruption that is generated by the politician's need for political funds does not translate easily into a willingness to forgo the constituency services that Diet members perform and that require an extensive and expensive organizational infrastructure.

Politicians obtain their campaign funds and money to finance their day-to-day political activities from four general sources: the party, the faction, direct business contributions, and personal resources. The channeling of political money through these four funding windows has been a perennial feature of LDP politics, as true for the party in the late 1980s as in 1955. But there has occurred an enormous change over time in the relative importance of these different funding sources.

Party support has never counted for a substantial portion of politician funding in any of Japan's parties except in the JCP and Kōmeitō, and it does not account for much today. In the 1986 election, the LDP gave each of its candidates ¥5 million (about $35,000) in a direct campaign contribution. It also provided so-called political activity support (*katsudōhi*) in the amount of ¥3 million to candidates who had cabinet experience, and ¥15 million to other incumbents and to nonincumbent candidates. This meant that each of the party's new candidates and those incumbents who had not yet been appointed to the cabinet received ¥20 million as the election approached—$130,000, more or less, depending on the exchange rate. That candidates consider this a relatively insignificant contribution to their funding needs is an indication of how expensive political life is in Japan.[25]

Only a few politicians depend to any substantial degree on their personal financial resources to fund their political activities and campaign expenses. The prewar tradition of the "well-fence politician" (*idobei seijika*), the landlord turned politician who spent so much of his own money on politics that he ended up with nothing but the fence and well of what used to be his extensive land holdings, is far removed from current political practices. But LDP politicians raise a larger share of their campaign funds on their own now than they did in previous years, for reasons that are explained below, and many borrow heavily from banks in order to do so. These debts are then usually repaid with contributions obtained after the election, oftentimes including major donations by the banks that have loaned the money.

It is the balance between reliance on faction leaders and on the business contributions LDP politicians obtain directly that has changed the most dramatically and significantly over the years of LDP rule. Traditionally, factional support has been the most crucial factor in enabling a candidate to put together a campaign war chest. And, conversely, the ability to raise the enormous sums of money needed to maintain a faction was the primary qualification for factional leadership.

But in recent years, and particularly since the passage of the 1975 revision of the law regulating political funds, individual politicians have raised an increasingly large share of their funds on their own. This is true for junior as well as senior politicians, although, as a general rule, the more senior a politician is the more he is expected to raise his own funds. Politicians with cabinet experience do not in principle receive any funds from their factions; in fact they are expected to raise funds *for* the faction.

The role of the faction in fund raising has shifted significantly. Its most important role, and one of the most central tasks of its leader, is to assist its members in raising money on their own. This involves providing entrée to potential donors and in other ways endorsing their fund-raising efforts, and assisting them in selling tickets to fund-raising parties, now one of the most popular fund-raising techniques in Japan. In today's LDP factions, not only the faction leader but all the midranking and senior faction members are expected to raise the money to pay for the faction's operations and to help new candidates with their funding needs. This pattern has increased the independence of individual Diet members vis-à-vis their faction bosses while keeping them dependent on the factional organization for access to political funds. Thus it has been a major factor in spurring the transformation of factions into collegial bodies that was mentioned in an earlier chapter.

Changing the Rules of the Funding Game

These changes in the pattern of political funding were not what Prime Minister Miki had in mind when he persuaded the Diet to revise the political funding law. Miki's purpose was to alter the traditional pattern of funding so that money would flow more to parties and less to factions and to individuals, and would come more from individual donors and less from large corporations than had been the case in the past.

The revised law set ceilings on the amount that corporations, unions, and industrial and other associations are permitted to contribute to parties, factions, and other political organizations, including organizations that act as funding windows for individual politicians. Ceilings on corporate contributions are determined by a formula linked to the corporation's level of capitalization. Companies capitalized at under ¥100 million may make contributions to political parties totaling no more than ¥7.5 million in any given year.[26] The ceiling for corporations capitalized at between ¥500 million and ¥1 billion is ¥30 million. From there the ceiling rises in ¥5 million increments for every ¥500 million in additional capitalization, to a maximum of ¥100 million in political party contributions for firms capitalized at ¥105 billion or more.[27]

Contributions by corporations, unions, and associations to factions and to individual politicians are regulated by a similar formula but in amounts that are one-half those allowed in political party contributions. In other words, the most the largest corporations are permitted to contribute to all factions and individual politicians combined is ¥50 million in any one year. Moreover, the law prohibits corporations, unions, or associations from giving more than ¥1.5 million (approximately $10,000) to any one faction or individual.

Because of a gaping loophole in the law, this restriction on contributions to particular factions and individuals has turned out to have less of an impact than might have been expected. The ceiling applies to contributions made to any single nonparty organization, but there are no restrictions on the number of organizations a single politician may establish. In 1979 some 2,357 organizations, including parties, factions, and individual politician support organizations, filed financial reports with the Home Ministry. By 1984 the number of such organizations had increased to 3,334.[28] This includes some minor parties and fringe groups, but it is mainly composed of multiple organizations of incumbent LDP Diet members. "New leader" Abe Shintarō, for example, collected money in 1984 through at least 27 different political organizations.[29] It need hardly be stressed that this proliferation of legally defined political organizations has made the task of tracing political contributions extremely complicated and has undercut the goal of achieving transparency that was one of the revised law's objectives.

By putting a ceiling on the amount of corporate contributions, the revised law sought to encourage a shift toward greater reliance on individual contributions. Individual donors are permitted to give up to ¥20 million to political parties and ¥10 million to factions and individual politicians, with a maximum contribution of ¥1.5 million to any single faction or individual politician. Moreover, the law offered a new incentive to individual donors by making contributions tax deductible up to an amount that, combined with an individual's other tax deductible contributions, would not exceed more than 25 percent of income for the year.

The revision failed, however, to accomplish its objective of shifting the source of political money away from corporations and toward individuals. Individual contributions accounted for a meager 6.6 percent of total contributions to all political organizations in 1984.[30] Even this figure is inflated, because many of the contributors are the parties' own Diet members. In the LDP, for example, every Diet member contributed ¥600,000 to the party that year.[31]

The law also failed to bring about a shift in the flow of money from factions to parties. Contributions to political parties have increased since 1975, but donations to factional and personal political organizations have grown at a faster rate. The LDP's income is dwarfed by the money raised by its factions and its individual politicians. Its income is also substantially less than that of the Japan Communist party, which since 1975 has had the highest legally reported income of all political parties.[32]

In 1984, the LDP's five major factions together collected over ¥4 billion in direct corporate contributions.[33] In addition, the party's "new leaders" Abe Shintarō, Takeshita Noboru, and Miyazawa Kiichi, and aspiring new leader Watanabe Michio, collected well over ¥2.5 billion, equal to almost two-thirds the amount collected by the regular factions.[34] Takeshita alone collected more money than the Tanaka faction of which he was a member, which testified both to Tanaka's declining power and to Takeshita's determination to take over leadership of the faction.

In fact, senior faction members with aspirations of taking over leadership of their factions play a particularly important role as faction fund raisers. The pattern plays itself out differently in different factions. In the Tanaka faction, Takeshita in 1984 donated ¥92 million to the faction and ¥20 million to Nikaidō Susumu, the faction's most senior leader. But this represented less than half the amount he had raised for the faction the previous year. Although he raised more money in 1984 than in 1983, in 1984 he put away ¥550 million for later use and disbursed the rest, mostly in ¥10-to-¥20-million donations directly to politicians in the Tanaka faction and in donations of from ¥100,000 to ¥1 million to Dietmen in other factions.

Like Takeshita, Abe Shintarō gave approximately 10 percent of his income (in this case ¥80 million) to the faction which in 1984 was still officially led by former Prime Minister Fukuda. He distributed the rest mainly to individual Fukuda faction politicians, including former Dietman defeated in the previous election and planning to run again.

Watanabe Michio, who aspires to succeed eventually to the leadership of the Nakasone faction, gave about a quarter of the funds he raised to the faction, and spent the rest in donations to politicians who are Watanabe loyalists. And Miyazawa Kiichi, who has had a better reputation for policy expertise than for skill in factional politics, gave more than 40 percent of the funds he raised to his faction to demonstrate, one assumes, that he has the wherewithal to be an effective faction leader.

The Changing Sources of Political Funds

Contributions to the LDP, factions, and individual politicians continue to come almost entirely from business, but there have been important changes in the relative importance to the LDP of different industries. During the economy's high-growth years, the three major contributors to the LDP were the steel industry, the electric power industry, and the city banks. But with the end of the era of high growth and the adoption of the revision of the political funds law—which occurred at about the same time—this pattern changed considerably. Contributions from the steel industry fell off dramatically: political contributions by Nippon Steel in 1976 were estimated to have dropped to one-tenth what they had been prior to the revision of the law one year earlier;[35] in 1975 the electric power companies stopped making political contributions altogether; and the relative importance of contributions by the thirteen city banks began to decline. LDP politicians turned increasingly to Japan's new growth industries—consumer electronics, securities and life insurance companies, and local banks. And they became particularly dependent on the support of the construction industry.

In 1979 the forty-six major construction companies that are members of the construction industry industrial association (Nikkenren) together contributed ¥760 million to the LDP. Other construction companies were reported as donating an additional ¥98 million. The total of ¥858 million was higher than the total amount donated by the thirteen city banks.[36] Construction industry political contributions declined with the cutbacks in public works spending that attended the adoption of restrictive fiscal policies after 1980. But this industry remains high on the list of contributors to the LDP and is almost certainly one of the largest sources of unreported funds obtained by LDP politicians at the local level to fund their election campaigns and local political activities.

In the LDP's early years, the big business community, the *zaikai*, was the major source of political contributions, and it channeled them to the LDP and party factions through Keidanren, the Federation of Economic Organizations, the main umbrella organization of the big business community. Keidanren continues to organize contributions by the *zaikai* by setting quotas to be met by the industrial associations and companies that are its members. But the relative importance of the *zaikai* in political funding has declined as companies not part of the traditional business establishment have grown in wealth and have become more important sources of funding than they were in earlier years.

This is true not only for legally reported contributions, which are but the tip of the iceberg of political contributions, but it is even more the case for political funds that go unreported. Not surprisingly, it is impossible to report hard data about Japan's underground political economy. That it is large and that a major source of funds are small, wealthy, and unincorporated provincial companies, particularly in the real estate and construction industries, is not in doubt. Rumors abound about the manipulation of stock prices and insider tips to leading politicians and other various and often imaginative methods that have been devised to funnel illegal political contributions. Speculation about the underground political economy is rife precisely because there is so little information available about it—and because scandals erupt frequently enough to indicate that it really does exist.

One of the new ways in which politicians and factions have gone after political funds since the 1975 revision of the funding law is by holding large fund-raising parties. These take various forms, the most popular being so-called *hagemasu kai*, parties to literally "cheer on" the particular politician being honored. There are also parties to celebrate the publication of a book written by a Diet member or his appointment to the cabinet. The list of possible excuses for holding a fund-raising party has grown at an explosive rate over the past decade.

The idea for these parties initially was taken from the American practice of fund-raising dinners. Virtually unknown in Japan before 1975, fund raisers are now a major source of income. Typically tickets to such events run to ¥30,000 (about $200) for a fairly well-established Diet member, ¥20,000 for a more junior backbencher. These are rarely if ever sit-down affairs. They are large receptions to which business corporations buy up blocks of tickets. It is not unusual for a well-established Dietman to sell three thousand or more ¥30,000 tickets for one of these parties. It is also symptomatic of the more collegial quality of factional relationships that has emerged in recent years that LDP politicians help sell tickets to each other's fund raisers.

Some idea of the weight that these parties have come to occupy in the funding picture in Japan is indicated by the following figures, which still underestimate the amount of money raised through this technique. In 1984 politicians

ranking among the top thirty recipients of political funds
reported income from fund raisers accounting for over ¥3
billion or $20 million, equal to about three-quarters of the
total amount of money raised by factions in direct corporate
contributions. The Nakasone faction raised ¥507 million
through fund raisers, the Kōmoto faction some ¥413 million. One upper house Diet member alone collected ¥450
million from fund-raising parties, and several other LDP
politicians also obtained millions of yen through this activity.[37]

Although money obtained through these parties is
supposed to be reported in one form or another as income,
the cost to companies of buying tickets to them is treated
as a business expense and not as a political contribution.
This provides a way around the legal ceiling on corporate
contributions. It has also helped create a situation in which
virtually every LDP politician is actively involved in fund
raising for himself, for his faction, and for other individual
politicians in his faction. This has enabled LDP politicians
to spread a wide net across the business community in so-
liciting funds, and it has contributed to the general fragmentation that now characterizes the LDP's solicitation of
political money (and that parallels the fragmentation of interest group activity discussed in chapter 3).

Opposition parties and individual politicians also have
adopted the fund-raiser approach, but nowhere with the
degree of success the LDP has had. The Democratic Socialist party raised ¥87 million from parties, and many individual politicians report fund-raiser income; but no opposition party politician raised as much as ¥20 million from
fund raisers in 1984.

One unintended consequence of the revision of the
political funding law has been to remove the buffer that long
had separated the LDP backbencher from the sources of much
of his political funding. In the past a large amount of the
money that flowed to LDP politicians came from the big
business establishment through the party and its factions.
The pattern of funding emphasized the big business com-

munity's interest in seeing the LDP remain in power. Contributions were aggregated through industrial associations and Keidanren in a way that separated them from particular policy issues and made it difficult for business to use them to pursue specific, narrow policy goals. It gave contributions instead the characteristic of a kind of insurance policy to keep the LDP in charge of the government.

Now that individual politicians depend more on their own fund-raising activities for a larger portion of their political funds, and as the relative importance of the *zaikai* as a funding source has declined, businessmen intent on securing concrete benefits and payoffs for their largess play a larger role than ever before in the funding picture. Thus, rather than reducing the role of money in Japanese politics, the revision of the law regulating political contributions seems to have provoked changes in funding patterns that well may have exacerbated the problems of political corruption.

The Decline of the Modern Party Model

The effort to use legal rules to encourage voters to focus on parties and their programs more than on candidates and their promises and thus create more modern parties has touched many aspects of political life besides election campaigning and political funding. It reached a climax of sorts in a decision taken by the Diet in 1982 to eliminate the national constituency in the upper house and replace it with a proportional representation system.

Members of the upper house, as noted in chapter 1, are elected in two districting systems. One hundred fifty-two are elected in prefecture-wide multimember constituencies; until 1982, 100 were elected in a national constituency (*zenkokuku*). Under this national constituency system, a voter cast his ballot for 1 of more than 100 candidates. The top 50 candidates (with half the total being elected every three years) emerging with the most votes were elected. This system led parties to recruit large numbers of celebrities, representatives of large religious organizations, and retiring bureaucrats who had the backing of major interest groups, since candidates with nationwide name recognition or the backing of powerful nationwide organizations were needed to compete effectively in what amounted to a national popularity contest.

Under the new system voters write the name of a political party rather than a candidate on their ballot. Parties win seats in proportion to their share of the vote, and candidates are elected in the order in which they are ranked on their party's list. For the individual candidate the crucial issue is how high he is placed on the party list.

Adoption of this new system thus created a new, and as it turned out extremely expensive, source of political competition in the LDP (and in the JSP and other parties as well, which present much shorter lists). In preparation for the 1986 election, the second upper house election in which the proportional representation system was used, the LDP tried to establish some objective criteria for regulating the competition for ranking on its list. To qualify for inclusion on the list, a candidate had to have recruited at least twenty thousand party members and one million (!) kōenkai members in 1985, and have held at least two public meetings in each of the country's forty-seven prefectures between August 1985 and February 1986.[38] How high on the list a candidate would be ranked would depend on the extent to which he exceeded these goals, and of course on factional bargaining, seniority, and other factors as well.

This set off an enormously expensive competition. One incumbent recruited three hundred thousand party members and four million kōenkai members; another got one hundred and thirty thousand party and five million kōenkai members. In many cases these politicians paid the party membership fees (which are ¥4,000 per year) in order to get people to agree to join. One incumbent admitted spending ¥750 million (something on the order of $5 million) on party fees.[39]

The new system has been used only twice but it already has proved extremely unpopular. In a poll taken among upper house members in April 1986, only 6 percent expressed support for continuing the system in its present form.[40] Nor has the proportional representation system generated any more enthusiasm among the general public than it has among political parties, since its major effect has been to deprive voters of the right to vote for the particular individual candidates they want to see in the Diet's upper house.

As with revisions of the election law and political funding law, reform of the upper house national constituency system did little to reduce the expense of professional political life or move Japan away from candidate-centered campaigns. What it did seem to do was to contribute to a general decline in public interest in issues of political reform.

This decline in interest in changing the way Japanese do things politically is surely in part the product of cynicism born of the failures of recent reform attempts. But it also seems to have something to do with a more profound shift in Japanese attitudes about the modernity of their own political system—and of their country.

In recent years there has been a tremendous increase among Japanese (and perhaps even more so among foreign observers of Japan) who believe that traditional Japanese ways of doing things are as modern and legitimate as the western ways that had long been held up as models for Japan to follow. While this shift in attitude has mainly characterized percpetions of Japanese business organization, it has begun to pervade political life as well. In earlier years, it was usual for Japanese scholars to denigrate LDP organization as backward and to dismiss conservative dominance as the product of the continuing political impact of premodern values. The recent positive assessment of the LDP and of Japan's one-party dominant system by Tokyo University political scientist Satō Seizaburō is emblematic of the change that has begun to occur.[41]

The decline in enthusiasm for reform may also owe

something to increased Japanese awareness that the notion of the modern political party as a programmatic, integrated mass party is not only hard to reconcile with traditional Japanese practices, but is equally hard to square with party politics as they have developed in recent years in the United States and in western Europe.

Contemporary politics in advanced industrialized democracies is almost everywhere characterized by the weakening of party identifications, the obscuring of clear and easily understandable party programs and ideologies as parties try to reach out to the broadest constituency possible, and the search by politicians for new ways to mobilize electoral support. There is something decidedly old-fashioned about the model of "modern" party organization that has been so widely accepted in Japan.

Indeed, as partisan attachments to political parties weaken in Japan's postindustrial society, the ties between individual politicians and the electorate that are structured through personal support organizations (*kōenkai*) may be assuming a new importance in linking voters and the government and in providing avenues for public political participation. It is not inconceivable that over time these organizations will be seen as possessing postmodern attributes, much as has been the case with forms of Japanese business organization that in earlier years were dismissed as backward and feudal.

In any case, it is unrealistic to expect that Japan will eventually adhere to western models of social and political organization and move away from a system in which local political organization is structured around individual politicians. Efforts to eradicate this kind of modern personalism from Japanese politics are not only somewhat futile. They also impede the process of meaningful political reform by demanding a wholesale change in the system rather than focusing attention on ways to control the excesses of the existing one.

Japan, now with a one-hundred-year history of parliamentary elections, has developed distinctive patterns of political organization that have proved to be remarkably resilient in the face of repeated efforts to change them. Changes have occurred, oftentimes in the most profound ways. But they have hardly taken the form that reformers had hoped for or that the model of the modern party embraced by the Japanese has called for. Japanese experience can only stand as an object lesson to anyone who wants to believe that the consequences of reform can be controlled, or even anticipated, in a highly developed and complex political system.

6.

THE CHANGING
JAPANESE VOTER

In the 1970s, as was noted in
an earlier chapter, it was widely thought that voting trends
were moving the party system toward a conservative-progressive parity (*hokaku hakuchū*). In the lower house elections held in 1976, 1979, and again in 1983, the LDP failed
to return a majority with its officially endorsed candidates.
It made a strong showing in the 1980 double election, the
first simultaneous election of members of both houses of
the Diet, winning 284 seats in the lower house. But this victory could plausibly be attributed to the combination of a
high voting rate produced by the novelty of the double election, and a large sympathy vote for the LDP resulting from
Prime Minister Ōhira's death in the middle of the campaign.

A double election was also held in 1986, and it produced a landslide LDP victory of unprecedented proportions. The party increased its representation in the lower
house by more than 50 seats, bringing its total to 304, the
largest number of seats it has ever controlled.[1] It did equally

well in the upper house election, its total of 70 successful candidates being the largest number it had ever elected in an upper house contest.

The LDP's share of the popular vote in the lower house race rose to 49.4 percent, the highest level it had reached in over twenty years, since the election held in 1963 when 54.7 percent of those voting chose LDP candidates. By prefecture, the LDP's popular vote ranged from a high of 78.4 percent in rural Aomori to a low of 25.4 percent in urban Kanagawa. It obtained over 50 percent of the vote in thirty-four prefectures and between 40 and 50 percent in nine others. It obtained more than a third of the vote in Tokyo (36.6 percent) and in Kyoto (35.0 percent) and less than 30 percent in only two prefectures, in the above-mentioned Kanagawa and in Osaka (27.4 percent).

The Socialist party suffered its worst defeat since 1949, electing only 20 members to the upper house and just 85 of its 141 lower house candidates. Among the losers were 27 of the party's 101 lower house incumbents who were running. For the first time the JSP won fewer seats in the lower house than the three centrist parties (the Kōmeitō, the DSP, and the SDL), which together elected 86 members. The party was shut out of fifty districts, a record high, and its share of the popular vote was an unprecedentedly low 17.2 percent.

The DSP also suffered heavy losses, winning only 26 lower house seats (compared to 38 in 1983) and securing only 6.4 percent of the vote (compared to 7.3 percent in the previous election). It was left without any representation at all in Tokyo for the first time in its history, its three incumbents and three new candidates there all going down to defeat.

The New Liberal Club's support continued to crumble. From a high point a decade earlier when it obtained 4.2 percent of the vote nationwide and elected 17 members in its first lower house contest, it was now reduced to 6 members and a meager 1.8 percent of the vote. As noted earlier, it disbanded soon after the election ended. The Social Democratic League elected 4 members with less than 1 percent of the popular vote.

The Kōmeitō and Communist parties managed to hold their own against the LDP onslaught. The Kōmeitō won only 2 seats less than the 58 it obtained in the prior lower house contest. The Communists returned 26 members, the same number elected in the previous race. Both parties' share of the nationwide popular vote declined slightly from the previous election in 1983 (from 10.1 to 9.4 percent for the Kōmeitō, and from 9.3 to 8.8 percent for the Communists), but generally both were able to hold their own, particularly in metropolitan districts where they have concentrated their organizational efforts and where they draw most of their support. This meant, however, that their support remained at levels initially reached in the 1970s. In Tokyo, for example, the Kōmeitō obtained the same 18.2 percent of the vote in the 1986 election as it did in the election held back in 1976. For the JCP, the 15.6 percent of the Tokyo vote it obtained in 1986 was virtually the same as the vote share it received a decade earlier, when 15.4 percent of those who voted in Japan's capital city chose Communist party candidates. But given the LDP's success in the 1986 election, these figures could be, and were, claimed to represent a victory of sorts.

To what extent could the LDP's resounding victory in this election be ascribed to the idiosyncrasies of the election district system and the double election ploy? Many observers believed that the LDP's success in 1980 was due to the fact that that year's double election was unprecedented, a view that seemed to be confirmed by the party's poor showing in the subsequent contest held in 1983. Could the 1986 results also be viewed as in some way aberrant?

The LDP expected the double election to raise the voting rate and thereby draw out to the polls LDP-inclined voters who might otherwise abstain. Recent elections seemed to demonstrate a close relationship between the voting rate and LDP performance. When the voting rate increased, as in the 1980 election, the LDP vote share also rose; when it declined, as it did in 1979 and 1983, so did the LDP's vote. In the election held in 1983, for example, the voting rate went down 6.6 percentage points. The LDP's share of the absolute vote (that is, its percentage of votes relative to the total electorate including those who did not vote) was 30.8 percent, down about four points from 34.9 percent in 1980. This decline amounted to almost two-thirds of the drop in the voter turnout between the two elections. In other words, for every three voters who cast ballots in 1980 but stayed home in 1983, probably two were people who had voted for the LDP in 1980.[2]

The voting rate of 71.4 percent in the 1986 election was higher than the record low 67.9 percent recorded in the previous 1983 race. But it was not as high as in the 1980 double election, when 74.5 percent of eligible voters went to the polls. Nor was it high by historical standards, being slightly below the 71.9 percent voting rate that is the average for all seventeen postwar lower house elections.

Although the voting rate fell short of the 1980 double election rate by 3.2 percentage points, the LDP's share of the popular vote was higher (by 1.5 points), and it won 20 seats more. Moreover, in Tokyo, where voter turnout was a relatively low 66.5 percent (compared to 68.9 percent in 1980), the LDP won 36.6 percent of the vote, an increase of 3.3 points over 1980, and 19 seats, the highest number ever. The increased voter turnout obviously helped the LDP, since it was the only party to significantly increase its vote over 1983. But in 1986, with the novelty of a double election having worn off and with nothing dramatic like the death of the incumbent prime minister to galvanize public interest, the double election ploy did not work in the sense of generating an unusually high voting rate.

Could the party's success in 1986 have been in part the consequence of its poor showing in 1983, when many of its candidates suffered narrow defeats? Invariably a number of candidates who come in just behind the last-placed winner (fourth in a three-member district, sixth in a five-member one, what in Japanese is called *jiten*) win the next time around, often in the top position, as a result of spending their full time from the day they are defeated until the next election building their local support organization and canvassing for votes.

In the 1983 election the LDP produced 61 *jiten* candidates. Forty-one of them ran in the 1986 contest, of whom 38 won. But it is not clear that being *jiten* was particularly important to these candidates' victories, since the success ratio for all LDP candidates (300 winners among 320 endorsed candidates) was equally high.

The high number of *jiten* candidates produced in the 1983 election is more relevant for explaining why the LDP did as poorly as it did in that earlier election than for explaining why it did so well in the one held in 1986. The LDP ran 339 candidates in 1983, more than in any election since 1967, its confidence high as a result of its victory in the previous double election in 1980 and because of public opinion polls that showed the popularity of both the party and Prime Minister Nakasone to be on the rise. But only a large increase in the voting rate could have brought victory to this large a number of LDP candidates. Instead the voting rate dipped, leaving 61 LDP *jiten* candidates who had vote totals that put them just behind the last-placed winners in their districts.

The question arises whether district reapportionment benefited the LDP. There were eight districts where the number of seats had been increased and seven that lost one seat each in the redistricting that took place just prior to the election. In the eight enlarged districts, the LDP picked up seven new seats. But the Communists also benefited from the redistricting, adding four new seats in these districts. The JSP and the NLC and an independent provided the losses. In the seven districts that were reduced in size, the JSP lost five seats and the LDP lost two. Overall, therefore, redistricting provided a net gain for the LDP of five seats.

The most persuasive evidence on behalf of the view that the 1986 election results were idiosyncratic and not reflective of long-term trends is that many voters who voted for the LDP would not have done so if they had anticipated the dimensions of the LDP victory. In a postelection *Asahi Shinbun* poll, 65 percent of respondents said that they believed that the LDP had won too many seats. Even among voters who had cast their ballots for LDP candidates, 53 percent said that they thought the LDP had won too many seats. Only 39 percent said that they thought it was good that the LDP had won a landslide victory.[3]

These data are entirely in accord with public opinion polls that show strong public support for narrow LDP majorities and for keeping the opposition in a position where it is able to operate as a brake on the ruling party. Forty-five percent of respondents to a 1984 Japan Broadcasting Company poll that is representative of the polling data said that they favored a narrow LDP majority. Another 35 percent supported "stable" LDP majorities. Only 10 percent expressed support for a coalition government that would exclude the LDP.[4]

It is not unreasonable to assume that after the LDP's poor performance in the 1983 election, many voters who abstained or voted for opposition party candidates in that election decided to give their vote to the LDP in 1986. Nor is it unreasonable to expect that the LDP will lose a substantial number of seats in the next election, even if its popularity among the public remains essentially unchanged. In the Japanese electoral system, quite minor variations in the voting rate and minor swings in the vote can produce major shifts in party performance. The JSP's 13 percent decline in its popular vote in 1986, for example, resulted in a 24 percent decline in its share of lower house seats. And the LDP's 7 percent increase in its popular vote resulted in a 16 percent increase in its share of seats. It would be surprising if the next election did not see some correction to the LDP's overshooting of its target in the 1986 contest.

But these factors alone do not explain the LDP's resounding electoral success. There is little reason to believe that the election's results were some kind of fluke. The size of the LDP victory was unexpected, but the party's success itself hardly came as a surprise. It confirmed what opinion polls had been showing: that LDP popularity had been increasing since the early 1980s and had risen by 1986 to a higher level than at any time since the party's founding thirty years earlier.

The LDP's Resurgence

Table 6.1 summarizes changes in party support as measured by *Asahi Shinbun* nationwide opinion surveys conducted between 1955 and 1986. Support for the LDP was remarkably constant from 1955 to the end of the 1970s, hovering around 45 percent. The growth in popularity of minor parties came almost entirely at the expense of the JSP. LDP support since 1980, however, has been consistently over 50 percent. In 1984 it was 54 percent on average; in 1985, 57 percent. And in a May 1986 *Asahi Shinbun* poll, it reached an unprecedentedly high level of 59.3 percent. Given these figures, it is not surprising that Prime Minister Nakasone was eager to call a lower house election or that he wanted a double election that might contribute to a higher than usual

TABLE 6.1. Party Popularity, 1956–1986 (In Percent)

	LDP	JSP	Kōmeitō	DSP	JCP	NLC	SDL
1955–1959	45.8	37.9	—	—	0.6	—	—
1960–1963	46.0	30.3	—	5.0	0.7	—	—
1964–1967	48.0	29.9	3.4	5.4	1.1	—	—
1968–1971	46.5	25.8	5.8	7.5	3.8	—	—
1972–1975	44.1	25.5	5.1	6.1	7.4	—	—
1976–1979	45.8	20.2	5.2	5.3	4.8	6.6	1.0
1980–1982	50.9	17.9	4.5	6.2	4.5	2.8	1.2
1983–1984	52.8	17.0	5.0	5.6	4.4	2.4	1.2
1985–1986	57.2	14.5	5.1	4.1	2.9	1.5	0.8

SOURCE: Compiled on the basis of opinion poll data provided by the *Asahi Shinbun*.

Note: The percentage figures represent the average percentages of all polls taken during the time periods indicated. The figure for 1985–1986 includes polls taken through May 1986.

voting rate and thereby bring out the reserves of LDP supporters who otherwise might not bother to vote.

Until 1979, as seen in table 6.2, the LDP's share of the popular vote declined with each succeeding lower house election, going from a high of 57.8 percent in 1958 to a low of 41.8 percent in 1976. But the 1979 election produced a significant turnabout, even though the nearly 3-percentage-point increase in the LDP's popular support was not translated into a larger number of seats. The party's vote share increased further in the 1980 election, and the share obtained in 1983, though less than in the previous race, was still higher than in any other lower house election in over a decade. And as noted, the 49.4 percent share obtained in the 1986 election was the highest in more than two decades.

Moreover, conservative party decline in the 1970s seems particularly steep because of the presence of the New Liberal Club. If the percentage of the vote obtained by the NLC is added to the LDP's vote share, the total conservative vote in the 1976 election turns out to have been less than 1 percentage point smaller than in the previous race in 1972; in 1983 the combined vote share was higher than in any election since 1967.

Furthermore, even as the LDP's vote share in lower house elections declined, the distance separating it and the

TABLE 6.2. Party Shares of the Valid Popular Vote, Lower House, 1958–1986 (In Percent)

	LDP	JSP	Kōmeitō	DSP	JCP	NLC	SDL	IND
1958	57.8	32.9	—	—	2.6	—	—	6.7
1960	57.6	27.6	—	8.8	2.9	—	—	3.2
1963	54.7	29.0	—	7.4	4.0	—	—	4.9
1967	48.8	27.9	5.4	7.4	4.8	—	—	5.8
1969	47.6	21.4	10.9	7.7	6.8	—	—	5.5
1972	46.9	21.9	8.5	7.0	10.5	—	—	5.3
1976	41.8	20.7	10.9	6.3	10.4	4.2	—	5.8
1979	44.6	19.7	9.8	6.8	10.4	3.0	0.7	5.0
1980	47.9	19.3	9.0	6.6	9.8	3.0	0.7	3.7
1983	45.8	19.5	10.1	7.3	9.3	2.4	0.7	5.0
1986	49.4	17.2	9.4	6.4	8.8	1.8	0.8	6.0

SOURCE: Ministry of Home Affairs data.

next largest party's share of the vote grew. In 1958 there were 24.9 percentage points separating the LDP and the JSP; in 1983 the gap was 26.3 points. This gap spread wider in the 1986 election, to 32.2 points.

An important factor in accounting for increased LDP electoral support has been changes in the voting behavior of Japanese voters who exhibit no strong party preferences. The LDP is not a party of strong supporters but, rather, a strong party of weak supporters. This is not entirely surprising since partisan attachments always have been relatively weak in Japan. One cross-national study of political participation, for example, found Japan to have the smallest percentage of strong party identifiers and the largest percentage of weak identifiers of all the countries surveyed (which included the United States, Austria, the Netherlands, and India).[5]

Data on party support in public opinion polls conducted by the *Asahi Shinbun* and many other polling agencies are based on responses to two questions. First, voters are asked what party they like the most. Those who offer no party name in response to this question comprise the group that is known in Japan as the "nonparty supporting strata" (*shiji seitō nashi sō*). These respondents are then asked a follow-up question which in the case of the *Asahi Shinbun* is phrased, "Leaving aside likes and dislikes, which one would you choose?" Only about 10 percent of respondents fail to give a party name in response to this question. Those who do choose a party comprise the group that is regarded as being weak party identifiers.[6]

According to *Asahi Shinbun* polls, between 1954 and 1961 some 40 percent of the electorate were part of the nonparty supporting strata. In the 1960s this percentage dropped to around thirty percent, but after 1970 it rose again to former levels.[7] In the July 1986 *Asahi Shinbun* poll it was 39.6 percent.[8]

But continuity in the size of the nonparty supporting electorate conceals an important change in its composition. There has been a shift, to borrow terms used by Walter Dean

Burnham, from old independents, exhibiting low levels of political interest and largely indifferent to parties, to new independents, politically attentive voters who consciously reject party affiliation.[9] In Japan old independents are primarily poorly educated older people living in rural and semirural areas who are protopartisans of the LDP, inasmuch as they are mobilized through traditional social networks to vote for LDP candidates. While not strong party supporters in a formal sense, they are "hard votes" for specific LDP politicians.[10] The new independents, by contrast, are most numerous among the young, the well-educated, and the urban.

According to *Asahi Shinbun* data, voters who indicated support for no party in the 1950s were drawn mainly from older voters who were either male farmers or women and who had low educational levels. By the 1970s, however, nonparty supporters were prevalent particularly among men and women in their twenties, white-collar workers and managers, and people with high educational levels.[11]

The rise of these new independents reflects a Japanese variation on the dealignment phenomenon—that is, the decline in party loyalties—evident in the United States and in most western European countries.[12] In Japan dealignment has occurred almost entirely on the left. The LDP's traditional support groups have remained steadfast in their support, while groups that were once the mainstay of the progressive camp now fill the ranks of Japan's new independents.

This process has been underway for two decades. It was already evident in the early 1970's that the opposition parties were being increasingly alienated from the public that had been traditionally opposed to the LDP.[13] But voters who left the JSP at that time had not yet abandoned the progressive camp. At the local level in particular, the decline of the JSP's popularity was paralleled by the success of independent candidates running with progressive party backing for governor and mayor in Japan's big cities and metropolitan prefectures.

From the mid-seventies, however, new independents began to shift their support increasingly to the LDP. In the *Asahi Shinbun* poll conducted in May 1986, when asked what party they liked, 32 percent of respondents first replied that they liked no party or did not know. In response to a follow-up question asking which one among existing parties they would choose, 65 percent named a party. Of these voters, 54 percent chose the LDP and 22 percent the JSP, while each of the other parties obtained 5 percent or less.[14] In another poll conducted two weeks prior to the 1986 election, 55 percent of respondents who said they supported no party and 66 percent of those who answered that they did not know said that they planned to vote for the LDP.[15]

It is not yet clear whether dealignment on the left is leading to a realignment on the right, i.e., turning independents into LDP partisans. There is some data that might be interpreted to suggest that this process is underway. According to *Yomiuri Shinbun* calculations based on its periodic public opinion surveys, for example, the number of independents declined by some 3.2 million between the 1983 and 1986 elections. This figure corresponds quite closely to the increase of 3.9 million in the LDP vote.[16] But the preponderance of evidence suggests that what is occurring in Japan, much as in the United States and elsewhere, is a general weakening of strong partisan feelings and party identification. Nationwide polls conducted by Japan's national newspapers show that upwards of 60 percent of Japanese voters do not decide who to vote for until close to election day.

Dealignment makes election outcomes less predictable than in a system in which most voters have strong party loyalties. But in Japan what is unpredictable is the margin of LDP victory. Most independents who do not vote for the LDP do not vote. They are not a swing vote in the usual sense in which that term is understood in western countries, voting for one party in one election, for a different party in another, with the hope that their vote will make a difference as to which party controls the government.

The processes of dealignment and the shift of the nonaligned voter toward support for the LDP has greatly reduced the gap in LDP support that used to exist between different age and occupational groups and between rural and urban voters. As a result, it has become increasingly difficult to distinguish the electoral choices of Japanese voters on the basis of how old they are, where they live, or what they do for a living.

Table 6.3 provides data on party support for the mid-1960s, the mid-1970s, and for 1986. The figures include both strong and weak party identifiers. In terms of age, voters in their twenties are now virtually indistinguishable from older voters in their support for the LDP. The life cycle theory of voting behavior—that voters start off supporting the left and grow more conservative as they get older—often has been overplayed in the Japanese case. More profound has been the stark generational change in voting behavior among new entrants into the electorate. In the early 1960s these young voters gave substantial support to the parties of the left; since the early 1970s they have been characterized, first, by the large number that rejects partisanship altogether and, among those who make a party choice, by support for the LDP.

This is true not only for young people generally but for university students who were in the 1960s a key element in the support of both the Socialist and Communist parties. In a survey conducted among University of Tokyo freshmen in 1983, 44.4 percent expressed no party preference or no opinion while 28.5 percent preferred the LDP, 10.5 percent the Socialist party, and 6.9 percent the JCP.[17] The survey also found that "liberal students are not drawn as strongly to leftist parties as conservative students are to conservative parties, a larger proportion remaining independent or even preferring conservative parties."[18]

This confirmed a conservative shift among University of Tokyo students that had been noticed initially in a poll conducted by the University's student newspaper in 1978. That survey found that among the 37.1 percent of Univer-

TABLE 6.3. Party Support in 1965, 1976, and 1986 (In Percent)

	LDP			JSP			Other Parties			No Party		
	1965	1978	1986	1965	1976	1986	1965	1976	1986	1965	1976	1986
Age												
20–24	38	38	55	45	21	9	11	23	20	6	18	16
25–29		40	62		27	12		24	14		9	12
30–34		42	59		25	15		21	14		12	12
35–39	41	45	54	42	31	17	10	15	16	7	9	13
40–49	45	45	55	34	26	15	9	18	18	12	11	12
50–59	53	47	60	26	23	19	8	19	12	13	11	9
60+	55	56	66	16	17	12	5	9	11	24	18	11
Sex												
Men	49	48	63	34	23	14	11	20	14	6	9	9
Women	42	43	56	35	25	15	7	17	15	16	15	14
Occupation												
Office workers	37	37	53	47	31	20	10	23	14	6	9	13
Managers	50	55	68	31	14	8	12	16	18	7	15	6

	1965	1976	1986	1965	1976	1986	1965	1976	1986	1965	1976	1986
Industrial workers	20	33	46	54	35	23	15	19	20	11	13	11
Service workers	35	43	58	43	26	13	11	16	16	11	15	13
Merchants & business owners	58	55	72	25	14	5	6	18	12	11	13	11
Self-employed	60	52	71	35	11	13	5	26	10	0	11	6
Farmers	59	62	74	19	17	9	5	13	8	17	8	9
Others	52	51	55	20	20	15	6	16	15	22	13	15
Residence												
Large cities	37	43	57	43	21	12	15	22	21	5	14	10
Medium cities	44	40	57	34	24	13	10	22	16	12	14	14
Small cities	48	47	62	35	28	16	6	14	12	11	11	11
Towns & villages	48	52	61	30	23	17	7	14	11	15	11	11
Overall	45	45	59	34	24	15	9	18	14	12	13	12

SOURCE: Data provided by the *Asahi Shinbun*.

Note: The figures for 1965 represent an average of the results of all polls taken in 1964, 1965 and 1966. Similarly the figures for 1976 are an average of poll data collected in 1975, 1976, and 1977. The figures for 1986 are from a poll conducted in May 1986.

sity of Tokyo freshmen who supported a political party, 45.2 percent favored the LDP, while support for the JCP was a mere 3.5 percent. The *Asahi Shinbun* reported this poll on its front page, commenting that "the left-wing University of Tokyo student who leads student protest movements may be becoming a myth."[19]

The significance of increased support for the LDP among young voters is heightened by the fact that the Japanese population is aging at a historically unprecedented rate. Coming years will see a falling off in the number of new entrants into the electorate and a growing proportion of voters among the oldest age groups. The LDP stands to benefit from this demographic trend. Many Japanese voters, like voters elsewhere, tend to continue to vote for their initial party of choice as they get older. One indication of this pattern in Japan is the fact that the JSP's support is now clustered among middle-aged voters instead of among young voters as it was in the 1960s. Also, while some voters become more conservative as they get older, there is no evidence to suggest that a significant number become more liberal.

Over the past two decades there has also been a sharp decrease in a rural-urban cleavage in party support. In 1966 a larger percentage of residents of large cities expressed support for the Socialist party than for the LDP. The LDP drew the support of a majority of residents of towns and villages, but public opinion surveys showed that less than 40 percent of people living in the country's largest cities supported it. In the mid-seventies, the LDP was still weak in large urban areas relative to its support levels in more rural parts of the country, though support for the Socialists in these urban centers had by then largely collapsed. A decade later LDP support, as measured by opinion polls, was nearly as high among residents of the country's largest cities as it was among those in its small towns and villages.

The nadir of LDP urban support occurred in the early and mid-1960s, when Japan was experiencing massive population movements from countryside to city. In 1965 some thirty prefectures (out of a total of forty-seven) experienced net population decline. The new urban dwellers produced by this population shift could not be reached by the LDP through its traditional approach of relying on the personal networks of community notables, since the new urbanites had few if any ties to these localities. On the other hand, their support was actively solicited by urban-based opposition parties. These parties could reach many of the new urban voters because of their links to union organizations or to Sōka Gakkai (which was and remains today an almost exclusively urban phenomenon), and by virtue of their support of local citizen movements that were seeking improved housing conditions, increased social services, and the like.

But the end of the high-growth era was accompanied by a settling down of Japan's urban population. Rural population decline slowed dramatically after 1970. In 1975 there was no prefecture experiencing net population loss from outward migration. Between 1975 and 1980 the only prefecture to experience a loss of population was Tokyo, which a decade earlier had been the fastest-growing prefecture. The growth in Tokyo's population since 1980 has not been due to a renewed increase in population exodus from rural areas, but seems to be produced primarily by suburbanites who now are able to afford to move closer to the metropolitan center and thereby reduce commuting time to work.

The settling down of the urban population has been accompanied by the growth of population in Japan's provinces. Japan's most rapidly growing areas are provincial cities, places where the LDP traditionally has been strong and where opposition parties other than the Socialists have only recently tried to establish themselves. They are cities whose new residents tend to come from nearby rural communities, either directly or by way of the so-called J turn, which is the term the Japanese use to refer to people who earlier had emigrated to metropolitan areas and now, rather than returning to their home villages (the U turn), return to a me-

dium-sized city offering employment opportunities and lo-
cated within a comfortable driving distance of their childhood
home.

The settling down of the urban population has resulted in the growth of urban neighborhoods that are relatively stable in terms of population and that are increasingly characterized by the kinds of extended networks of
personal relations, school and family ties, and active neigh-
borhood associations (*chōnaikai*) that traditionally have provided major channels for LDP politician access to the electorate in small towns in the countryside.

This settling down has also occurred in the context
of an important shift in public attitudes about welfare state
policies brought about by oil shocks and the slowdown in
economic growth. In the early 1970s progressive party
administrations came to power in one urban center after another, only to find that the economic dislocations provoked
by the first oil shock not only made it impossible for them
to fulfill their promises, but confronted them with a voter
backlash over their spending policies. Some opposition
leaders tried to jump on the bandwagon of small government and joined the "reconsidering welfare" debate that
erupted in the mid-seventies, as was noted in chapter 2. But
these efforts were half-hearted and unconvincing. By the
end of the decade the LDP had restored its leadership in
almost all of Japan's major cities, leaving the opposition in
full retreat.

In terms of electoral performance, the LDP draws a
considerably smaller share of the popular vote in metropolitan districts than in smaller cities or rural areas. In the
1986 election it obtained 35 percent of the popular vote in
metropolitan districts, compared to 60 percent in provincial
cities and 63 percent in rural constituencies. But the gap
between its support as measured by survey data and its share
of the vote in lower house elections is largely the product
of district size and the number of parties in the competition.
Metropolitan districts are mostly four- and five-member districts where all the opposition parties are active and where

a candidate can be elected with as little as 10 percent of the vote.[20] LDP enthusiasm for a single-member constituency system derives from the knowledge that the smaller the district, the fewer the opportunities for minor parties to be successful, whatever the district's demographics might be.

Although people living in densely populated urban areas confront problems of housing, congestion, pollution, and the lack of adequate leisure facilities, levels of satisfaction with urban life are remarkably high. The image of densely populated, highly urbanized metropolitan areas as a mass society of isolated, alienated individuals could hardly be at greater variance with the reality of urban life in Japan. Figure 6.1, which is based on a 1982 poll and describes feelings of attachment or belonging (*aichaku*) in cities of varying sizes and characteristics, is one illustration of this reality. Positive feelings run almost as high in metropolitan Tokyo and the Tokyo bedtown of Urawa as they do in the smaller and more placid cities of Morioka and Yonezawa.[21] Some 83 percent of Tokyo dwellers responding to this poll said they were either very attached or at least fairly attached to the city, while only 3 percent had unambiguously negative feelings about life there.

Relative satisfaction with life in Tokyo does not necessarily translate into satisfaction with the LDP. But it does not offer grounds, either, for a political movement based on the idea that urban dwellers are alienated and hostile. The appropriate image is not of alienation but of what Murakami Yasusuke has characterized as a "new middle mass,"[22] a large urban population of relatively affluent people who tend to define their political interests in terms of protecting the gains in living standards that they have achieved since they (or their parents) migrated to these urban centers two decades ago.

The decreasing salience of an urban-rural cleavage in Japanese party preferences has been paralleled by a sharp weakening of distinctions in party support between different occupational groups. Of particular note is the shift in party preferences of Japan's blue-collar labor force.

Socialist party support among these voters has decreased at a rapid rate. The JSP was supported by more than
half of blue-collar workers in the early 1960s. By the middle
of the seventies it drew the support of no more than a third
of these workers. In the mid-eighties it could claim the support of only a fifth of these blue-collar voters. For the LDP,

FIGURE 6.1. Levels of Attachment (*aichaku*) to Residential Area

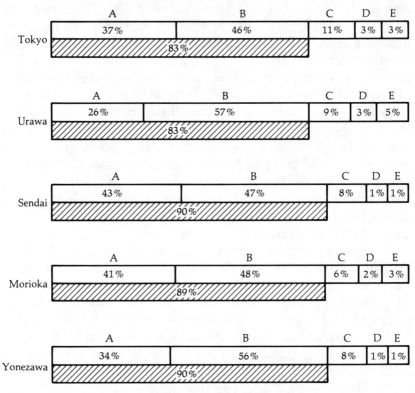

SOURCE: Sōrifu Kōhōshitsu, *Gekkan Yoron Chōsa* (Tokyo: Sōrifu Kōhōshitsu, August 1982).

Code:
A – Very attached
B – Fairly attached
C – Not very attached
D – Not attached at all
E – Don't know

the figures moved in the opposite direction. It drew the support of only a fifth of blue-collar workers in the early sixties but 46 percent in 1986, according to the *Asahi Shinbun* poll cited in table 6.3.

Survey data (from 1978) for the Tokyo metropolitan area, replicated in table 6.4, reveal a pattern of party support by occupational groups that is similar to the one reflected in the nationwide aggregate data. As would be expected, the LDP is especially popular among managers, sales personnel (over half of whom in this survey are retail shop owners and other independent small-scale businessmen), and service industry personnel (beauticians, cooks, owners of dry cleaning stores, etc). But it also obtained impressive support from blue-collar workers, and the support of nearly half of the college students surveyed. The only category in this poll where the JSP outpolled the LDP was among workers in transportation and communication, industries which have been predominantly in the public sector. These industries have been characterized by the presence of strong Socialist party supporting unions, such as the national railway workers (Kokurō), private railway workers (Shitetsu Rōren), and telecommunications workers (Zendentsū). The privatization of the telecommunications industry in 1985,

TABLE 6.4. Party Support by Occupation, Tokyo Metropolitan Area, 1978 (In Percent)

Occupation	LDP	JSP	Kōmeitō	DSP	JCP	NLC
Specialists, technicians	28	19	5	11	6	12
Managers	45	16	4	11	1	11
Office workers	33	20	4	7	3	11
Sales & marketing personnel	45	12	8	4	4	14
Transportation & communication personnel	27	35	4	6	8	6
Industrial workers	38	16	12	5	4	8
Service workers	47	4	10	5	1	14
Students	49	11	6	5	3	3
Retired persons	44	16	9	4	2	6
Unemployed	31	13	25	—	—	—
Other	33	13	10	5	1	9
Total	38	16	7	7	3	10

SOURCE: Hayashi Chikio, *Seiji Ishiki No Kanjō Kōzō No Kenkyū*, p. 34.

however, and of the national railways in 1987 have gravely weakened these two unions and their ability to secure votes for the JSP, as discussed further below.

A series of opinion surveys conducted among union members over the past several years provides further evidence of the decline in Socialist party working class support, and also lends credence to the thesis that dealignment, rather than a major increase in the number of voters who identify strongly with the LDP, is the most salient characteristic of contemporary Japanese voter attitudes. These surveys asked respondents who said that they supported no party whether they considered themselves to be progressive independents, conservative independents or just independents. The results of surveys conducted in 1978, 1982, and 1986 are replicated in table 6.5. What is particularly striking is the sharp decline over time in JSP support and in the percentage of progressive independents, and the rise in the percentage of respondents who say that they are independents, but neither progressive nor conservative. The highest percentage of these "neutral" independents, 41 percent, is among the 20- to 24-year-old group. The LDP obtains its highest levels of support from people between the ages of 20 and 34; the JSP is most popular among union members over the age of 35.

The Decline of Labor Union Militancy

Underlying the decline in working class support for the JSP reflected in the survey data is the immense weakening of the Japanese labor movement. The JSP has never had much success mobilizing nonunionized employees of small and medium-sized business firms. It has been a party of the labor elite, workers in large unionized firms and in the public sector.

The party's union base has been eroded in several ways. For one thing, there has been a general decline in union membership in Japan, as there has been in the United

TABLE 6.5. Party Support by Union Members (In Percent)

	LDP	JSP	Kōmeitō	DSP	JCP	NLC	Other	None (Independent)			NA
								Cons.	Prog.	Neut.	
1978	9.8	33.3	1.4	7.7	3.1	1.8	0.8	8.9	18.0	12.4	2.8
1982	8.3	25.9	2.3	10.3	3.0	1.1	0.6	10.8	17.6	18.6	1.7
1985	10.9	24.8	2.6	12.3	2.0	0.5	2.8	9.1	12.5	20.3	2.2
Age in 1985											
20–24	15.8	16.9	3.5	5.2	1.1	0.5	2.2	8.2	4.9	40.9	0.8
25–29	11.9	14.8	2.6	7.5	1.1	0.7	3.2	14.4	14.4	28.5	1.0
30–34	12.3	21.3	1.8	10.9	1.6	0.8	3.3	10.8	17.4	18.9	1.0
35–39	8.8	27.9	2.0	12.6	2.2	0.6	3.1	10.4	16.2	14.3	1.8
40–44	9.9	29.1	2.5	19.0	2.5	0.8	3.1	8.5	12.4	9.8	2.8
45–49	11.1	28.0	3.8	20.2	3.8	0.2	3.5	4.7	12.0	10.7	2.0
50–54	12.3	36.1	2.1	17.0	2.6	0.3	2.1	8.2	8.5	8.5	4.7
55+	9.2	43.4	4.0	11.6	3.5	0.0	0.6	6.1	9.8	7.6	1.7

SOURCE: Rōdōchōsa Kyōgikai, "Soshiki Rōdōsha No Shakai Seiji Ishiki," pp. 20–30.
Note: NA—No Answer.

States in recent years. Union membership hovered around 35 percent of the labor force until 1975, but has been in steady decline since then. In 1984 it fell below 30 percent for the first time and was at 28.9 percent at the end of 1985. Though this is still a considerably higher percentage of the labor force than the estimated 15 percent of workers organized into unions in the United States, there is no sign that the downward trend in union membership in Japan soon will be reversed.

The decline in union membership has been accompanied by a sharp falling off in political radicalism by the once powerful wing of the union movement associated with the JSP. Sōhyō, the JSP-supporting national labor umbrella organization, was in the 1950s the strongest force in the labor movement and was dominated by a leadership that continually reiterated its commitment to Marxism and to political struggle to bring down the capitalist order. By the end of the 1960's Sōhyō's Marxist appeal rang hollow to union members in private industries that had grown and prospered during the years of high growth. And from the mid-1970s on its leadership of annual so-called spring struggles for higher wages was weakened by the slowdown in growth, the readiness of company-based unions to accept low increases in wage levels, and the resistance of unions at the company and industry level to following Sōhyō's guidelines in formulating their spring struggle demands.

Although Sōhyō remains the largest federation by far of Japan's four so-called national centers—its nearly four and a half million members comprising 35 percent of all organized workers—it has lost much of its vitality. Like the Socialist party itself, it has found itself in the hands of a leadership unable to articulate new approaches and surviving through its readiness to forge compromises that paper over fundamental differences within the organization. The Marxist rhetoric that characterized Sōhyō in the 1950s has all but disappeared, but the organization has not yet found anything to replace it.

Moreover, Sōhyō increasingly has become the vehicle

for the expression of the interests of public sector unions which now account for over 60 percent of its total membership. Dōmei, the smaller federation that was formed soon after Nishio led his faction out of the JSP to form the Democratic Socialist party, and that provides the organizational backing for the DSP, represents only 17 percent of union members. Nevertheless, it represents more union members in the private sector of the economy than does Sōhyō, as seen in table 6.6.

Public sector unions in Japan are centralized, and they have sought to realize their demands by exercising political influence on the Diet, resorting to strikes which take the form of "strikes for the right to strike" (*suto ken suto*) to get around the legal ban on strikes by public sector workers, and generally acting out their conflicts with the authorities in the public arena. Privatization, however, both decentralizes these unions and exerts tremendous pressures on them to privatize their conflicts with management and seek accommodation along lines common to private sector company unionism in Japan.

The privatization of the telecommunications monopoly in 1985 led the All Japan Telecommunications Workers' Union (Zendentsū), with its 270,000 members, out of the Council of Public Corporation Workers' Union (Kōrōkyō). Kōrōkyō, which prior to Zendentso's departure had 830,000

TABLE 6.6. Labor Union National Centers (Numbers of Members, in Thousands)

	Sōhyō	Dōmei	Chūritsu Rōren	Shin-Sanbetsu	Other	Total
Public Sector	2,646	144	0.04	3	233	3,025
Union Members	(88%)	(4.8%)				
Private Sector	1,719	2,016	1,557	58	4,588	9,393
Union Members	(18%)	(22%)	(13%)			
Total Union	4,365	2,161	1,557	61	4,821	12,418
Members	(35%)	(17%)	(12%)	(0.5%)	(38%)	
Zenminrōkyō						
Members	1,229	1,540	1,203	58	1,198	5,156

SOURCE: Nihon Rōdō Kyōkai, *Rōdō Undō Hakusho*, 1986, pp. 337 and 525.

members and is the heart of the Sōhyō organization, also lost the 30,000-member All Monopoly Corporation Workers' Union (Zensenbai) with the privatization of the tobacco monopoly. It has now had to accept the privatization of the national railways, which threatens to devastate the public sector union movement in Japan.

The National Railway Workers Union (Kokurō), one of the most powerful unions in Sōhyō and one of the major pillars of union support for the JSP, engaged in a futile effort to stop privatization that resulted in defections from within its own ranks and confrontation with other smaller unions of public railway workers. Its membership plummeted. In the three months from April to June 1986, Kokurō lost 10,000 members. Between 1980 and 1986 its membership was reduced by a third, from 250,270 to 155,723. And then in less than a year it was cut again by half. In March 1987, one month before the national railway system was privatized and divided into several regional companies, Kokurō had only 62,000 members.[23]

In an effort to survive privatization, Dōrō, the union of railway engineers, and until recently one of the most politically radical unions in Sōhyō, accepted the government's plans for privatization. It joined hands with Tetsurō, a small DSP-supporting "second union" that had been formed to counter the influence of Kokurō, and at its July 1986 convention decided to withdraw from Sōhyō.[24] To make things worse for the JSP, one of the consequences of the drive for administrative reform was a change in the law to require national railway employees to resign from their employment in the railways if elected to city, town, or village assemblies. (They had long been required to resign from the railways if elected to prefectural assemblies.) This has greatly weakened Kokurō's power at the local level and its ability to gather votes for the JSP.[25]

Public sector unions that do not face the threat of privatization have been weakened as well. The Union of Local Government Employees (Jichirō), with 1.27 million members the largest union in Sōhyō, has been bearing the brunt of public anger over the high salaries and lavish retirement benefits enjoyed by many local government workers and has been hurt by a concerted government campaign to reduce both the number of such workers and their benefits. (Between 1975 and 1985 Jichirō membership declined by more than 80,000.)

The Japan Teachers Union (Nikkyōso) has been weakened by a sharp decline in membership among new teachers,[26] and by Prime Minister Nakasone's success in taking the initiative in championing educational reform. This has left Nikkyōso in the hapless position of criticizing both the existing educational system and efforts to reform it, without being able itself to articulate a reform program capable of generating public interest. This once powerful union has been all but shunted to the sidelines as the Japanese consider making far-reaching educational reforms.

At fundamental odds with the public sector unions over Sōhyō's tactics and goals are the private sector unions that remain in Sōhyō, led by the steel workers, one of that organization's most militant unions at one time. Although Sōhyō has maintained an official policy of exclusive support for the JSP, many of its private sector unions support DSP and Kōmeitō candidates and advocate the unification of the labor movement into one national center that would not be aligned with any political party. Like private sector unions in Dōmei, these private sector Sōhyō unions generally subscribe to the theory that the union movement should concern itself with seeking economic gains within the existing political system and eschew direct involvement in political struggles. In the context of Japanese business organization, this often means that "moderate" union leadership is simply passive, promanagement company unionism.

Over the past decade private sector unions have strengthened their ties with each other despite their division into competing national centers. This trend culminated in December 1982 in the formation of the Zenminrōkyō (the National Council of Private Sector Unions, Zenkoku Minkan Rōdō Kumiai Kyōgikai), a development of considerable potential consequence both for the union movement and for the political parties that have been closely linked to it. As of November 1985, Zenminrōkyō had a membership of fifty-five unions with 5.2 million members (including seventeen major private sector unions in Sōhyō), accounting for 54.6 percent of unionized workers in the private sector.

Zenminrōkyō was founded with the express purpose of creating a new unified national center of private sector unions. At its fourth congress in November 1985, it decided to transform itself from being a "Council" into a federation (or "national center," in Japanese) at its sixth congress in 1987. Dōmei, Chūritsu Rōren (a federation dominated by one of the prime movers of the movement to unify private sector unions, the Electrical Workers' Union, Denki Rōren), and the small Shinsanbetsu have pledged to dissolve their organizations when Zenminrōkyō establishes itself as a national center of the union movement.

In order to avoid seeing many of its private sector unions leave the federation, Sōhyō has taken the position that the transformation of Zenminrōkyō into a federation is a "transitional" step toward the goal of completely unifying the union movement (i.e., including public sector unions), and that Sōhyō unions in the private sector would be permitted to hold dual membership in the two federations until that occurs. Zenminrōkyō has set 1989 as its target date for bringing public sector unions under its wing. Sōhyō at its 1986 convention declared that its target was to effect the complete unification of the labor movement by 1990.[27] But these are difficult if not impossible goals to reach, given the intense opposition of most public sector unions to a merger that would greatly weaken their influence in the union movement.

Zenminrōkyō also agreed at its 1985 convention that as a federation it would not link itself to any political party or lend campaign support to any candidates, leaving it up to each constituent union to make its own decisions on political support. If such a position actually were to be adopted by a unified national center, it would mean a sharp break with the existing formal pattern of union-party relations whereby Sōhyō gives exclusive support to the JSP, and Dōmei to the DSP. But the adoption of a stance of neutrality vis-à-vis the issue of party support would not be as much of a change from current practices as one might think, inasmuch as meaningful support is given to candidates by individual unions rather than by their national centers. The absence of national center support would no doubt make things somewhat more difficult for both the JSP and DSP, particularly if it led constituent unions to adopt the same policy. But the net effect of a stance of political party neutrality by a new union federation would be to accelerate the present trend toward the deradicalization, indeed the depoliticization, of the Japanese labor movement.

These developments must make one ponder why blue-collar workers give as much support to the JSP (and to the DSP) as they do. Partly it is a matter of habit: it is reasonable to assume that more middle-aged workers support the JSP than do young workers because these older voters are simply continuing to vote the way they have always voted.

This support also has a great deal to do with the prevalence of union leaders as JSP and DSP candidates. Union-based candidates receive the lion's share of union campaign contributions. They also are able, as nonunion candidates are not, to appeal to union members' organizational loyalties and to argue the advantages of having "one of our own" in the Diet.

In an interesting survey conducted by the federation of unions in the Nippon Steel Corporation, respondents were asked to explain why they participated in election campaigns. The results are replicated in table 6.7. Half of the total number of respondents (48.9 percent) indicated that they participated in election campaigns. Of this group, 69 percent indicated that they took part either because they "were performing their role as union members" or because they "were responding to requests from above." This passive participation was particularly pronounced among female union members, virtually all of whom are graduates of high school or junior college working for a few years before marriage: over 60 percent said they participated because they were asked to do so by someone from above.

Participation for explicitly political goals was lowest among the youngest voting age workers and highest among the oldest workers. The single largest response offered by workers in their 20s was that they were asked to participate by superiors. For people over the age of 30, the most frequently offered reason was their sense of obligation to perform one's union-related duties. The relatively high percentage of those over 45 who said that they participated either to have their personal views reflected in politics or to further the cause of the union movement in general is probably the reflection of attitudes forged in the 1950s, when the steelworkers' union was in the forefront of a movement committed to radical political change.

TABLE 6.7. Union Members' Reasons for Participating In Election Campaigns (In Percent)

	A	B	C	D	E	F
Age						
20–24	6.8	9.8	14.4	52.3	16.7	0.0
25–29	7.6	12.4	30.9	38.7	9.7	0.7
30–34	9.7	9.7	39.4	30.9	10.0	0.3
35–39	7.6	10.0	39.0	33.4	9.0	1.0
40–44	7.8	9.7	42.7	30.2	9.0	0.6
45–49	12.8	13.0	36.2	28.1	8.7	1.2
50+	14.7	13.2	34.0	26.1	10.6	1.5
Sex						
Men	9.3	11.0	36.2	32.8	9.8	0.8
Women	7.1	4.8	16.7	60.7	10.7	0.0

SOURCE: Shin Nihon Seitetsu Rōdō Kumiai Rengōkai, *Seiji Ishiki Chōsa,* Chōsa Jihō, no. 16 (Tokyo: Shinnittetsu Rōsō Rengokai, February 1979).
Code:
A—I felt that I participated directly in order to have my views reflected in politics.
B—I felt that by participating I would be contributing to the development of the union movement.
C—I felt that I performed a role incurred by membership in the union organization.
D—I felt that I participated because I was asked to do so from above.
E—I did not have any particular reason.
F—No answer.

The Limits of Patron-Client Relations

Despite the lack of strong working class support for leftist parties, analyses of Japanese voting behavior often have persisted in focusing on socioeconomic status. This is partly due to the lack of politically significant differences of race, ethnicity, language, regionalism, religion (with the singular exception of Sōka Gakkai, as noted below), or virtually any of the other social cleavages that are so deeply imbedded in western party systems. It might be reasonable to hypothesize that partisanship based on one's socioeconomic status would, if anything, be particularly pronounced in a developed market economy like Japan's where there is a less than equal distribution of wealth and an absence of the kinds of sharp cleavages that crosscut class differences in other advanced capitalist societies. The cross-national study of political participation organized by Verba, Nie, and Kim is just one of many studies that takes this position, arguing that "the absence of clear subcultural cleavages suggest emphasis on occupational characteristics in Japan."[28]

Pursuit of the seeming logic of this hypothesis invariably leads to an analysis of why there is so much apparently deviant behavior on the part of the Japanese working class in not supporting working class parties in greater numbers. Verba, Nie, and Kim raise but do not adequately deal with this question. Instead they cite others who claim that the reasons have to do with the pervasiveness of personal networks and their ability to overwhelm class-based interests.[29]

The importance of personality and of networks of personal relationships in Japanese politics is not in dispute. LDP politicians typically organize large numbers of voters into their own support organizations, *kōenkai*, that perform many of the functions that in other countries are carried out by local party organizations. These organizations are built both out of personal relationships between the Diet politician and voters, and on top of the personal support bases established by prefectural, city, town, and village assemblymen and mayors. While local politicians, who have a vested interest in convincing Diet politicians of their vote-getting powers, may sometimes exaggerate their ability to deliver the votes of their supporters, there is no question but that they are key elements in the personal political machines that every LDP politician constructs.

But it is not helpful to view these individual-based organizations as a variant on political clientelism. Central to any meaningful definition of clientelism is the notion that a relationship of exchange is involved between persons of radically different power resources.[30] But unlike the situation in many Latin American or Southeast Asian countries where clientelism is strong—and unlike the situation in pre-war Japan—the politician or his local supporter in contemporary Japan is not a powerful landlord demanding compliance with his political decisions in exchange for something that is of basic importance to his clients. The postwar land reform effectively eradicated the economic basis for such clientelist relationships.

The politician today is much more a supplicant, promising to deliver more pork barrel than his competitor. Ties of sentiment based on family, marriage, school relationships, favors to be repaid, and so on are crucial to forging bonds between politician and voter—which is why second-generation politicians are so numerous and why almost all politicians are natives of the districts from which they stand for election. Furthermore, as long as the politician is able to deliver on his promises to a reasonable degree, these bonds will help him fend off even competitors who have the resources to outbid him but who lack local personal ties that are as extensive. But politicians who prove themselves to be ineffective in providing what the Japanese like to call a "pipe" from the center to the locality to serve local interests find these ties of sentiment to be fragile indeed.

Nor, incidentally, does it make very much sense to view this organizational mode as feudal, as does much Japanese scholarship and public commentary. It is true enough that the social relationships imbedded in Japanese local political organizations have features similar to what Marc Block has identified as characteristic of social relationships in feudal society: "a vast system of personal relationships whose intersecting threads [run] from one level of the social structure to another."[31] But it makes no more sense to characterize Japan as "feudal" for that reason than it would be to characterize western feudal society as "modern" in the Japanese sense. And, in any case, there is no reason to believe that Japan will rid itself of its supposedly feudal remnants.

Moreover, no matter how skillfully the LDP has manipulated social networks to provide a solid base of support that cuts across conventional social cleavages, this manipulation alone does not explain the increase in LDP support—or the even more impressive decrease in Socialist support—that has occurred in recent years. Nor does it explain why the LDP has been able to increase its support among voters who are not caught up in LDP-linked social networks. The view that the LDP owes its success primarily to its ability to exploit webs of social relationships is also contradicted by the fact that its popularity has risen along with heightened public interest in issues that transcend parochial constituency concerns. Although reliable survey data on this subject are elusive, more Japanese voters both in rural and urban settings seem to take into account the personalities of party leaders and national and international policy issues in making their voting choices today than a decade ago. Theories of patron-client relations do not help explain these developments.

The relevance of socioeconomic status to the party preferences of the Japanese electorate has been further obfuscated by the emergence in Japan of a society in which something on the order of 90 percent of the working-age population considers itself to be "in the middle." Most Japanese today, as did most Americans and Europeans in the late 1960s,[32] see themselves as roughly middle class. This is not, as many Japanese believe, a uniquely Japanese phenomenon. Nor is the absence of strong class differentiation in Japan culturally rooted and therefore quasi-permanent, as some like to argue. The emergence of a "middle mass" in Japan was the product of the rapid spread of affluence in a society made extraordinarily mobile by the dislocations produced by war and by the reforms of the early postwar years. It therefore would not be surprising to see the social structure become less fluid and develop new rigidities as a result of poor economic performance over a considerable period of time, increased unemployment, or merely the inevitable settling down of the society that comes with economic success and social and political stability.

The argument has been made that the impact of affluence and of postindustrial values on party preferences in European politics has been blunted because patterns of political partisanship were frozen in the early years of the party system, a phenomenon especially relevant for explaining why working class parties have continued to be supported by people who in their self-perception are part of the broad middle of society.[33] This theory has appeared less convincing in the 1980s, given the surge in conservative party support among working class voters in Great Britain, the United States, and elsewhere, than it did in the 1960s. But at the least, longtime party loyalties contributed to inhibiting or retarding the processes of dealignment that are now occurring in nearly all modern democracies.

In Japan, however, the party system did not stabilize in the early years of industrialization. Working class parties, in particular, were not given full freedom to organize until after the end of the Pacific War. They then tried to do so in a period of frenetic social and economic change. With the absence of traditional patterns of political loyalties to hold working class voters to them, Japan's Socialist and Communist parties have faced enormous problems in building or even holding on to their support among the constituencies whose interests they claim to represent.

The impressive shifts in partisan preferences among Japan's voters that have been noted in this discussion—

namely, dealignment on the left and an increase in LDP support—result from a combination of long-term social changes, public perceptions of the political opportunity structure, and specific environmental factors. Clearly many Japanese, regardless of where they live or how they earn their livelihood, are motivated politically by a desire to protect the enormous gains in living standards made during the past decades, and by an uneasiness about future prospects given lower growth rates and a more unstable international environment now than the country enjoyed in the 1960s.

Concern for protecting the achievements of the past thirty years partly explains why the LDP has done better in the comparatively adverse economic and international environment of recent years that it did in the halcyon days of high economic growth. The feeling that it is imprudent to change horses in midstream, especially when traversing a particularly treacherous passage, is very strong with Japanese voters. Voters may be dismayed by revelations of corruption in the LDP but continue to regard it as the only party capable of governing. As a result, the opposition has done best when times were good and the popular mood was upbeat about the future. Under those circumstances more people are willing to vent their concern over the "quality" of politics.

There is also the matter of the real choices the Japanese voter has when he goes to the polls. The choice is not between several parties, each representing "a body of men," in Edmund Burke's famous definition of parties, "united for promoting by their joint endeavors the national interest, upon some particular principle in which they are all agreed."[34] It is a choice among individual candidates whose appeals are far removed from principles and from the national (rather than the local) interest, and among political parties distinguished by the fact that all but one have been parties of protest for about as long as most voters can remember. Voters who go to the polls, in other words, are constrained in their choices by the particular individual candidates and parties that are in the competition, and by the reality of one-party dominance. Looking for expressions of class interests or value orientations in party choice is fairly futile in a system which has only one broad-based governing party and a number of small protest parties.

The Political Ramifications of Changing Values

The failure of conventional indicators to reveal differences in party choices among the Japanese electorate has led a number of Japanese scholars to explore variability in lifestyles, belief systems, and various value orientations as possible sources of differences in political partisanship.[35] These analysts have correlated with political party preferences attitudes toward religion, aesthetics, company paternalism, nationalism, individualism, and a range of other value indicators. The methodology has been innovative and imaginative, but the result has been a profile of a Japanese electorate remarkably homogeneous in its value orientations: supporters of Japan's various political parties, despite the wide spectrum of ideologies and programs these parties represent, embrace strikingly similar values and attitudes. Diversity in Japanese views does not correlate closely with patterns of party support.

The one exception is religion, where Kōmeitō supporters are clearly outside the bounds of the dominant value consensus. While only 9 percent of LDP supporters, 5 percent of supporters of the JSP, and no supporters of the Communist party indicated that they engage in religious activity, some 46 percent of Kōmeitō supporters responded that they do. "Belief in religion" ranges from 9 percent for the Communists to 29 percent for LDP supporters, but the figure for Kōmeitō supporters is 83 percent.[36]

Other than confirming that the Kōmeitō represents members of the Sōka Gakkai, the distribution of value and attitudinal differences among the Japanese public fails to reveal the presence of any significant subcultures that might plausibly explain variations in party preferences. For example, Hayashi correlates party preferences with attitudes about company paternalism. Respondents were asked whether they would rather work for a boss "who gets involved in your private life" (*ninjō kachō*) or for one with whom contact was limited to business hours and professional matters. The range of preference for the *ninjō kachō* was from 73 percent of Communist party supporters to 83 percent of LDP supporters. Table 6.8 summarizes the results of Hayashi's analysis of the relationship between value orientations and party support and shows that the range of differences in value orientations among supporters of different parties is exceedingly narrow.

Communist and LDP supporters, as might be expected, tend to occupy the extremes on most variables, while JSP supporters almost invariably are at the middle of the range, but the distance separating them is small. One of the

TABLE 6.8. Value Orientation and Party Support (In Percent)

	LDP	JSP	DSP	Kōmeitō	JCP	No Party
Achievement orientation	72	76	72	74	78	73
Company paternalism	83	82	76	78	73	82
Religious-like spirit	82	77	72	94	68	70
Japanese aesthetics	92	91	91	89	87	88
Support for dominant values	82	82	78	84	77	78

SOURCE: Hayashi Chikio, "Nihonjin No Ishiki Wa Seitō Shiji Betsu Ni Dō Chigau Ka," in Nihonjin Kenkyūkai, ed., *Shiji Seitō Betsu Nihonjin Shūdan*, p. 15.

Notes: **Achievement orientation** measured by the percentage of respondents who agreed that a company should employ the person who does best on the company entrance examination rather than the child of a company colleague. **Company paternalism** measured by the percentage of respondents who favored working for a *ninjō kachō*, a boss who would involve himself in the worker's private life. **Religious-like spirit** measured by the percentage of respondents who said that they valued a religious-like spirit (*shūkyōteki na kokoro*) regardless of whether they believed in a religion or not. **Japanese aesthetics** measured by the percentage of respondents who said they preferred Japanese gardens to western gardens.

features of Communist party supporters, for example, is the high value they tend to place on individualism and western values. These values tend to be embraced more by younger than older voters, but the relatively high support for individualism among JCP voters holds even when one controls for age. Here again, however, the degree of difference between JCP and LDP supporters is relatively narrow. Moreover, the strength of individualist values among JCP supporters means only that a higher percentage of Communist party supporters than of supporters of other parties emphasize these values. It does not mean that people who hold these values primarily support the JCP which, after all, obtains only a small share of the electorate's support. This data relating individualism to party identification also lends support to the view that part of the Communist party's appeal derives not from its collectivist ideology but from its being perceived as a channel for the expression of nonconformist behavior.

In terms of basic attitudes, no party, with the exception of the Kōmeitō on issues regarding religion, is the object of support of a group that embraces a range of opinions clearly at variance with the majority opinion in the society. This is in stark contrast, for example, to the picture of subcultural integration and exclusivity presented by Richard Hamilton in *Affluence and the Worker in Fourth Republic France*. Hamilton describes how supporters of the French Communist party (the PCF) comprise a discrete subculture with shared attitudes about life, work, and human relationships distinct from those who are not part of their world. The burden of Hamilton's argument is that the existence of this subculture has helped protect the PCF's base of support in the face of increasing affluence. It suggests a provocative contrast with Japan, where the absence of deeply rooted social cleavages means that no working class party has been able to enjoy the buffer-like effects that deep and long-held values can create against the impact of changes in the material well-being of its supporters and in the narrowing of class differences.

The absence of clear subcultural differences in contemporary Japan also points to one of the most fundamental changes in the character of the Japanese polity to occur over the past thirty years. This is the breakdown of the conservative-progressive cleavage. And that, in turn, reflects the end of a long era during which the Japanese electorate was deeply divided over fundamental values relating to Japaneseness and modernity.

The expectation that economic development would bring about an increase in the number of urban wage earners embracing modern values and a decline in farmers with their traditional (i.e., feudal) values was the fundamental assumption that underlay the predictions of the 1950s that the progressives would eventually capture governmental power. Thus, it was thought that a majority of voters would come to identify themselves as modern-oriented progressives rather than as tradition-bound conservatives. Watanuki Jōji captured the essence of this value cleavage in his notion of Japan being divided by a "cultural politics."

Later Watanuki rather lamely defended his theory as being "not wholly wrong."[37] But the theory was more significant than that. It identified a key feature of the Japanese body politic during the first twenty years of the postwar period. What Watanuki failed to anticipate—indeed what all predictions of growing progressive party strength failed to recognize—was that Japanese economic success and the end of American hegemony in world affairs would precipitate a breakdown of this value cleavage and leave the LDP, with all of its traditionalist orientations, the defender of the successes of Japan's modernization.

Changing Japanese perceptions of the relationship between Japaneseness and modernity are particularly well illuminated by the interesting work of the sociologist Tsujimura Akira on changes in postwar Japan's popular culture. Tsujimura analyzed shifts in the themes of books appearing on Japan's best-seller lists from the early postwar years until the end of the 1970s. In the 1950s the most popular books were those highly critical of indigenous Japanese mores and values. They differed among themselves in terms of their political orientations and prescriptions for change, some arguing that Japan's salvation lay in the adoption of Marxist socialism, others that success would come only with modernization along essentially American lines. But whatever their ideological bent, the common element in the books that rose to the top of the best-seller list in this decade was what Tsujimura calls a "reject Japan thesis" (*nihon hitei ron*).

The rejection of Japanese indigenous political values and practices as backward, as well as the coexistence of western liberal and Marxist ideology in the same political camp, were central features of Japan's political culture during this decade. There was a widespread belief that the Socialists and the Communists comprised a camp of modern citizens struggling to overcome a traditionalist majority, and that to be modern meant to fight against a dominant traditionalist culture.

Tsujimura points out that the 1960s, that decade of double-digit economic growth rates and rapid increases in the standard of living, saw the enormous popularity of a spate of so-called how to books, practical and functional guides to getting rich, speaking better English, having a more exciting social life, and in general getting the most out of the opportunities opened up by Japan's new-found prosperity. The decade was a transitional one in which earlier debates about modernization were waning but in which new perspectives had not yet crystallized.

The transitional qualities of the period that Tsujimura emphasizes were manifested politically in the beginnings of the decomposition of the conservative-progressive dichotomy. New centrist parties such as the Kōmeitō and the Democratic Socialists emerged, and there was a move away from party support among voters who had been the stalwarts of the progressive parties. But given the transitional quality of the time, these new independents, when they voted, tended to support candidates backed by opposition parties, as mentioned earlier. It was a decade in which the processes of dealignment on the left were in an early stage:

voters who were no longer supporters of the Socialists were still part of the progressive camp.

The 1970s became the decade of the *nihonjin ron*, the Japanese national character debate. Instead of rejecting Japanese ways of doing things, many of the books the Japanese were reading were extolling for the most part the positive virtues of Japanese approaches and the compatibility of indigenous Japanese practices with modern, indeed postindustrial, life. The *nihon hitei ron*, the "reject Japan thesis" of the 1950s, had been transformed in less than two decades to a new *nihon kōtei ron*, the "affirm Japan thesis." It was fitting, if not a little ironic, that in place of the Japanese-authored books propounding the importance of emulating foreign countries that headed the best-seller lists in the 1950s, the book that rose to the top of the best-seller chart in the late 1970s that best captured the new Japanese mood and the shift in attitudes about the compatibility of modernity and Japaneseness was the Japanese language translation of Ezra Vogel's *Japan as Number One*.[38]

These changes in public attitudes also became clearly visible in the political trends that gathered strength from the middle of the 1970s onward: in the increased popularity of the LDP, the decline in Socialist support, and in Japan's centrist parties' disengagement from the progressive camp and their search for an opening to the right. Even talk about the need for party modernization or the backwardness of factions began to disappear from political debate, as noted in chapter 5. The notion that people embracing modern values were a minority in a country ruled by a political party responsive to the interests of old, traditionalist middle classes had lost its credibility. The LDP became identified with defense of the new Japan, while the Socialists became increasingly viewed as musty and backward looking.

The emergence of the modern sector of Japanese society as the dominant majority undercut the basis for the cultural politics out of which the conservative-progressive cleavage had arisen. Economic success—and the intense interest of the rest of the world in learning how Japan achieved it—has tremendously eroded a Japanese perception of a contradiction between Japaneseness and modernity. This amounts to a fundamental change in Japan's political culture, one that is at the heart of the disintegration of the progressive camp and the new surge in support for the LDP.

EPILOGUE: THE JAPANESE WAY OF POLITICS

The basic theme of this book has been the Japanese capacity to combine change with political stability. For more than three decades the Liberal Democratic party alone has held power in Japan. Not only has it never lost a national election; there has never been a Diet election in which anyone, in the LDP or the opposition, has assumed anything but that the LDP would return victorious. The only question has been the size of its victory. Thus defeat has come to mean to the LDP winning less than a "secure" majority, and the usual democratic political drama of struggles for power between leaders of different parties has been replaced by power struggles between leaders of discrete, well-organized factions within the LDP.

But this umbrella of one-party LDP rule has provided a cover for an enormous range of political changes, not the least of which has been the change in the LDP itself: in its organization, its electoral bases of support, its role in government decision-making processes, and its policy orientations. Over time the LDP has become a differentiated, complex organization. Factions, which continue to play critical roles in recruiting the nation's top political leadership, have changed considerably in their internal organization from what they were in the early years of LDP rule. As they have moved through successive generations of leaders, their initial pattern of strong patron-client relationships centered around a single powerful faction boss has been replaced by a more complex set of authority relationships. Changes in laws regulating political funding, the high cost of political life itself, growth in the size of factions as each has sought to maximize its share of party and governmental power, and the attenuated emotional bonds and prevalence of more pragmatic ties between faction leaders and the party's backbenchers have helped turn factions into something other than the personal coteries of supporters of particular party leaders.

This more collegial structure does not necessarily mean greater factional cohesiveness, however. The most cohesive factional structure is one in which each member believes that he owes an allegiance to the faction's leader that cannot be broken under almost any circumstance. That sense of loyalty is much diminished in today's LDP factions. In its place there are various subsets of much less intense loyalties between senior faction members and particular individuals who they helped recruit into the faction and with whom they have especially close relationships. It is not inconceivable that future succession struggles will reveal the existence of what amounts to factions-within-factions, and that rivalries for leadership might well strain factional cohesion and produce splits, for a time at least, and an increase in the number of factions in the LDP system. But the election district system and the informal rules that have developed within the LDP to determine who shall hold powerful party and government positions are factors that bolster factional unity, in spite of these internally generated divisive pressures.

The development of what amounts to a body of common law to regulate recruitment of LDP Diet members into party posts and the cabinet; the evolution of factions into more collegial organizations; and the ability of many long-term incumbent Diet members to pass on a considerable share of their personal support to their chosen successors have helped produce important changes in the characteristics of Japanese political leadership. As we have seen, there has been an extraordinary increase in the number of second-generation politicians, many of whom have a more cos-mopolitan background than has been typical of men seek-ing political careers in Japan but lack both the policy ex-pertise of the bureaucrat-turned-politician and the political skills and down-home touch of Japan's long line of colorful and powerful professional politicians.

Japan's new leaders are less able to amass the kind of power that traditionally has been associated with faction bosses, and they have weaker personal ties to the profes-sional bureaucracy. But some of them have a more inter-nationalist world view than their predecessors and are more inclined to involve themselves in a wider range of policy issues than has usually been the case with LDP leaders. Whether they will prove up to the task of effectively exer-cising the responsibilities that will inevitably be thrown upon them, however, is one of the major imponderables of the next decade of Japanese politics.

The pattern of leadership instability within the con-text of a stable party system that was so characteristic of Japanese politics in the years between the retirement of Prime Minister Satō in 1972 and the arrival of the Nakasone administration in 1983 is likely to be a recurring feature of Japanese politics in the post-Nakasone period. The LDP's instinct for survival and its recognition that the party lead-er's personal popularity can make a significant difference in the party's electoral performance have created a situation in which public opinion finds its way at least indirectly into the back rooms of LDP power brokering. The public has little say about who rises to factional leadership and, given the failure of the party presidential primary system to open the selection process to the general public in a meaningful way, its influence over which faction leader becomes prime minister is limited and indirect. But the public clearly plays an important role in determining how long a prime minister stays in power, and it forces anyone who wants that top office to seek enough popularity with the voters to demonstrate to the party that he will at the least not weaken the party's electoral strength.

In Japan's one-party dominant system, a change in the LDP's leadership, and thus of the prime minister, has come to be treated as a major change of style and even of policy orientation. Thus staid and conservative Prime Minister Satō was replaced by the aggressive "computerized bulldozer" Tanaka, who, later engulfed in scandal, was succeeded by "clean" Miki. Suzuki Zenkō, whose policy expertise was confined almost entirely to fish, was succeeded by Nakasone Yasuhiro, an outspoken politician with an interest in and knowledge of international politics unparalleled in a Japanese prime minister since the early postwar years of Prime Minister Yoshida. There is less difference in basic policy orientation than meets the eye in this passing of power among the LDP's leaders. But there is no doubt that the transfer of power among faction leaders has provided the LDP with the opportunity to break with an unpopular administration without itself losing power, and it has provided an opportunity to push party policy in new directions.

As the LDP's organization has evolved and become transformed over the more than thirty years of the party's rule, so has its base of support. The party continues to the present day to represent the interests of the rural electorate, but it also has become the most popular party among the new urban middle class. That is, like ruling parties in most large industrialized democracies, the LDP has become broad based, encompassing plural and often conflicting interests and emphasizing pragmatic responses to concrete policy issues while downplaying ideology and a comprehensive world view.

There is little doubt that the LDP could survive as Japan's ruling party in the event of a one-man-one-vote reapportionment and even of the complete liberalization of rice and other agricultural commodities, particularly if the two were to occur simultaneously. What would not survive such changes—and one reason why they are likely to be implemented only slowly and in a piecemeal fashion—are the political careers of many LDP Diet members elected in Japan's rural constituencies. The party was almost entirely rural-based in its early years. Thus its most powerful politicians, whose seniority largely derives from the fact that they have been in office the longest, are almost all from districts that have strong agricultural lobbies.

The argument is sometimes advanced that the way for Japan's weak political opposition to increase its support would be for it to adopt the stance of being an "urban" party and to challenge the LDP's supposed rural orientation. Besides the fact that this is a practical impossibility for the JSP, which depends almost as much on rural voters for its support as does the LDP, the perception of a sharp and deep urban-rural cleavage in Japan and an image of the LDP as a rural party are more appropriate to the 1960s than to the 1980s.

It does not make much sense to argue the desirability of an urban party in a country in which even rural areas are urbanized; where a majority of farmers earn most of their income in off-farm occupations; where affluence has meant that urbanites spend an ever-smaller share of their disposable income on staples such as rice (and thus are not as sensitive to high commodity prices as foreign exporters of agricultural goods think they should be); and where many urban dwellers have close relatives and a strong sense of roots in rural communities.

Urban Americans put up with government subsidies to producers of dairy products, sugar, corn, and other commodities that are considerably more expensive than government subsidies to Japanese farmers. In the United States in fiscal year 1986, the cost to the government of agricultural subsidies amounted to a record $25.8 billion. Unlike in Japan, where a ceiling has been put on agricultural subsidies as well as other government expenditures, American government spending on agricultural subsidies has been increasing. The previous high was recorded in 1983 when $18 billion was spent to subsidize farmer income.[1]

Yet Americans do not take to the streets to demand lower prices, nor do they demand a choice between a "pro-farm" and a "pro-city" party. It is not peculiar that urban Japanese act likewise. An urban party would repel voters who for reasons of self-interest or sentiment favor continued government support for people engaged full or part time in farming, without necessarily attracting many others for whom agricultural policy is at best a secondary issue. The LDP has been successful precisely because it has been willing and able to evolve into a broad-based party embracing diverse and to some extent conflicting interests. It is not likely that the opposition could increase its strength by opting for a narrower base of representation.

Indeed, it is difficult to see what the opposition might do that would substantially improve its prospects. The coalescence of all of the noncommunist oppostion parties into one party might help. It would eliminate the electoral competition that now exists between the several parties, enable them to pool their financial and organizational resources, and perhaps permit them to attract talent that in Japan's present political situation invariably gravitates to the LDP.

There are fewer obstacles to such party union now than at any previous time. The traditional ideological differences between the DSP and the JSP have been reduced by the JSP's formal scuttling of its Marxist pretensions, and the move toward unification among Japan's major labor union umbrella organizations removes one of the major reasons for the existence of two labor-backed political parties. Moreover, the Kōmeitō, though functioning as the political arm of the Sōka Gakkai and dependent on that religious group for its organizational muscle, has downplayed its religious ties, developed a pragmatic and flexible policy orientation, and become increasingly open in indicating its readiness to consider party merger.

But there are formidable obstacles to opposition party union. Personal enmities and distrust run deep; conflicts between incumbents from different parties elected from the same districts are not trivial; and there remain fundamental differences over important policy issues, particularly in regard to Japanese security policy. Neither the JSP nor the DSP appears to have the energy to vigorously pursue a new and innovative course, while the Kōmeitō is too closely identified with the Sōka Gakkai to be the central pivot of a new opposition party. In the absence of a considerable degree of confidence that merger would lead to electoral success, there are precious few incentives for opposition party politicians to exchange the opportunity to exercise power within their own small party for the uncertainties that merger would bring. This is particularly true since Japan's system of LDP rule does not entirely shut out opposition party politicians from participation in decision making or completely prevent them from obtaining benefits for their constituents.

There is little the political opposition can do to win political power. The question is whether the LDP will do something to lose it. Surely one way to lose it would be to let the public's confidence in the LDP's competence be shaken. This conceivably could be brought about by a deep and prolonged economic recession, particularly if such a recession occurred in the context of a perceived decline in the LDP's ability to skillfully manage relations with the United States.

The LDP has not yet faced such a situation. The dislocations brought about by the oil shock in the early 1970s were widely viewed as having been provoked by forces well beyond Japanese control, and the policy response—to encourage Japanese industry to import less and export more—enabled the government to do more of what it had long been expert at doing. Social strife was precluded by an expansive bond-financed fiscal policy that served both to ward off unemployment and to spread the benefits of the welfare state among the society's burgeoning middle class.

But Japan can no longer respond to economic adversity by adopting aggressively export-oriented growth policies, nor is there public support for once again running up enormous fiscal deficits. Precisely because Japan's unemployment rate has been well under 3 percent, a rapid increase to a 6 or 7 percent rate could be politically more damaging to the LDP than considerably higher levels of unemployment have been for ruling parties in other countries where a 6 percent unemployment rate has come to be regarded as low. Criticism of the LDP government in the event of serious economic problems is all the more likely as protectionist pressures from abroad, the flow of Japanese capital overseas, and the comparatively high cost of Japanese labor drive Japanese industry to move more production offshore and open it to charges that it is exporting jobs and "hollowing out" domestic Japanese industry.

But it must be remembered that democratic politics is a matter of choice among available alternatives, and that in Japan this choice is widely perceived as being between one party long experienced at governing and others for whom politics has been the politics of protest against those who exercise power. It is not impossible to change these perceptions, but nonetheless it would be extraordinarily difficult to do so, particularly when the structure of the LDP makes it possible for the party's own faction leaders to dissociate themselves almost entirely from the policies of the incumbent prime minister and to steal the thunder of the opposition parties if it appears that the policies they are advocating are drawing large public support.

For the foreseeable future at least, the end of LDP rule, if it is to occur at all, is most likely to result from a split within the LDP itself. Since the early 1970s the LDP has come perilously close to a split on more than one occasion. In each instance the precipitating factor was not a

camp, revitalizing the parties there and making the system more competitive again.

The modern Japanese political system has thus devised its own set of checks and balances, one in which Diet boycotts by the opposition, the mobilization of press opinion and interest group organizations to oppose LDP policy, and LDP fear of an electoral backlash act as powerful constraints on the ruling party. The operation of this system of checks and balances was given eloquent testimony in the months following the LDP's enormous 1986 election victory, when Prime Minister Nakasone, despite his party's commanding majority in both houses, was unable to get the Diet to adopt a bill that provided for a new, and intensely unpopular, national sales tax.

The contemporary Japanese political system has had a centrist orientation; it was kept on center during the first phase of LDP dominance by the standoff between the LDP and the progressive parties; later, the emergence of a multi-party system, the breakdown of the cultural politics of earlier years, and the end of the LDP's secure majority in the Diet facilitated a pattern of compromise between the LDP and its opposition and created a strong centripetal thrust in the political system. The centrist thrust of the system has remained strong even in the third phase of LDP dominance, because LDP leaders recognize that to try to oppose it would create political turmoil and threaten the party's overriding goal of remaining the only party in power.

Political change in Japan over these past several decades has not come about by bureaucratic fiat or by the imposition of an elite consensus on a submissive public. Rather it has been largely the product of the responsiveness of the political system to shifting public demands, a responsiveness that in turn has been produced by the LDP's determination to return electoral majorities and retain political power.

This picture of a party-centered politics is at sharp variance with popular stereotypes of Japanese political power, which either locate power almost entirely in the career bureaucracy or in an elite composed mainly of bureaucrats and representatives of big business. But these stereotypes are fundamentally flawed, not because they emphasize the considerable power of bureaucrats or the business community but because they fail to place these actors and institutions in the context of a democratic political system in which those who hold ultimate power are accountable to the electorate.

To put parties at the center of the political system does not mean that parties "do" everything; parties are not structured, in Japan any more than in any other industrialized and democratic country, to process the great preponderance of government decisions. But what sets democracies—including Japan's democracy—apart from other political systems is the ability of citizens to organize into groups to represent their interests vis-à-vis the state and the opportunity that elections provide for the electorate to pass judgment on government. This exerts a profound and pervasive influence over all political actors and all processes of government.

Models of bureaucratic dominance are mostly drawn from the early years of LDP rule when there existed an overwhelming public consensus on the desirability of rapid industrialization and high GNP growth, and when the party's organization was rudimentary and its most important leaders drawn largely from among senior bureaucrats. Even in that period, bureaucratic behavior was characterized by a considerable amount of anticipatory response, as professional bureaucrats sought to avoid alienating the elected political leadership and endeavored to retain as much of their traditional power and autonomy as they could in a new political system in which they were formally responsible to the Diet and to the political parties that controlled it. But it should be recognized that bureaucratic power, especially on issues relating to the national economy, was enormous. Agreement on the nation's economic goals in those years was so profound that economic policy decisions were regarded as largely administrative rather than political issues and few dissented from the view that they could be handled best by

Japan's capable administrators in the professional bureaucracy.

LDP leaders saw their task as working with the bureaucracy in pursuit of common goals, resolving contentious issues of foreign policy, articulating and mobilizing
public support for the nation's economic goals, and making
sure that their party's Diet members had fair access to government resources to dispense to their constituents. The
typical LDP backbencher saw little reason for raising his sights
much above his local district and concentrated his energies
on maintaining the "pipe" through which benefits would
pass from the central government to his district and to his
supporters. Thus LDP politicians (and opposition party politicians on a smaller scale) spent most of their time engaged
in "petition politics," welcoming constituents and representatives of local interest groups to their Diet offices, listening
to their requests, and helping them secure benefits from the
government.

This pattern has changed in important ways in recent
years. LDP backbenchers still spend a great deal of their
time in petition politics, but the growth, liberalization, and
internationalization of the economy have greatly expanded
and complicated the range of issues that are the focus of
constituent concerns. This has forced even the most parochial of LDP politicians to become interested in issues that
formerly were considered the preserve of the professional
bureaucracy.

The broad public consensus on the desirability of rapid
growth over and above everything else has given way to a
much less uniform set of goals that reflects a growing pluralism and a fragmentation of political interests in Japanese
society. This fragmentation does not set Japan apart from
other advanced industrialized democracies and does not merit
treatment as a unique Japan Problem.[3] It does produce a
considerable degree of political immobility, to be sure, by
making it difficult for the government to secure support for
policy shifts that are not equitable to all constituencies. As
we have seen, the LDP's tenacious hold on a policy of zero

and minus ceiling budgets was to a considerable extent the product of its inability to make hard choices that would have an unequal impact on different interests.

But the fragmentation of political power is a feature of political life in all modern industrialized democracies. Japan would be peculiar, and it would be difficult to see how it could sustain a political democracy, if power were not diffused. The political problem that confronts Japan is much the same one that bedevils the United States; namely, how to get elected politicians to support policies that are necessary for the society's long-term health, but that involve sacrifices and arouse the intense opposition of sizeable voting groups. In Japan this problem is complicated by the fact that the social coalition that backs the LDP has become so broad that virtually every significant group has its *zoku* working to protect its interests.

Bureaucratic institutions remain important power centers, and bureaucrats have fought hard to resist the cutting back of their authority. Bureaucratic intransigence, moreover, derives not simply from a desire to preserve power but from long-held attitudes about the proper role of the state. The election law, with its myriad restrictions and regulations, is indicative of the ways in which the state involves itself in society, and the resistance of Home Ministry bureaucrats to liberalizing the law is typical of bureaucratic attitudes toward administrative reform. These long-established and deeply ingrained attitudes about the proper relationship between state and society are changing, but the process is bound to be slow and to leave the bureaucracy with considerably more authority than Americans, at least, coming from a very different tradition, expect civil servants to have.

What is incontrovertible, however, is that the campaign for administrative reform and deregulation and the steady liberalization of the Japanese economy have thrown bureaucratic institutions on the defensive and increased the role of the LDP. This expanded LDP role in policymaking is symbolized by the increased intervention of *zoku* in the decision-making processes of different ministries and by the larger role now played by the party's top leadership in making a wide range of decisions involving economic policy and other matters. Bureaucratic-party relations are characterized both by cooperation and by competition, but the most important characteristics of the relationship as it has evolved in recent years are the acceptance by both the party and the buraucracy of the right of the other to participate in making the government's decisions, and a propensity for working closely together in doing so.

Greater politician involvement in decision making has made the policy process more complex and cumbersome, but also more open and transparent. It also may have the effect of speeding up government decision making on many important issues. The Japanese preference for extensive prior consultation before arriving at a decision—what is generally referred to as *nemawashi* in Japanese—does not necessarily have to be as time-consuming as it is usually portrayed as being. Slow decision making by the government is not the manifestation of a general cultural trait, but is typical of bureaucratic behavior, particularly when the bureaucracy in question is characterized by as a high a degree of sectionalism and interministerial competition as in Japan. Foreign pressure is often effective in getting the Japanese government to make a policy decision, not because Japanese are peculiarly responsive to threats and hectoring—like other people, they deeply resent such behavior—but because it drives issues into the political arena and thus brings into play the views of political leaders attuned to the game of compromise, deal making, and getting things done.

But politician involvement in Japanese policy decisions also carries in its wake many of the same problems that can be observed in congressional decision making in the United States, namely, an overwhelming concern for the impact the issue will have on the interests of the congressman's own constituents, a penchant for political grandstanding, and oftentimes a lack of real expertise. Despite all of the publicity recently given to Diet member expertise, most ibers lack independent sources of information and and thus remain poorly informed on many issues. ledge is power, the Japanese bureaucracy retains a ɛrable amount of it, despite the increase in the LDP's role ᴵᴵ policymaking.

Nonetheless, contemporary Japanese politics is characterized by increased party involvement in the policy process. A parallel trend of perhaps even greater importance in terms of the evolution of Japan's political democracy, however, is the decreasing role of the state in the economy and in the society at large. Japanese society is becoming increasingly autonomous, a process that further economic liberalization can only promote. Japanese business is now strong, jealous of its independence, divided in its interests, and no longer in need of state help as it was in the early postwar economic growth years. On the contrary, many businessmen now view the bureaucracy, with its tradition of regulation and its desire to prevent the erosion of its power, as a hindrance rather than an aid. There is a growing dissensus between big business and bureaucratic institutions, and the processes of liberalization, internationalization, and government deregulation are reducing the bureaucracy's ability to impose its definition of national interests on the business community and on the society more generally.

It has become something of a cliché to say that the United States and Japan are linked by their common commitment to democratic values and by the similarities in their political systems. But like all good clichés, this one is rooted in a fundamental truth. That truth is not that Japan and the United States are alike in the structure of their parties or in their decision-making processes. Nor is it a matter of the Japanese slowly but surely becoming more like Americans in the practice of their politics. To the extent that there is convergence in the political and economic life of the advanced industrialized democratic countries, that convergence is Japanizing the West as much as it is Americanizing Japan.

The truth is that Japan, like the United States, has woven the threads of democratic political life—civil liberties, open elections, competitive politics, and responsible government—into the fabric of the nation's social structure to create a stable political system that echoes universal values and behavior while at the same time being utterly unique. And that is what is most significant about the Japanese way of politics.

APPENDIX: RESULTS OF LOWER HOUSE ELECTIONS, 1946–1986

Party	A Votes	B % of Vote	C % of Voters	D Seats	E Candidates
April 10, 1946					
Progressive	10,350,530	18.7	13.5	94	376
Liberal	13,505,746	24.4	17.6	141	485
Cooperative	1,799,764	3.2	2.3	14	92
Socialist	9,924,930	17.9	12.9	93	331
Communist	2,135,757	3.9	2.8	5	143
Minor	6,488,032	11.7	8.4	38	570
Independent	11,244,120	20.1	14.5	81	773
Total	55,448,879		72.1	466	2770
April 25, 1947					
Democratic	2,960,270	10.8	7.2	126	338
Liberal	7,312,524	26.7	17.9	131	324
National Coop.	1,915,948	7.0	4.7	31	110
Socialist	7,176,882	26.2	17.5	143	284
Communist	1,002,883	3.7	2.5	4	120
Minor	1,389,416	5.1	3.4	18	141
Independent	1,603,684	5.9	3.9	13	250
Total	27,361,607		66.9	466	1567
January 23, 1949					
Democratic	4,798,354	15.7	11.4	69	211
Dem. Liberal	13,420,269	43.9	31.9	264	417
National Coop.	1,041,879	3.4	2.5	14	63
Socialist	4,129,794	13.5	9.8	48	186
Labor-Farmer	606,840	2.0	1.4	7	46
Communist	2,984,780	9.8	7.1	35	115
Minor	1,602,496	5.2	3.8	17	116
Independent	2,008,109	6.6	4.8	12	210
Total	30,592,521		72.7	466	1364

October 1, 1952

	Votes	%	%	Seats	Cand.
Reform	6,421,094	18.2	13.7	85	210
Liberal	16,937,225	47.9	36.2	240	475
Cooperative	390,015	1.1	0.8	2	28
Left Socialist	3,493,970	9.9	7.5	54	96
Right Socialist	4,013,872	11.4	8.6	57	109
Labor-Farmer	261,190	0.7	0.6	4	11
Communist	896,764	2.5	1.9	0	107
Minor	559,021	1.6	1.2	5	41
Independent	2,363,553	6.7	5.1	19	165
Total	35,336,704		75.6	466	1242

April 19, 1953

	Votes	%	%	Seats	Cand.
Reform	6,186,232	17.9	13.1	76	169
Hatoyama Lib.	3,054,688	8.8	6.5	35	102
Yoshida Lib.	13,476,428	38.9	28.6	199	316
Left Socialist	4,516,714	13.1	9.6	72	108
Right Socialist	4,677,833	13.5	9.9	66	117
Labor-Farmer	358,773	1.0	0.8	5	12
Communist	655,990	1.9	1.4	1	85
Minor	152,050	0.4	0.3	1	13
Independent	1,523,737	4.4	3.2	11	105
Total	34,602,445		73.5	466	1027

February 2, 1955

	Votes	%	%	Seats	Cand.
Democrat	13,536,044	36.6	27.5	185	286
Liberal	9,849,457	26.6	20.0	112	248
Left Socialist	5,683,311	15.4	11.5	89	121
Right Socialist	5,129,594	13.9	10.4	67	122
Labor Farmer	357,611	1.0	0.7	4	16
Communist	733,121	2.0	1.5	2	60
Minor	496,614	1.3	1.0	2	37
Independent	1,229,082	3.3	2.5	6	127
Total	37,014,837		75.2	467	1017

Party	A Votes	B % of Vote	C % of Voters	D Seats	E Candidates
May 22, 1958					
LDP	22,976,846	57.8	44.2	287	413
JSP	13,033,993	32.8	25.1	166	246
JCP	1,012,035	2.5	1.9	1	114
Minor & Ind.	2,668,786	6.7	5.2	13	178
Total	39,751,661		76.4	467	951
November 20, 1960					
LDP	22,740,271	57.6	41.9	296	399
JSP	10,887,134	27.6	20.0	145	186
DSP	3,464,147	8.8	6.4	17	105
JCP	1,156,723	2.9	2.1	3	118
Minor & Ind.	1,260,846	3.2	2.4	6	132
Total	39,509,123		72.7	467	940
November 21, 1963					
LDP	22,423,915	54.7	38.5	283	359
JSP	11,906,766	29.0	20.4	144	198
DSP	3,023,302	7.4	5.2	23	59
JCP	1,646,477	4.0	2.8	5	118
Minor & Ind.	2,016,078	4.9	3.5	12	183
Total	41,016,540		70.4	467	917
January 19, 1967					
LDP	22,447,838	48.8	35.6	277	342
JSP	12,826,103	27.9	20.4	140	209
DSP	3,404,463	7.4	5.4	30	60
JCP	2,190,563	4.8	3.5	5	123

Party	Votes	%	%	Seats	Candidates
Kōmeitō	2,472,371	5.4	3.9	25	32
Minor & Ind.	2,655,232	5.8	4.3	9	151
Total	45,996,573		73.0	486	917
December 12, 1969					
LDP	22,381,570	47.6	32.3	288	328
JSP	10,074,100	21.4	14.5	90	183
DSP	3,636,590	7.7	5.3	31	68
JCP	3,199,031	6.8	4.6	14	123
Kōmeitō	5,124,666	10.9	7.4	47	76
Minor & Ind.	2,573,933	5.5	3.7	16	167
Total	46,989,892		67.8	486	945
December 10, 1972					
LDP	24,563,199	46.9	33.3	271	339
JSP	11,478,742	21.9	15.6	118	161
DSP	3,660,953	7.0	5.0	19	65
JCP	5,496,827	10.5	7.5	38	122
Kōmeitō	4,436,755	8.5	6.0	29	59
Minor & Ind.	2,788,601	5.3	3.8	14	149
Total	52,425,078		71.1	491	895
December 5, 1976					
LDP	23,653,624	41.8	30.4	257	319
NLC	2,363,984	4.2	3.0	17	25
JSP	11,713,005	20.7	15.0	123	162
DSP	3,554,075	6.3	4.6	29	51
JCP	5,878,192	10.4	7.3	19	128
Kōmeitō	6,177,300	10.9	7.9	55	84
Minor & Ind.	3,272,575	5.8	4.2	11	130
Total	56,612,755		73.5	511	899

Party	A Votes	B % of Vote	C % of Voters	D Seats	E Candidates
October 7, 1979					
LDP	24,084,130	44.6	35.0	248	322
NLC	1,631,811	3.0	2.0	4	31
JSP	10,643,449	19.7	13.0	107	157
DSP	3,663,691	6.8	4.6	35	53
JCP	5,625,526	10.4	7.0	39	128
Kōmeitō	5,282,682	9.8	6.6	57	64
SDL	368,660	0.7	0.5	2	7
Minor & Ind.	2,710,166	5.0	3.4	19	129
Total	54,010,119		68.0	511	891
June 22, 1980					
LDP	28,262,441	47.9	34.9	286	310
NLC	1,766,396	3.0	2.2	12	25
JSP	11,400,747	19.3	14.1	107	149
DSP	3,896,728	6.6	4.8	32	50
JCP	5,803,613	9.8	7.2	29	129
Kōmeitō	5,329,924	9.0	6.6	33	64
SDL	402,832	0.7	0.5	3	5
Minor & Ind.	2,166,135	3.7	2.7	11	103
Total	59,028,834		74.6	511	835

SOURCE: Figures for 1946–1976 elections from Ishikawa Masumi, *Sengo Seiji Kōzō Shi*, pp. 214–215; figures for subsequent elections from Seiji Kōhō Sentā, *Seiji Handobukku* (Tokyo: Seiji Kōhō Sentā, various years) and *Asahi Shinbun*.

December 18, 1983

	Votes				
LDP	25,982,781	45.8	30.8	250	339
NLC	1,341,584	2.4	1.6	8	17
JSP	11,065,080	19.5	13.1	112	144
DSP	4,129,907	7.3	4.9	38	54
JCP	5,302,485	9.3	6.3	26	129
Kōmeitō	5,745,750	10.1	6.8	58	59
SDL	381,045	0.7	0.5	3	4
Minor & Ind.	2,831,058	5.0	3.4	16	102
Total	56,779,690		67.9	511	848

July 6, 1986

	Votes				
LDP	29,875,501	49.4	34.6	300	320
NLC	1,114,800	1.8	1.2	6	12
JSP	10,412,584	17.2	12.1	85	138
DSP	3,895,858	6.4	4.5	26	56
JCP	5,313,246	8.8	6.2	26	129
Kōmeitō	5,701,277	9.4	6.6	56	61
SDL	499,670	0.8	0.5	4	5
Minor & Ind.	3,635,670	6.0	4.2	9	117
Total	60,448,609		71.4	512	838

NOTES

1. THE TRANSFORMATION OF THE JAPANESE POLITICAL PARTY SYSTEM

1. See Joji Watanuki, "Patterns of Politics in Present-Day Japan," in Lipset and Rokkan, eds., *Party Systems and Voter Alignments,* pp. 447–466.

2. See Packard, *Protest in Tokyo.*

3. For an account, see Baerwald, *The Purge of Japanese Leaders.* For an excellent analysis of the purge of Diet politicians, see Ishikawa, *Sengo Seiji Kōzō Shi,* pp. 1–12.

4. Baerwald, *The Purge of Japanese Leaders,* p. 20.

5. See Kawai, *Japan's American Interlude,* p. 94, and also the comments of Prime Minister Yoshida in Yoshida, p. 165.

6. Another nine were elected to the upper house. Thirty-eight of the eighty-five non-IRAA-recommended candidates were successful in the first postwar election of 1946. In total, 30.3 percent of all the candidates elected to the Diet in 1942 were elected at least once in the postwar period. See Ishikawa, *Sengo Seiji Kōzō Shi,* p. 8.

7. See Scalapino, *The Japanese Communist Movement,* pp. 84–85.

8. Yoshida, *Memoirs,* p. 240.

9. These are the figures cited by Prime Minister Yoshida. See Yoshida, *Memoirs,* p. 241.

10. Hatoyama was released from the purge in August 1951. See Hatoyama, *Hatoyama Ichirō Kaisōroku,* p. 51.

11. Yoshida comments somewhat elliptically: "Mr. Hatoyama probably imagined that my tenure as president of the Liberal Party would last only until the opportunity came for him to re-enter public life and resume that position; I myself certainly had no idea at that time that I should retain the presidency of the party, and the Premiership, for very long" (*Memoirs,* p. 75).

12. Since the LDP came to power there have been only four people appointed to the cabinet who were not members of the Diet at the time. Fujiyama Aiichirō was foreign minister in the Kishi cabinet in 1957 (and was elected to the Diet in the next election); Nagai Michio was made education minister by Prime Minister Miki in 1974; Ushiba Nobuhiko was minister for external economic relations in the Fukuda cabinet in 1977; and Ōkita Saburō served as foreign minister in the Ōhira cabinet in 1979.

13. SCAP had favored a unicameral legislature and it was only at the insistence of the Japanese that an upper house was created. Its members are elected for six-year terms; half are selected at a time, in elections held every three years. Two different constituency systems are used: 152 members are elected in prefecture-wide districts, and another 100 are elected in a proportional representation system that is described in chapter 5.

For an excellent historical analysis of the upper house, see Herbert Passin, "The House of Councillors: Promise and Achievement," in Blaker, ed., *Japan At the Polls*, pp. 1–45.

14. The 1946 election was the only one since the adoption of this system in 1925 to use a different electoral system. In that year, the country was divided into large districts electing up to fourteen members each. In districts electing three or fewer members, voters had one ballot; in districts electing from four to ten members, each voter could cast two votes; and in districts electing eleven or more members, voters were given three ballots.

This was the first election to be held after the granting of the suffrage to women in 1946, and the only one to the present day in which large numbers of women ran and were elected. (Thirty-nine women were elected. In 1986, the number was seven.) Some analysts argue that the electoral system directly contributed to their success, with many women voters in urban areas giving one of their two or three votes to female candidates. See for example Nakamura and Kamijō, *Sengo Nihon Seiji Shi*, p. 55.

15. See Harari, *The Politics of Labor Legislation in Japan*, pp. 63–66.

16. On this Morito-Inamura debate, see Cole, Totten, and Uyehara, *Socialist Parties in Postwar Japan*, pp. 26–31. There is an excellent analysis in Japanese in Sasada, *Nihon Shakaitō*, vol. 1, pp. 137–146. Ideological differences within the JSP are discussed in chapter 4.

17. According to one of the participants in that CEC meeting, Sone Eki, the "real right-wingers" in the CEC—including himself and Nishimura Eiichi, who was later to become chairman of the Democratic Socialist party—wanted to vote in favor of both treaties. They were dissuaded by the argument that to do so would weaken the right's ability to get support for the A Plan. See Sone, *Watakushi No Memoāru*, p. 168.

18. See Sartori, *Parties and Party Systems*, pp. 131–144.

19. See for example the discussion of the similarities between the JSP and the Italian Socialist party (PSI) in Stockwin, *The Japanese Socialist Party and Neutralism*, pp. 145–154.

20. The LDP has tried on several occasions to change Japan's multimember, single-entry ballot system into a simple first-past-the-post district system in the belief that this would further increase its representation. All of the opposition parties, which assess the implications of a single-member district system in the same way, have been fiercely against its adoption.

21. Of the forty-three seats at stake in Tokyo's eleven constituencies in 1976, the LDP won fourteen (32.5 percent) and the JSP won eight (18.6 percent). The Kōmeitō did better than the JSP, winning ten seats (23.3 percent), and the Communist party took four seats. Three went to the New Liberal club, two to the DSP, and there were two successful independents.

22. In the 1976 election the LDP won 41.8 and the JSP 20.7 percent of the vote; other parties obtained 31.8 percent, and independents accounted for the remaining 5.7 percent.

23. Terry MacDougall has calculated that in 1974 over 41 percent of all Japanese lived in prefectures or cities having progressive chief executives, meaning governors and mayors elected with the support of the opposition parties and not the LDP. Cited in Scott Flanagan, "Electoral Change in Japan: An Overview," in Steiner, Krauss, and Flanagan, eds., *Political Opposition and Local Politics*, p. 44.

24. Between 1960 and 1965, all twenty-seven cities with more than 300,000 residents experienced population increases. On the other hand, 95 percent of towns and villages with less than 5,000 residents and 86 percent of municipalities with under 30,000 people experienced declines in population. During this time period the rate of population increase was highest in Kanagawa (28.7 percent), followed by Saitama (24.1 percent), Osaka (20.9 percent), Chiba (17.2 percent), Aichi (14.1 percent), Tokyo (12.2 percent), and Hyōgo (10.3 percent). See Masumi, *Gendai Seiji*, vol. 2, p. 450.

25. The major charge against Nishio was that he violated party policy calling for the immediate abolition of the Security Treaty, by arguing that the JSP should not simply oppose the treaty but offer its own concrete alternative. Nishio was also accused of having agreed to serve on a Japan-China (Taiwan) Cooperation Committee; of having been involved in forming "second unions," i.e., unions created to compete with established Sōhyō-affiliated ones; and of having given a speech at the Defense College and having written an article for a student publication there in which he said that the struggle today was not between capitalism and socialism, but between democracy and communism. See Nakamura and Kamijō, *Sengo Nihon Seiji Shi*, pp. 149–150. For Nishio's explanation of the events leading to his departure from the JSP, see his *Seiji Oboegaki*, pp. 335–350. The left wing's position is reflected in Gekkan Shakaitō, *Nihon Shakaitō No Sanjūnen*, vol. 2, pp. 276–292.

26. Quoted in Nakamura and Kamijō, *Sengo Nihon Seiji Shi*, p. 252.

27. See White, *The Soka Gakkai and Mass Society*, and also Dator, *Soka Gakkai*, pp. 12–15.

28. For a history of the party to the middle of the 1970s, see Toyama, *Kōmeitō Giin Dan*.

29. See for a good example Naitō, *Kōmeitō No Sugao*.

30. This was the so-called obstruction of free speech and publication incident (*genron, shuppan bōgai jiken*). The book at issue was political commentator Fujiwara Hirotatsu's *Sōka Gakkai O Kiru*, published in English as *I Denounce Soka Gakkai*.

31. The Kōmeitō's share of the popular vote in the 1976 election was 10.91 percent; in 1983 it was 10.12 percent; and in 1986, 9.4 percent.

32. See for example Nihonjin Kenkyūkai, ed., *Shiji Seitō Betsu Nihonjin Shūdan*, p. 178. See also Hayashi, ed., *Nihonjin No Seiji Kankaku*, p. 20.

33. The only national election in which the JCP won a substantial number of seats in the early postwar years was in the 1949 lower house election, when it increased its representation from 4 to 35 members. This was the election, as noted earlier, that reduced the Socialist's representation from 143 to 48 seats. In the next election, in 1952, the JCP's representation was reduced to zero.

34. Scalapino, *The Japanese Communist Movement*, p. 176.

35. Japan Communist Party, *The Sixteenth Congress of the Japanese Communist Party* (Tokyo: Japan Press Service, 1982). p. 118.

36. See Japan Communist Party, "Manifesto."

37. In the following election in 1976, the JCP won only seventeen seats, though its share of the popular vote (10.38 percent) was about the same as it had been in the previous race. In 1979, with 10.42 percent of the vote, it won thirty-nine seats, its high point to the present day. It won twenty-nine seats in 1980, twenty-six in 1983, and twenty-seven in 1986.

38. *Asahi Shinbun* poll of February 17, 1977, cited in Kawamura, *Seitō No Hōkai*, p. 93.

39. Cited in Karube Kiyoshi, "Nihonjin Wa Dono Yō Ni Shite Shiji Seitō O Kimeru Ka," in Nihonjin Kenkyūkai, ed., *Shiji Seitō Betsu Nihonjin Shūdan*, pp. 78–79.

40. See Tominomori, *Sengo Hoshutō Shi*, p. 216. Although Tominomori's prediction proved wrong, this book overall is a balanced historical account of postwar conservative politics.

41. Quoted in *Asahi Shinbun*, August 16, 1986.

42. Ōhira, as it turned out, did not need the NLC's votes. On the first ballot he received 135 votes to Fukuda's 125. On the second and deciding ballot, Ōhira received 138 to Fukuda's 121 votes.

43. *Asahi Shinbun*, August 15, 1986.

44. Bringing the NLC's history to a close during his time in office must have been no small source of satisfaction for Prime Minister Nakasone. Not only had he been the LDP secretary-general who had to accept the resignation of the six LDP Diet members who left the party ten years earlier, but he was the head of the faction founded by Kōno Yōhei's father, Kōno Ichirō.

45. The LDP's share of the popular vote declined by 5.1 percentage points from the previous 1972 election. The NLC vote was 4.2 percent. The combined vote for all opposition parties increased by only 0.4 points. Independents accounted for the remainder.

46. For an analysis of the Diet during this phase of LDP dominance, see Baerwald, *Japan's Parliament*.

47. Fourteen of the lower house's sixteen standing committees have an even number of members. Since committee chairmen are allowed to vote only to break a tie, a party must command a majority of two seats in each of these fourteen committees if it is to control both the chairmanship and the majority of seats. In the 1970s, when the lower house had 511 seats, the LDP needed 271 members to control the chairmanships and majorities on all committees.

48. T. J. Pempel, "Uneasy Toward Autonomy," in Suleiman, ed., *Parliaments and Parliamentarians*, p. 140.

49. Ellis S. Krauss, "Conflict in the Diet: Toward Conflict Management in Parliamentary Politics," in Krauss, Rohlen, and Steinhoff, eds., *Conflict in Japan*, p. 260.

50. Kakizawa Koji, "The Diet and the Bureaucracy: The Budget," in Valeo and Morrison, eds., *The Diet and Congress*, p. 95.

51. Satō and Matsuzaki, "The Liberal Democrats' Conciliatory Reign," p. 31.

52. The figures are taken from Satō and Matsuzaki, *Jimintō Seiken*, p. 287.

53. Satō and Matsuzaki, *Jimintō Seiken*, p. 131. See also Krauss, "Conflict in the Diet," p. 272.

54. Satō and Matsuzaki, "The Liberal Democrats' Conciliatory Reign," p. 28.

55. Krauss, "Conflict in the Diet," p. 257.

56. Satō and Matsuzaki, "The Liberal Democrats' Conciliatory Reign," p. 28.

57. Under the constitution the Diet must be convoked within thirty days from the date of the general election (Article 54). Upon convocation the cabinet is required to resign en masse (Article 70). The house must then elect a new prime minister before conducting any other business (Article 67).

58. The constitution provides that in the case of passage of a nonconfidence resolution, the cabinet shall resign en masse unless the house is dissolved within ten days (Article 69). The house can also be dissolved and elections called at any time at the prime minister's discretion. Under this constitution, only the Diet elected in December 1972 served a full four-year term.

59. In 1953 the campaign period for lower and upper house elections coincided, but voting for the upper house took place five days after the lower house election.

60. For an account of this incident, see Yomiuri, " 'Nikaidō Kūdetā.' "

2. THE LIBERAL DEMOCRATIC PARTY: PERPETUATING DOMINANCE

1. According to an *Asahi Shinbun* poll of May 7, 1986, 17.7 percent of LDP supporters live in the eleven largest metropolitan cities; 28.1 percent live in other cities with populations of more than 100,000; 27.9 percent live in smaller cities; and 26.1 percent in towns and villages. Unpublished data made available to the author by the *Asahi Shinbun*.

2. The *Asahi Shinbun* divides lower house election districts into four categories, according to a formula that combines the percentage of the labor force in agriculture and population density. According to this system, in 1986 there were thirty-three metropolitan districts (with 139 seats), thirty-two urban districts (130 seats), forty-three semiurban districts (167 seats), and twenty-two rural districts (76 seats). The *Mainichi Shinbun* divides districts into five categories. At the time of the 1986 election, these included twenty-three metropolitan (92 seats), thirty-three urban (137 seats), twenty-one semiurban (84 seats), twenty-nine semirural (108 seats), and twenty-four rural districts (91 seats). See *Asahi Shinbun* and *Mainichi Shinbun*, July 8, 1986.

3. Imai Ken'ichi, "Japan's Changing Industrial Structure," in Yamamura, ed., *Policy and Trade Issues of the Japanese Economy*, p. 51. Italics are mine.

4. For a particularly interesting account of Prime Minister Ikeda's thinking about the future of the agricultural labor force, see Itō Masaya, *Ikeda Hayato*.

5. In 1962, per capita rice consumption reached its peak of 118.3 kilo-

grams; it steadily declined thereafter, and in 1979 it was down to 79.8 kilograms. The share of the average household's monthly expenditures for food spent on rice decreased from 28.3 percent in 1955 to 9.3 percent in 1977. See Yoshimi Kuroda, "The Present State of Agriculture in Japan," in Castle and Hemmi, eds., *U.S.-Japanese Agricultural Trade Relations*, p. 101.

6. Michael W. Donneley, "Japan's Rice Economy," in Krauss, Rohlen, and Steinhoff, eds., *Conflict in Japan*, p. 350.

7. Nōrin Suisan Gyōsei Kenkyūkai, *Nōrin Suisan* (Tokyo: Gyōsei, 1983), vol. 1, p. 170. See also Kuroda, "Agriculture in Japan," p. 101.

8. Sōrifu Tōkeikyoku, *Nihon Tōkei Nenkan* (Tokyo: Nihon Tōkei Kyōkai and Mainichi Shinbunsha, 1983).

9. This "three-chan agriculture" refers to the *ojii-chan* (grandpa), *obā-chan* (grandma), and *okā-chan* (mother) who work the farm while the father is off working somewhere else.

10. *Nihon Tōkei Nenkan*, 1983.

11. Egaitsu Fumio, "Japanese Agricultural Policy," in Castle and Hemmi, *Agricultural Trade Relations*, p. 174.

12. *Ibid.*, p. 174.

13. Tachibana, *Nōkyō*, p. 17.

14. Hirose, *Hojokin To Seikentō*, pp. 94–95.

15. Cited in Tachibana, *Nōkyō*, p. 315, and in Masumi, *Gendai Seiji*, vol. 2, p. 474.

16. On this point see Noguchi, *Zaisei Kiki No Kōzō*, pp. 161–162.

17. On this point see Campbell, *Contemporary Japanese Budget Politics*.

18. For an early example of writing on the "postparty age," see Keizai Hyōron, *Datsu Seitō Jidai*. For a discussion of the dealignment-realignment issue, see Dalton, Flanagan, and Beck, eds., *Electoral Change*.

19. See Matsushita, *Shibiru Minimamu No Shisō*, p. 272.

20. Kakuei Tanaka, *Building a New Japan*, p. 70.

21. The highest popularity rating previously achieved by an LDP prime minister was Prime Minister Ikeda's 51 percent. Tanaka's popularity was even higher than was Prime Minister Yoshida's immediately after the signing of the San Francisco Peace Treaty, when it reached 58 percent. See Asahi Shinbunsha, *Nihonjin No Seiji Ishiki*, p. 67.

22. These figures are from *Asahi Shinbun* polls and are reproduced in *Nihonjin No Seiji Ishiki*, pp. 67–71.

23. Quoted in Asahi Shinbunsha, *Asahi Nenkan, 1975 Nen Han*, (Tokyo: Asahi Shinbunsha, 1975), p. 34.

24. See Kumon, Okamoto, and Taniguchi, *Zaisei Tōyūshi*, p. 61; Hirose, *Hojokin To Seikentō*, pp. 40–49; and Masumi, *Gendai Seiji*, vol. 2, pp. 486–488.

25. *Nihon Tōkei Nenkan*, 1985.

26. An indication of the importance of public works spending in Japan compared to other industrialized countries can be found by comparing the share of gross capital formation to GNP accounted for by government spending. In Japan this figure was 5.4 percent of GNP in 1983. In the U.S. the figure was 1.5 percent, and in West Germany 3.1 percent. The only country that begins to approach Japan in public works spending is Italy, where the comparable figure was 4.3 percent. Data from Japan's Ministry of Finance Budget Bureau, *The Budget in Brief, 1986* (Tokyo: Ministry of Finance, 1986), p. 45.

27. Comparable figures for the United States are 32.7 percent (in 1979), for Great Britain, 44.3 percent (in 1980), and for West Germany, 45 percent (in 1980). See Ōkurashō, *Zaisei No Genjō To Tenbō*. It might be noted, however, that the Reagan revolution has brought about an increase in the GNP share accounted for by government spending in the United States, while the Japanese government has been able to reduce its share slightly. Data comparing FY1984 for Japan and FY1983 for the United States show total general government expenditures at 33 percent for Japan and 37.8 percent for the United States. Both countries spend almost the same GNP share on social security transfers (11.1 percent in Japan and 11.9 percent in the United States). The gap is in government final consumption expenditures—19.0 percent for the United States, compared with 9.8 percent for Japan.

28. The use of a ceiling in formulating budget requests was introduced in 1960. From then until FY1965, ministries were required in compiling their budget requests to ask for no more than a 50 percent increase over the budget they had received the previous year. The ceiling was then reduced to a 30 percent increase, and from FY1968–FY1975 the maximum request was 25 percent more than the previous year's budget. Thereafter it was steadily reduced until it reached zero at the end of the decade. See the Ministry of Finance, *The Budget in Brief, 1986*, pp. 83–85.

29. In FY1984, 1985, and 1986, this ceiling was −10 percent. Investment-related expenditures, however, were kept to a somewhat higher ceiling of −5 percent. The technical details of setting ceilings—officially known as guidelines for estimate budget requests—are summarized in the Ministry of Finance, *The Budget in Brief, 1986*.

30. Quoted in Asahi Shinbunsha, *Asahi Nenkan, 1976* (Tokyo: Asahi Shinbunsha, 1977), p. 495.

31. Quoted *ibid.*

32. Quoted *ibid.*

3. THE LIBERAL DEMOCRATIC PARTY: THE ORGANIZATION OF POLITICAL POWER

1. This is well explained in Thayer, *How the Conservatives Rule Japan*, pp. 15–57.

2. Watanabe, *Habatsu*, pp. 2–3.

3. The factional breakdown as of November 21, 1986 was as follows:

Faction	Lower House	Upper House	Total
Tanaka	86	54	140
Miyazawa	60	29	89
Nakasone	62	25	87
Abe	56	28	84
Kōmoto	28	6	34
Unaffiliated	15	2	17
Total	307	144	451

SOURCE: Data provided author by political desk of the *Tokyo Shinbun*.
See also Seiji Kōhō Sentā, *Seiji Handobukku*, (Tokyo: Seiji Kōhō Sentā, 1986).

4. The Fukuda faction had two members each in Gumma 2, Chiba 3, and Yamaguchi 1. The Tanaka faction had two members in Shizuoka 3 and in Saga. There were two Suzuki faction members in Hiroshima 2.

5. To the six districts mentioned in the previous note were added three in which the Tanaka faction elected two members each: Aomori 2, Ibaraki 1, and Gifu 1.

6. Satō and Matsuzaki, *Jimintō Seiken*, p. 79. This volume offers a excellent detailed analysis of the LDP's organization and brings together an enormous amount of data which I have relied on heavily in this chapter.

7. See Nihon Keizai Shinbunsha, *Jimintō Seichōkai*, pp. 120–122. Hereafter referred to as Nikkei, *Jimintō Seichōkai*.

8. Kakizawa Koji, "The Diet and the Bureaucracy," in Valeo and Morrison, eds., *The Diet and Congress*, p. 80.

9. Watanabe, *Habatsu*, p. 188.

10. This is pointed out by Satō and Matsuzaki, *Jimintō Seiken*, p. 48.

11. The two nonbureaucrats during this time were the first two post-1955 prime ministers, Hatoyama and Ishibashi. Succeeding Ishbashi as prime minister were the former bureaucrats Kishi Nobusuke (February 1957–July 1959); Ikeda Hayato (July 1959–November 1964); and Satō Eisaku (November 1964–July 1972).

12. T. J. Pempel, "Uneasy Toward Autonomy," in Suleiman, ed., *Parliaments and Parliamentarians*, p. 142.

13. Scalapino and Masumi, *Parties and Politics*, p. 57.

14. *Ibid.*, p. 167.

15. There were also three former bureaucrats elected on the DSP ticket and two in the JSP. These are my calculations based on data in Seiji Kōhō Sentā, *Seiji Handobukku*, 1984.

16. The political recruitment of bureaucrats is not a uniquely Japanese phenomenon by any means. About one-quarter of parliamentarians in Sweden, West Germany, and France also come from the bureaucracy. See Putnam, *The Comparative Study of Political Elites*, p. 50. This work is cited in Naka, *Giin No Kōsei*, p. 90.

17. The figures are calculated on the basis of data provided in Satō and Matsuzaki, *Jimintō Seiken*, p. 233.

18. *Ibid.*, p. 42.

19. *Ibid.*

20. *Ibid.*, p. 230. Miyazawa Kiichi was made cabinet minister (director of the Economic Planning Agency) in 1966 after only one lower house election victory, but he had already served two terms in the upper house.

21. Nakasone began a career in the Ministry of Home Affairs but he left early and was elected to the Diet when he was 28 years old. He was the youngest Diet member at the time.

22. See Nikkei, *Jimintō Seichōkai*, p. 2.

23. Calculated on the basis of data in *Seiji Handobukku*, 1984.

24. *Asahi Shinbun*, July 8, 1986.

25. Scalapino and Masumi, for example, devote considerable attention to career background analysis in their 1962 book, *Parties and Politics in Contemporary Japan*, but do not mention the second-generation-politician phenomenon.

26. Naka, *Giin No Kōsei*, p. 84.

27. *Asahi Shinbun*, July 8, 1986.

28. The rest of this group is accounted for by businessmen (eleven members), journalists (eight), professional people (nine), and six others about whom information is incomplete.

29. The career backgrounds of opposition party Diet members are discussed in Gerald L. Curtis, "The Opposition," in Passin, ed., *A Season of Voting*, pp. 43–80. Both the JSP and DSP are heavily dependent on the unions, the Kōmeitō relies entirely on the Sōka Gakkai, and the Communists draw their candidates from party activists in the unions (particularly in the anti-JSP faction of the Teachers Union) and from lawyers and local citizen movement activists.

30. Kishi, the second oldest of ten brothers and sisters in the Satō family, had been adopted into the family of his father's elder brother who had three daughters but no male heir. Adoption of this kind is quite common in Japan, but the name situation is particularly complicated in this case. The father of Kishi (and of Satō Eisaku) had been born in the Kishi family and was adopted into the Satō family.

31. See Tachibana, "Tanaka Kakuei Kenkyū." The Lockheed scandal had nothing to do with Tanaka's resignation; evidence of his involvement in it did not surface until 1976 during the administration of his successor, Miki Takeo.

32. From 1956 to 1962, each prefectural chapter sent two voting delegates to the party convention. The rules were amended in the 1962 convention to give each prefecture four delegates, while reducing the number of delegates with the right to vote from two to one. Until 1971 the president's term was two years, with no limit on the number of times he could be reelected. In 1971 the term was extended to three years, and a new rule was adopted that required a two-thirds affirmative vote of all LDP Dietmen to have a third term. In January 1977 the length of the term was reduced from three years to two. See Masumi, *Gendai Seiji*, vol. 2, pp. 331–332.

33. A few months after the primary, in January 1983, Nakagawa committed suicide. His faction was taken over for a brief time by Ishihara Shintarō and eventually disbanded.

34. For an excellent account of the revival negotiations process see Campbell, *Contemporary Japanese Budget Politics*, pp. 172–199.

35. Curtis and Ishikawa, *Doken Kokka Nippon*, p. 35.

36. On this particular issue see *Nihon Keizai Shinbun*, March 28, 1985 and *Japan Economic Journal*, July 16, 1985.

37. In 1983 there were 17 divisions and 93 commissions (*chōsakai*), committees (*iinkai*), and special committees (*tokubetsu iinkai*). There was also one discussion group (*kondankai*, on commodity markets), and one project team (on the system for approving textbooks used in public schools). See Nikkei, *Jimintō Seichōkai*, pp. 209–222, for a listing of these groups and their chairmen and vice chairmen.

38. The commission on the tax system is discussed in Nikkei, *Jimintō Seichōkai*, pp. 70–74.

4. THE JAPANESE SOCIALIST PARTY: PERPETUAL OPPOSITION

1. For details see Gerald L. Curtis, "The Opposition," in Passin, ed., *A Season of Voting*, pp. 43–54.

2. Totten, *The Social Democratic Movement in Prewar Japan*, p. vii.

3. Originally published in the January 1963 issue of *Chūō Kōron*, Ishida's article, "Hoshuseitō No Bijon," is reprinted, along with his reflections on it twenty years later, in Ishida, *Watakushi No Seikai Shōwa Shi*, pp. 122–128.

4. See *Nihon Shakaitō No Shinsengen*, published in pamphlet form by Nihon Shakaitō Chūō Honbu Soshiki Kyoku, April 20, 1986.

5. The Heiminsha was the publishing house for the *Heimin Shinbun* (The Commoners' Newspaper), created in 1904 as a journal of antiwar opinion. It was the major gathering place for socialists at the time.

6. See Kawakami Tamio, "Shakaishugi, Museifushugi, Kyōsanshugi" in Kimura, ed., *Shakai Shisō Tokuhon*, p. 169.

7. In his only reference to Japan in his famous book on political parties, Robert Michels noted that "the presence of bourgeous elements in the proletarian movement organized to form a political party is a historical fact, and one which may be noted wherever the political movement of the international working class is attentively observed. This phenomenon reproduces itself wherever the socialist tree throws out new branches, as may be seen, for example, in Japan and Brazil." Michels, *Political Parties*, p. 231.

8. Yamakawa and Sakisaka, *Yamakawa Hitoshi Jiden*, p. 378.

9. *Ibid.*, p. 406.

10. The Socialist party was the first party to be formed after the war, its official inauguration date being November 2, 1945.

11. Even while he was criticizing the party for relying on foreign ideas and sources to make their arguments, Asukata could not resist looking to a European source to legitimize his own position, noting that in his first year in office as party chairman, he had strengthened the party's role in ideological training by expanding the activities of the party headquarters school and prefecture and branch schools. "We learned this," Asukata notes, "from the Italian Communist party." See Asukata, "Jichi To Bunken," p. 44.

12. This incident brought jail terms of from one to two years to a number of socialist leaders for carrying to a welcoming party for a comrade just released from jail a red flag inscribed with the characters meaning "anarchy communism" (*museifu kyōsan*).

13. As a result of this incident, Kōtoku Shūsui and eleven others went to the gallows for allegedly plotting to kill the emperor. See Notehelfer, *Kotoku Shusui*.

14. See McKenzie, *Comintern and World Revolution*, p. 49.

15. Lichtheim, *Marxism in Modern France*, p. 33.

16. Satō Noboru, "Shakaishugi Kyōkai Hihan No Jōshiki," p. 56.

17. See Yamakawa and Sakisaka, *Yamakawa Hitoshi Jiden*, p. 369ff.

18. Ōsugi and his wife were murdered by the police in September 1923 in the aftermath of the Tokyo earthquake. See Stanley, *Ōsugi Sakae*.

19. Yamakawa Hitoshi, "Musan Kaikyū No Hōkō Tenkan," *Zen'ei*, August 1922; cited in Beckmann and Okubo, *The Japanese Communist Party*, p. 53.

20. Nihon Shakaitō, *Nijūnen No Kiroku*, pp. 38–39.

21. Quoted in Takahashi Hikohiro, *Shakai Minshushugi Seitō*, p. 136.

22. Nihon Shakaitō, *Nijūnen No Kiroku*, p. 173.

23. See *Shakaishugi E No Michi* in Nihon Shakaitō, *Nijūnen No Kiroku*, pp. 486–487.

24. Nihon Shakaitō Chihō Giindan Zenkoku Kaigi, *Tō Kaikaku E No Teigen,* December 1974, unpublished.

25. Kawakami Tamio, "Shakaishugi, Museifushugi, Kyōsanshugi," in Kimura, ed., *Shakai Shiso Tokuhon,* p. 184.

26. For a list of its original members, see Chūma, " 'Dokyumento' Shakaishugi Kyōkai," p. 146.

27. Quoted in Chūma, " 'Dokyumento,' " p. 146.

28. For a profile of Sakisaka and his activities at Miike see Olsen, "A Japanese Marxist," in his *Dimensions of Japan,* pp. 203–224. For an analysis of the Miike strike, see Cook, "Political Action and Trade Unions," pp. 103–121. The events leading to the strike were as follows: In August 1959 the Mitsui Company, which owned six of the country's largest colleries, decided to bring about a "rationalization" of its work force by calling for the voluntary retirement of 5,000 of its 35,000 workers. This went smoothly enough in five of the six mines. But at the sixth, at Miike, where there were 14,000 union members, only 1,000 miners offered to quit rather than the 2,000 the company wanted to have leave. The company then "nominated" another 1,200 workers, including 300 union activists, for retirement. With this, the union called on its members to strike; the company, in turn, locked out the organized workers. This was followed by the creation of a second union sympathetic to management and by the introduction of nonunion workers brought in through subcontractors. The Miike struggle was on in full force.

29. Ōta Kaoru, for example, then chairman of Sōhyō and a major opponent of structural reform, quotes Garaudy at length in attacking the structural reform group. See Ōta Kaoru, "Shakaitō No Kōzō Kaikakuron Ni Taisuru Nanatsu No Gimon," January 1, 1961, in Nihon Shakaitō, *Nijūnen No Kiroku,* pp. 259–270.

30. Sakisaka's critique of structural reform is best stated in "Shakaishugi No Joken To Kōzō Kaikaku Ron," February 5, 1961, in Nihon Shakaitō, *Nijūnen No Kiroku,* pp. 284–289. Sakisaka's argument was the same as Rosa Luxemburg's criticism of Bernstein's revisionism: "If we do not hold that the contradictions of capitalism drive it to its doom, we give up the Marxist tenet of the 'objective necessity' for socialism. If we argue, as Bernstein does, that we cannot count on a capitalist collapse, we must give up all hope for a Socialist future." Quoted in Gay, *The Dilemma of Democratic Socialism,* pp. 260–261.

31. Asanuma's famous statement during a visit to Peking that "American imperialism is the common enemy of Japan and China" was a piece of leftist rhetoric intended primarily to help him secure the support of the pro-Chinese Suzuki faction in his quest for the party chairmanship.

32. Koyama and Shimizu, *Nihon Shakaitō Shi,* p. 227.

33. See Sasaki Kōzō, "Tō No Shisei O Tadasu," in Nihon Shakaitō, *Nijūnen No Kiroku,* p. 303.

34. *Ibid.,* p. 305.

35. *Ibid.,* p. 305.

36. The tactic was first used on December 13, 1947, when Sasaki's mentor, Suzuki Mosaburō, led the party's left wing in issuing a statement declaring that it had become a *tōnai yatō,* or "inner-party opposition party," and reserved to itself the right to criticize the coalition government. Not long thereafter the left

brought down the government by voting against the budget it submitted to the Budget Committee chaired by Suzuki.

37. At the November 1962 congress, the party adopted a resolution sponsored by Sasaki Kōzō that bitterly critized Eda for his Eda Vision. Taking this as a vote of nonconfidence, Eda resigned from the post of secretary-general. But party activists who had supported this resolution were not prepared to vote for Sasaki for secretary-general and instead voted with the "right," giving the position to Narita.

38. "By the socialist revolution in the Soviet Union in 1917 the first socialist state in world history was established. Since then, over the past forty years, thirteen countries, 35 percent of the world's population, have established socialist systems in Eastern Europe, China, Korea, North Vietnam. . . . These socialist systems . . . are demonstrating more and more their superiority." *Shakaishugi E No Michi*, reprinted in Nihon Shakaitō, *Nijūnen No Kiroku*, p. 466.

39. *Ibid.*, p. 486.

40. See Katsumata Seiichi, "Shingi Keika To Kore Kara No Kadai," postscript to *Shakaishugi E No Michi*, pamphlet (Tokyo: Nihon Shakaito Shuppan Kyoku, 1966), p. 93. See also Katsumata, *Shakaishugi E No Michi To Gendai*, pp. 144–145.

41. Narita, it will be remembered, first became secretary-general in 1962 as the candidate of the structural reform group, beating out Sasaki Kōzō. He then moved steadily to the left (i.e., toward alliance with Sasaki) as power swung in that direction. He became party chairman in 1969, a post he held until 1977, longer than any other chairman in the party's history. See Ishikawa, "Tayōsei No Naka No Tanjun Na Tōsō," p. 14.

42. Nishio, *Seiji Oboegaki*, p. 61.

43. Quoted in Ishikawa, "Tayōsei No Naka No Tanjun No Tōsō," p. 14.

44. Roth, *The Social Democrats in Imperial Germany*, p. 186.

45. Cited in Haga, "Iinchō No Joken," p. 138.

46. Quoted in Chalmers, *The Social Democratic Party of Germany*, p. 87.

47. See Shimizu and Ōta, "Gendai Shakaishugi Ronsō," p. 33.

48. See Sasaki, *Shakaishugitekiteki Seiken*, p. 2.

49. On this point see Najita, *Hara Kei*, p. 5ff.

50. Shakaishugi Kyōkai, *Shakaishugi Kyōkai Tēze*, p. 136.

51. See Tanaka Naoki, "Shakaitō Seinenkon Wa Nani O Mezasu Ka."

52. *Shaseidō's* English-language name is the Japan League of Socialist Youth. It is affiliated with the Soviet-sponsored World Youth Federation.

53. Quoted in "Shakaitō O Gyūjiru Shakaishugi Kyōkai," *Asahi Jānaru*, December 27, 1974, p. 14.

54. Asukata, "Jichi To Bunken De Arata No Tōsō O," p. 45.

55. For an example of Asukata's skill in manipulating this rhetoric, see Asukata, "Minshushugi No Saisei to Shakaitō No Hōkō."

56. Cobban, *A History of Modern France*, vol. 3, p. 225.

5. CAMPAIGNING, FINANCING, AND THE MODERN PARTY

1. For an analysis of *kōenkai*, see Curtis, *Election Campaigning Japanese Style*, pp. 126–151.

2. In the party's early years Kōmeitō Diet members were required to turn

over their salaries to the party which then paid them a stipend, a policy which is still followed in the JCP, and which is intended to keep the Diet member subordinate to the party. In recent years, however, Kōmeitō Diet members have been permitted to retain their entire Diet earnings; several Diet members in the party also have created their own personal support organizations and have developed independent sources of political funds.

3. See Duverger, *Political Parties.*

4. The relationship between the expansion of the suffrage and the development of membership parties in Britain was actually pointed out at the turn of the century by M. Ostrogorski. See his *Democracy and the Organization of Political Parties,* p. 279.

5. Asahi Shinbun, *Seitō To Habatsu,* p. 198.

6. On the counterorganizational tendencies of party systems in advanced industrialized democracies, see Epstein, *Political Parties in Western Democracies.*

7. Both Ashida and Nishio were convicted in lower court trials, but ten years later both were acquitted on appeal. As it turned out, none of those tried for involvement in this case ever went to jail. Fukuda was not indicted. For a description of this and the other scandals mentioned below and a thoughtful analysis of Japanese political corruption, see Murobushi, *Oshoku No Kōzō.*

8. See Gendai Seiji Mondai Kenkyūkai, *Jimintō Gigoku Shi* pp. 62–70.

9. For an account see Fujita, *Shiina Saitei.*

10. This is the way Shiina characterized the situation in his memorandum announcing his recommendation of Miki. The memorandum is reprinted in Fujita, *Shiina Saitei,* pp. 122–123.

11. In 1963, as head of a commission appointed by Prime Minister Ikeda to make proposals for party reform, Miki was responsible for a famous report calling for party modernization and the "unconditional abolition of party factions." The Miki report and a history of the party's reform proposals during its first ten years are included in a chapter entitled "Tō Kindaika No Ayumi" (The Course of Party Modernization) in Jijū Minshutō, *Jiyū Minshutō Jūnen No Ayumi,* pp. 243–264.

12. The campaign to oust Miki actually had begun in June when Miki insisted on pursuing a revision and strengthening of the antimonopoly law. See Tominomori, *Sengo Hoshutō Shi,* pp. 203–205.

13. In particular, the 1975 reforms followed closely proposals made in 1968 by the Fifth Commission on the Election System established by Prime Minister Satō in response to the "black mist" scandals. These proposals were never drafted into legislation because of LDP demands that they be linked to the adoption of a single-member constituency system.

14. Jichishō Senkyobu, *Chikujō Kaisetsu Kōshoku Senkyo Hō,* p. 921. This is a 1,400-page article-by-article analysis of the election law by officials in the election bureau of the Ministry of Home Affairs.

The Ministry of Home Affairs (*Jichishō*), incidentally, used to be called in English the Local Autonomy Ministry. Several years ago, however, it adopted the Home Ministry appellation as its official English name, the same name used by its prewar predecessor, the *Naimushō.*

15. See the explanation of the background to the 1962 revision in Jichishō Senkyobu, *Chikujō Kaisetsu Kōshoku Senkyo Hō,* pp. 909–916.

16. Each party is permitted 1,500 posters for each election district plus 75 more for each additional candidate in a district where a party runs more than one.

17. Iwata, *Wakariyasui Kōshoku Senkyo Hō*, p. 189. This book, written by a senior official in the Home Ministry, is a kind of official guide to the revised Election Law.

18. That is, the prohibition of all activity outside of the official campaign period intended to obtain votes for a particular candidate in a specific election. In the immediate postwar period the minimum official campaign period was thirty days. In 1952 it was reduced to twenty-five days. In 1958 it was further shortened to twenty days. And in a revision of the law in 1982, it was reduced to fifteen days. In theory the official campaign period can run as long as forty days under current law, but the LDP invariably opts for the shortest possible campaign period. In the 1986 election it was the minimum fifteen days.

19. Iwata, *Wakariyasui Kōshoku Senkyo Hō*, p. 130. See also Jichishō Senkyo-bu, *Shūgiin Senkyo No Tebiki*, p. 114.

20. Prior to 1950 separate laws governed elections for various offices in Japan. In 1950 these were consolidated into one Public Offices Election Law.

21. Iwata, *Wakariyasui Kōshoku Senkyo Hō*, p. 112.

22. Jichishō Senkyobu, *Chikujō Kaisetsu Kōshoku Senkyo Hō*, p. 624.

23. Similar figures are reported in articles in major newspapers, as cited in Kishimoto, *Tokuhon, Nihon No Gikai Seiji*, pp. 238–241.

24. Alexander, *Financing Politics*, p. 9.

25. The Socialist party provided no set amount of support for its candidates in 1986, leaving it largely up to each individual to secure his own support from labor union organizations. The DSP provided each of its candidates ¥3 million in campaign funds.

26. Technically, contributions to the LDP are made to the National Political Association (Kokumin Seiji Kyōkai), which is registered with the Ministry of Home Affairs as the LDP's official funding organization. The official Home Ministry exegesis of the revised law is available in Jichishō Senkyobu, *Kaisei Seiji Shikin Kisei Hō Kaisetsu*.

27. The formula for setting the ceiling on union contributions is based on the number of union members. It is ¥7.5 million for unions with less than 50,000 members and goes up in increments from there to a maximum of ¥100 million for unions or union federations with half a million members or more.

The formula for industrial and other associations is based on the total amount of annual expenditures. Organizations whose previous year's expenditures were under ¥20 million can give ¥7.5 million. The amount rises in increments to a maximum of ¥100 million for associations with a previous year's expenditure of ¥460 million or more.

28. Jichishō Senkyobu, *Seiji Dantai Meibo*.

29. *Mainichi Shinbun*, September 3, 1985.

30. *Ibid.*

31. All organizations that receive political funds are required to file publicly available annual reports with the Ministry of Home Affairs. Unless otherwise specified, all figures about political funding cited in this chapter are taken from these reports. See *Kanpō, Gogai Tokushū 13go*, 7 vols., September 3, 1985,

and reports in the *Mainichi Shinbun* and *Nihon Keizai Shinbun* of September 3, 1985.

32. In 1984, for example, LDP income was ¥13.2 billion compared to ¥21.7 billion for the JCP. The Kōmeitō reported income of ¥9.3 billion. The figures were ¥6.3 billion, ¥1.7 billion, and ¥420 million for the JSP, DSP, and NLC respectively.

33. The breakdown is as follows: Fukuda, ¥1.18 billion; Nakasone, ¥1.09 billion; Kōmoto, ¥920 million; Tanaka, ¥820 million; Suzuki, ¥290 million.

34. Takeshita obtained ¥924 million; Abe ¥759 million; Watanabe ¥599 million, and Miyazawa ¥417 million, for a total of ¥2,699 million.

35. *Asahi Shinbun*, September 16, 1976.

36. See Hirose, *Hojokin To Seikentō*, pp. 236–238.

37. There were seven political organizations reporting fund-raising party income of over ¥100 million: Nakasone faction, ¥507 million; upper house member Tamaki Kazuo, ¥445 million; Kōmoto faction, ¥412 million; Fukuda faction, ¥352 million; Takeshita Noboru, ¥326 million; upper house member Itoyama Eitarō, ¥228 million; and lower house member (and then chairman of the LDP policy affairs research council) Fujio Masayuki, ¥217 million.

38. *Asahi Shinbun*, June 15, 1986.

39. *Ibid.*

40. *Asahi Shinbun*, June 18, 1986.

41. See Satō and Matsuzaki, *Jimintō Seiken.*

6. THE CHANGING JAPANESE VOTER

1. As a percentage, this total number equalled the share of Diet seats (59.3 percent) obtained in 1969. In the 1958, 1960, and 1963 elections, when the lower house had fewer seats, the LDP obtained over 60 percent. The figure for 1986 results includes four independents who joined the LDP as soon as they were elected.

2. For a further exposition of the relationship between the absolute voting rate—or to look at it from the other side, the abstention rate—and the LDP vote, see Arai, "Why the Liberal Democrats Barely Survived," and Satō Seizaburo, "The Shifting Political Spectrum," pp. 27–28.

3. *Asahi Shinbun*, August 8, 1986.

4. See Arai, "Why the Liberal Democrats Barely Survived," p. 16.

5. Verba, Nie, and Kim, *Participation and Political Equality*, pp. 98–100.

6. In Japanese the distinction between strong and weak support is drawn by using the term *shiji* (support, as in *Jimintō shiji*) for strong identifiers, and *shoku* (the word for color, as in *Shakaitō shoku*) for weak ones.

7. See Asahi Shinbunsha, *Nihonjin No Seiji Ishiki*, p. 177.

8. *Asahi Shinbun*, July 5, 1986.

9. See Burnham, *Critical Elections*, pp. 127–128.

10. For a discussion of the concept of the hard vote see Curtis, *Election Campaigning*, pp. 38–40.

11. Asahi Shinbunsha, *Nihonjin No Seiji Ishiki*, pp. 179–184. Between 1955 and 1965 there were more women than men who expressed support for no party. Supporters of no party were highest among women over sixty, then among those

over fifty, and then among those over forty. By the early 1970s, however, the percentage of men in their twenties and thirties supporting no party began to exceed the percentage of elderly women making no party choice. Similarly, with regard to educational levels, among all people with more than thirteen years of education, the percentage who support no party has been higher since 1970 than the percentage of all those with less than thirteen years of education who support no party. Before 1960 the situation was the reverse.

12. On this subject see Dalton, Flanagan, and Beck, eds., *Electoral Change in Advanced Industrial Democracies*.

13. See Curtis, "Conservative Dominance in Japanese Politics," p. 246.

14. The figures for the other parties were: NLC, 5.6 percent; Kōmeitō, 5.4 percent; DSP, 5.1 percent; JCP, 4.4 percent; and 3.0 percent for the SDL. Based on unpublished opinion poll data provided by the *Asahi Shinbun* for poll conducted May 7 and 8, 1986.

15. See *Asahi Shinbun*, July 3, 1986.

16. See *Yomiuri Shinbun*, July 7, 1986.

17. The figures for the other parties were 0.4 percent for the Kōmeitō, 2.5 percent for the DSP, 5.1 percent for the NLC, and 1.8 percent for the SDL. See Takashi Inoguchi and Ikuo Kabashima, "The Status Quo Student Elite," in Watanuki et al., eds., *Electoral Behavior in the 1983 Japanese Elections*, p. 106.

18. *Ibid*, p. 110.

19. The results of this poll and the *Asahi Shinbun* article of June 27, 1978 are noted *Ibid.*, p. 106.

20. The winner with the lowest percentage of the vote in the 1986 lower house election was a Socialist in Fukushima 2's five-member district. He won with 9.6 percent of the vote. There are one six-member, thirteen five-member, eleven four-member, and eight three-member metropolitan constituencies, according to the classification system used by the *Asahi Shinbun*.

21. In a 1985 Prime Minister's Office poll which asked about attachment in a slightly different way (giving respondents a choice between yes, no, or can't say), 72.8 percent of respondents nationwide said they had "feelings of attachment," 10.6 percent said they did not, and 16.6 percent were ambivalent. For residents in the eleven largest cities, the figures were 68.8 percent expressing feelings of attachment, 10.6 percent not having such feelings, and 16.6 percent being unable to say. Among respondents in towns and villages, the comparable figures were 81.1 percent, 6.7 percent, and 12.1 percent. See Sōrifu Kōhōshitsu, *Gekkan Yoron Chōsa*, May 1985, p. 16.

22. Murakami, *Shinchūkan Taishū No Jidai*.

23. *Japan Times*, March 2, 1987.

24. See *Asahi Shinbun*, July 11, 1986 for a report on the July conventions of Dōrō and Tetsurō, which were their last conventions as public sector unions.

25. Symbolic and symptomatic of this decline in Kokurō's vote-getting powers was the defeat in the 1986 lower house election of JSP Diet member Tomizuka Mitsu, former secretary-general of Kokurō and, just prior to being elected to the Diet for the first time in 1983, secretary-general of Sōhyō.

26. According to Education Ministry figures, Nikkyōso membership now comprises only 50 percent of those who qualify for membership. See *Asahi Shinbun*, August 8, 1986.

27. *Asahi Shinbun*, July 17, 1986.

28. Verba et al., *Participation and Political Equality*, p. 193.

29. Verba et al. mention in particular Flanagan and Richardson, *Japanese Electoral Behavior*.

30. The best statement of the theory of clientelist politics is Powell, "Peasant Society and Clientelist Politics," in Schmidt et al., eds., *Friends, Followers, and Factions*, pp. 147–160.

31. Quoted in Giddens, *The Class Structure of the Advanced Societies*, p. 83.

32. See for example the survey data reported in Inglehart, *The Silent Revolution*, p. 210.

33. See Seymour M. Lipset and Stein Rokkan, "Cleavage Structures, Party Systems, and Voter Alignments," in Lipset and Rokkan, eds., *Party Systems and Voter Alignments*, pp. 50–55.

34. Edmund Burke, cited in Sartori, *Parties and Party Systems*, p. 9.

35. The most important work has been done by Hayashi Chikio, Akuto Hiroshi, and others associated with a group called the Nihonjin Kenkyūkai (The Study Group on Japanese National Character). The two major studies produced by this group are: Nihonjin Kenkyūkai, *Shiji Seitō Betsu Nihonjin Shūdan*, and Hayashi Chikio, *Nihonjin No Seiji Kankaku*.

36. The data on religion are as follows:

Party	Believe in a religion	Engage in religious activity	Do not believe in a religion but believe in a religious spirit	Total
Kōmeitō	83%	46%	11%	94%
LDP	29	9	53	82
No Party	18	6	52	70
JSP	17	5	60	77
DSP	16	5	56	72
JCP	9	0	59	68

SOURCE: Hayashi Chikio, "Nihonjin No Ishiki Wa Seitō Shiji Betsu Ni Dō Chigau Ka," in Nihonjin Kenkyūkai, ed., *Shiji Seitō Betsu Nihonjin Shūdan*, p. 16.

37. Watanuki, *Japanese Politics*, p. 7.

38. Vogel's *Japan as Number One* was published in Japanese by TBS Britannica Company in 1979, the same year it was published in English by Harvard University Press.

EPILOGUE: THE JAPANESE WAY OF POLITICS

1. Figures on American subsidy payments provided by the Economic Analysis Staff, Office of the Assistant Secretary for Economics, U.S. Department of Agriculture.

2. The smallest of the four major LDP factions in the lower house are the Miyazawa Faction, with 60 members, and the Abe Faction, with 56. The number of members of these smallest major factions, added to the total number of Kōmeitō

and DSP lower house members, comes to 204, while the larger Tanaka, Nakasone, and Kōmoto factions and LDP independents together account for only 195
lower house members. Thus the combination of any two major factions plus the
Kōmeitō and DSP would outnumber those remaining in the LDP.

    3. See Van Wolferen, "The Japan Problem."

SELECTED
BIBLIOGRAPHY

Alexander, Herbert E. *Financing Politics: Money, Elections, and Political Reform*. 2d ed. Washington: Congressional Quarterly Press, 1980.

Andō Jinbei, Iwatare Sukio, and Gerald L. Curtis. "Shakaitō Ni Deguchi Wa Aru Ka." *Asahi Jānaru*, February 11, 1977, pp. 90–97.

Arai Kunio. "Why the Liberal Democrats Barely Survived." *Japan Echo* (September 1984), 11(2):10–16.

Asahi Shinbun. *Seitō To Habatsu*. Tokyo: Asahi Shinbunsha, 1968.

Asahi Shinbun Senkyo Honbu. *Senkyo Taikan, Dai 35 Kai Sōsenkyo*. Tokyo: Asahi Shinbunsha, 1980.

Asahi Shinbunsha Yoron Chōsashitsu. *Nihonjin No Seiji Ishiki, Asahi Shinbun Yoron Chōsa No Sanjūnen*. Tokyo: Asahi Shinbunsha, 1976.

Ashimura Kosuke. "Nihon No Rōdō Kumiai To Seitō." *Keiei To Rōdō* (September 1974), no. 9, pp. 17–33.

Asukata Ichio. "Jichi To Bunken De Arata Na Tōsō O." *Ekonomisto*, January 16, 1979, pp. 44–47.

Asukata Ichio. "Minshushugi No Saisei To Shakaitō No Hōkō." *Sekai*, July 1976, pp. 109–120.

Asukata Ichio. "Shakaitō Saisei E No Teigen." *Asahi Jānaru*, December 16, 1977, pp. 6–13.

Baerwald, Hans. *Japan's Parliament: An Introduction*. Cambridge: Cambridge University Press, 1974.

Baerwald, Hans. *The Purge of Japanese Leaders Under the Occupation*. Berkeley and Los Angeles: University of California Press, 1959.

Barnds, William J., ed. *Japan and the United States: Challenges and Opportunities.* New York: New York University Press, for the Council of Foreign Relations, 1979.

Beckmann, George, and Genji Okubo. *The Japanese Communist Party, 1922–1945.* Stanford: Stanford University Press, 1969.

Berger, Gordon Mark. *Parties Out of Power in Japan, 1931–1941.* Princeton: Princeton University Press, 1977.

Blackmer, Donald. *Unity in Diversity: Italian Communism and the Communist World.* Cambridge: MIT Press, 1968.

Blaker, Michael K., ed. *Japan at the Polls: The House of Councillors Election of 1974.* Washington: American Enterprise Institute, 1976.

Burnham, Walter Dean. *Critical Elections and the Mainsprings of American Politics.* New York: Norton, 1970.

Campbell, John Creighton. *Contemporary Japanese Budget Politics.* Berkeley and Los Angeles: University of California Press, 1977.

Castle, Emery N. and Kenzo Hemmi, eds., with Sally A. Skillings. *U.S.-Japanese Agricultural Trade Relations.* Baltimore: Johns Hopkins University Press, for Resources for the Future, 1982.

Chalmers, Douglas A. *The Social Democratic Party of Germany: From Working Class Movement to Modern Political Party.* Yale Studies in Political Science, no. 10. New Haven: Yale University Press, 1964.

Chūma Kiyofuku. "'Dokyumento' Shakaishugi Kyōkai." *Chūō Kōron,* August 1976, pp. 144–155.

Cobban, Alfred. *A History of Modern France.* Vol. 3, *1871–1962.* 3d ed. London: Penguin Books, 1965.

Cole, Allan B., George O. Totten, and Cecil H. Uyehara. *Socialist Parties in Postwar Japan.* New Haven: Yale University Press, 1966.

Cook, Alice H. "Political Action and Trade Unions: A Case Study of the Coal Miners in Japan." *Monumenta Nipponica* (1967), 24(1–2): 103–121.

Curtis, Gerald L. "Conservative Dominance in Japanese Politics." *Current History* (April 1971), 60(356):207–212.

Curtis, Gerald L. *Election Campaigning Japanese Style.* New York: Columbia University Press, 1971. Reprint. Tokyo: Kodansha International, 1983.

Curtis, Gerald L. "Sanjūnenkan No Henshin." *Gendai No Riron,* November 1982, pp. 33–36.

Curtis, Gerald L. and Ishikawa Masumi. *Doken Kokka Nippon.* Tokyo: Kōbunsha, 1984.

Dalton, Russell J., Scott C. Flanagan, and Paul Allen Beck, eds. *Electoral Change in Advanced Industrial Democracies: Realignment or Dealignment?* Princeton: Princeton University Press, 1984.

Dator, James Allen. *Soka Gakkai: Builders of the Third Civilization.* Seattle: University of Washington Press, 1969.

Duverger, Maurice. *Political Parties: Their Organization and Activity in the Modern State*. New York: Wiley, 1967.

Eda Saburō. *Nihon No Shakaishugi*. Tokyo: Nihon Hyōronsha, 1967.

Eda Saburō. "Nihon No Shakaishugi Ni Tsuite." *Ekonomisuto*, October 28, 1962, pp. 317–325.

Epstein, Leon D. *Political Parties in Western Democracies*. 1967. Reprint. New Brunswick, N.J.: Transaction Books, 1980.

Flanagan, Scott C. and Bradley M. Richardson. *Japanese Electoral Behavior: Social Cleavages, Social Networks, and Partisanship*. Professional Papers in Contemporary Political Sociology. Beverly Hills: Sage Publications, 1977.

Fujita Yoshiro. *Shiina Saitei*. Tokyo: Sankei Shuppan, 1979.

Fujiwara Hirotatsu. *Sōka Gakkai O Kiru*. Tokyo: Nisshin Hōdō, 1969. Published in English as *I Denounce Soka Gakkai*. Tokyo: Nisshin Hōdō, 1970.

Fukui, Haruhiro. *Party in Power: The Japanese Liberal Democrats and Policy Making*. Berkeley and Los Angeles: University of California Press, 1970.

Fukutake Tadashi. *Nihon Shakai No Kōzō*. Tokyo: Tokyo Daigaku Shuppankai, 1981.

Furusawa Ken'ichi. *Fukuda Takeo To Nihon Keizai*. Tokyo: Kōdansha, 1983.

Gay, Peter. *The Dilemma of Democratic Socialism: Eduard Bernstein's Challenge to Marx*. New York: Columbia University Press, 1954.

Gekkan Shakaitō Henshūbu. *Nihon Shakaitō No Sanjūnen*. 3 vols. Tokyo: Nihon Shakaitō Chūō Honbu Kikanshi Kyoku, 1975.

Gendai Seiji Mondai Kenkyūkai. *Jimintō Gigoku Shi*. Tokyo: Gendai Hyōronsha, 1979.

Giddens, Anthony. *The Class Structure of the Advanced Societies*. New York: Harper and Row, Torchbooks, 1973.

Gotō Motō, Uchida Kenzō, and Ishiwaka Masumi. *Sengo Hoshu Seiji No Kiseki*. Tokyo: Iwanami Shoten, 1982.

Haga Yasushi. "Iinchō No Joken." *Bungei Shunjū* (February 1978), 56(2):134–142.

Hamilton, Richard. *Affluence and the Worker in Fourth Republic France*. Princeton: Princeton University Press, 1967.

Harari, Ehud. *The Politics of Labor Legislation in Japan: National-International Interaction*. Berkeley and Los Angeles: University of California Press, 1973.

Hatoyama Ichirō. *Hatoyama Ichirō Kaisōroku*. Tokyo: Bungei Shunjū, 1957.

Hayashi Chikio. *Seiji Ishiki No Kanjō Kōzō No Kenkyū*. Tokyo: Tōkei Sūri Kenkyūjo, 1979.

Hayashi Chikio, ed. *Nihonjin No Seiji Kankaku*. Nihonjin Kenkyū, no. 6. Tokyo: Idemitsu Shoten, 1983.

Hirose Michisada. *Hojokin To Seikentō*. Tokyo: Asahi Shinbunsha, 1981.

Ide Yoshinori. *Nihon Kanryō Sei To Gyōsei Bunka.* Tokyo: Tokyo Daigaku Shuppankai, 1982.

Ike, Nobutaka. *A Theory of Japanese Democracy.* Boulder: Westview Press, 1978.

Inglehart, Ronald. *The Silent Revolution: Changing Values and Political Styles Among Western Publics.* Princeton: Princeton University Press, 1977.

Inuta Mitsuru. *Nihonjin No Kaiso Ishiki, "Chūryū" No Yoimikata, Toraekata.* Kyoto: PHP Kenkyūjo, 1982.

Ishida Hirohide. *Watakushi No Seikai Shōwa Shi.* Tokyo: Tōyō Keizai Shinpōsha, 1986.

Ishikawa Masumi. " 'Chūdō' Ni Taoreta Eda Saburō." *Asahi Jānaru* (June 3, 1977), 19(23):88–91.

Ishikawa Masumi. *Dēta Sengo Seiji Shi.* Tokyo: Iwanami Shoten, 1984.

Ishikawa Masumi. *Nihon Seiji No Ima.* Tokyo: Gendai No Rironsha, 1981.

Ishikawa Masumi. *Sengo Seiji Kōzō Shi.* Tokyo: Nihon Hyōronsha, 1978.

Ishikawa Masumi. "Tayōsei No Naka No Tanjun No Tōsō." *Asahi Jānaru* (August 29, 1975), 17(37):12–16.

Ishizaki Tadao. *Nihon No Shotoku To Tomi No Bunpai.* Tokyo: Tōyō Keizai Shinposha, 1983.

Itō Masaya. *Ikeda Hayato, Sono Sei To Shi.* Tokyo: Shiseidō, 1974.

Itō Masaya. *Jimintō Sengoku Shi.* Tokyo: Asahi Sonorama, 1983.

Itō Masaya. *Shin Jimintō Sengoku Shi.* Tokyo: Asahi Sonorama, 1983.

Itō Mitsuharu. *Hoshu To Kakushin No Nihonteki Kōzō.* Tokyo: Chikuma Shobō, 1970.

Iwata Osamu. *Wakariyasui Kōshoku Senkyo Hō.* Tokyo: Gyōsei, 1979.

Japan Communist Party. "Manifesto of Freedom and Democracy." *Japan Echo* (Winter 1976), 3(4):85–95.

Jichishō Senkyobu. *Chikujō Kaisetsu Kōshoku Senkyo Hō.* Tokyo: Seikei Shoin, 1985.

Jichishō Senkyobu. *Kaisei Seiji Shikin Kisei Hō Kaisetsu.* Tokyo: Chihō Zaimu Kyōkai, 1976.

Jichishō Senkyobu. *Seiji Dantai Meibo.* Tokyo: Jichishō Senkyobu, 1985.

Jichishō Senkyobu. *Shūgiin Senkyo No Tebiki.* Rev. ed. Tokyo: Gyōsei, 1986.

Jiyū Minshutō. *Jiyū Minshutō Jūnen No Ayumi.* Tokyo: Jiyū Minshutō, 1966.

Johnson, Chalmers, *MITI and the Japanese Miracle: The Growth of Industrial Policy, 1925–1975.* Stanford: Stanford University Press, 1982.

Johnson, Chalmers. "Structural Corruption, and the Advent of Machine Politics in Japan." *The Journal of Japanese Studies* (Winter 1986), 12(1):1–28.

Johnson, D. Gale, Kenzo Hemmi, and Pierre Lardinois. *Agricultural Policy and Trade: Adjusting Domestic Programs in an International Framework.* New York: New York University Press, for the Trilateral Commission, 1985.

Kaminogō Toshiaki. *Shakaitō Sōsō Kōshinkyoku.* Tokyo: Gendaishi Shuppankai, 1976.

Katō Hirohisa. *Shūsan Dōjitsu Senkyo No Takakuteki Bunseki.* Tokyo: Seiji Kōhō Sentā, 1980.

Katsumata Seiichi. *Shakaishugi E No Michi To Gendai.* Tokyo: Nihon Shakaitō Chūō Honbu Kikanshi Kyoku, 1977.

Kawabata Masahisa. *Kominterum To Nihon.* Tokyo: Hōritsu Bunkasha, 1982.

Kawai, Kazuo. *Japan's American Interlude.* Chicago: University of Chicago Press, 1960.

Kawakami Tadao. *Kiro Ni Tatsu Nihon Shakaitō.* Tokyo: Shakai Hyōronsha, 1981.

Kawamura Yuzuru. *Seitō No Hōkai: Shinjiyū Kurabu Zasetsu No Kiseki.* Tokyo: Ōesu Shuppan, 1980.

Keizai Hyōron (bessatsu). *Datsu Seitō Jidai No Seiji.* Tokyo: Nihon Hyōronsha, 1971.

Kijima Masamichi. *Kōzō Kaikaku Ha.* Tokyo: Gendai No Rironsha, 1979.

Kimura Takeyasu, ed. *Shakai Shisō Tokuhon.* Tokyo: Tōyō Keizai Shinpōsha, 1958.

Kishimoto Kōichi. *Tokuhon, Nihon No Gikai Seiji.* Tokyo: Gyōsei Mondai Kenkyūjo, 1983.

Kōhei Shinsaku. *Tenkanki No Seiji Ishiki, Kawaru Nihonjin No Tōhyo Kōdō.* Tokyo: Keiō Tsūshin, 1979.

Kōno Mitsu. *Nihon Shakai Seitō Shi.* Tokyo: Chūō Kōronsha, 1960.

Koyama Hirotake and Shimizu Shinzō. *Nihon Shakaitō Shi.* Tokyo: Haga Shoten, 1965.

Krauss, Ellis S., Thomas P. Rohlen, and Patricia G. Steinhoff, eds. *Conflict in Japan.* Honolulu: University of Hawaii Press, 1984.

Kumon Hiroshi, Okamoto Yoshiji, and Taniguchi Yoneo. *Zusetsu, Zaisei Tōyūshi.* Tokyo: Tōyō Keizai Shinposha, 1983.

Kyōgoku Jun'ichi. *Nihon No Seiji.* Tokyo: Tokyo Daigaku Shuppankai, 1983.

Large, Stephen S. *Organized Workers and Socialist Politics in Interwar Japan.* Cambridge: Cambridge University Press, 1981.

Lichtheim, George. *Marxism in Modern France.* New York: Columbia University Press, 1966.

Lipset, Seymour M. and Stein Rokkan, eds. *Party Systems and Voter Alignments: Cross National Perspectives.* New York: The Free Press, 1967.

McKean, Margaret A. *Environmental Protest and Citizen Politics in Japan.* Berkeley and Los Angeles: University of California Press, 1981.

McKenzie, Kermit E. *Comintern and World Revolution, 1928–1943: The Shaping of a Doctrine.* New York: Columbia University Press, 1964.

Masamura Kimihiro. *Sengo Shi.* 2 vols. Tokyo: Chikuma Shobō, 1985.

Masumi Junnosuke. *Gendai Seiji, 1955 Nen Igo.* 2 vols. Tokyo: Tokyo Daigaku Shuppankai, 1985.

Masumi Junnosuke. *Sengo Seiji, 1945–1955*. 2 vols. Tokyo: Tokyo Daigaku Shuppankai, 1983.

Matsushita Keiichi. *Shibiru Minimamu No Shisō*. Tokyo: Tokyo Daigaku Shuppankai, 1971.

Michels, Robert. *Political Parties: A Sociological Study of the Oligarchical Tendencies of Modern Democracies*. 1911. Reprint. New York: The Free Press, 1962.

Miyake Ichirō. *Seitō Shiji No Bunseki*. Tokyo: Sōbunsha, 1985.

Miyazaki Yoshimasa. *Hatoyama Ichirō*. Tokyo: Jiji Tsūshinsha, 1985.

Moore, Joe. *Japanese Workers and the Struggle for Power, 1945–1947*. Madison: University of Wisconsin Press, 1983.

Motoi Hisao. *Nihon Rōdō Undō Shi*. Tokyo: Rōmu Gyōsei Kenkyūjo, 1983.

Murakami Yasusuke. *Shinchūkan Taishū No Jidai*. Tokyo: Chūō Kōronsha, 1984.

Murakawa Ichirō. *Nihon No Seisaku Kettei Katei*. Tokyo: Gyōsei, 1985.

Muramatsu Michio. *Sengo Nihon No Kanryō Sei*. Tokyo: Tōyō Keizai Shinpōsha, 1981.

Murobushi Tetsurō. *Oshoku No Kōzō*. Tokyo: Iwanami Shoten, 1981.

Naitō Kunio. *Kōmeitō No Sugao, Kono Kyodai Na Shinja Shūdan E No Gimon*. Tokyo: Ēru Shuppansha, 1969.

Najita, Tetsuo. *Hara Kei in the Politics of Compromise*. Cambridge: Harvard University Press, 1967.

Naka Hisao, ed. *Kokkai Gin No Kōsei To Henka*. Tokyo: Seiji Kōhō Sentā, 1980.

Nakamura Kikuo and Kamijō Sueo. *Sengo Nihon Seiji Shi*. Tokyo: Yūshindō, 1973.

Nakasone Yasuhiro. *Atarashii Hoshu No Ronri*. Tokyo: Kōdansha, 1978.

Nara Nobuyuki. "Shakaitō Ni Tenbō Wa Aru No Ka?" *Chūō Kōron*, August 1979, pp. 140–154.

Nihon Hōsō Kyōkai Hōsō Yoron Chōsajo. *Dai Ni Nihonjin No Ishiki—NHK Yoron Chōsa*. Tokyo: Shiseidō, 1980.

Nihonjin Kenkyūkai, ed. *Shiji Seitō Betsu Nihonjin Shūdan*. Nihonjin Kenkyū, no. 2. Tokyo: Shiseidō, 1975.

Nihon Keizai Shinbunsha. *Jimintō Seichōkai*. Tokyo: Nihon Keizai Shinbun, 1983.

Nihon Seiji Gakkai. *Gojūgonen Taisei No Keisei To Hōkai*. Tokyo: Iwanami Shoten, 1977.

Nihon Shakaitō. *Nihon Shakaitō Nijūnen No Kiroku*. Tokyo: Nihon Shakaitō Kikanshi Shuppan Kyoku, 1965.

Nihon Shakaitō Chūō Tōgakkō and Nihon Shakaitō Shakaishugi Riron Iinkai. *Nihon Ni Okeru Shakaishugi E No Michi*. Tokyo: Shakai Shinpō, 1965.

Nishihira Shigeki. *Nihon No Senkyo*. Tokyo: Shiseidō, 1972.

Nishijima Hisashi. *Kōmeitō*. Tokyo: Sekkasha, 1968.

Nishio Suehiro. *Nishio Suehiro No Seiji Oboegaki.* Tokyo: Mainichi Shinbunsha, 1968.
Noguchi, Yukio. "Japan's Fiscal Crisis." *Japanese Economic Studies* (Spring 1982), 10(3):53–83.
Noguchi, Yukio. "Restructuring Public Finances." *Economic Eye*, March 1981, pp. 4–7.
Noguchi Yukio. *Zaisei Kiki No Kōzō.* Tokyo: Tōyō Keizai Shinposha, 1982.
Notehelfer, F. G. *Kotoku Shusui: Portrait of a Japanese Radical.* Cambridge: Cambridge University Press, 1977.
Ōkurashō. *Zaisei No Genjō To Tenbō.* Tokyo: Ōkurashō, 1983.
Olsen, Lawrence. *Dimensions of Japan.* New York: American Universities Field Staff, 1963.
Ostrogorski, M. *Democracy and the Organization of Political Parties.* Abr. ed. Seymour Martin Lipset, ed. New York: Quadrangle Books, 1964.
Ōta Kaoru, Ishikawa Makoto, and Iwai Akira. *Kiki Ni Tatsu Sōhyō.* Tokyo: Shakai Hyōronsha, 1985.
Packard, George. *Protest in Tokyo: The Security Crisis of 1960.* Princeton: Princeton University Press, 1966.
Passin, Herbert, ed. *A Season of Voting: The Japanese Elections of 1976 and 1977.* Washington, D.C.: American Enterprise Institute, 1979.
Pempel, T. J. *Policy and Politics in Japan: Creative Conservatism.* Philadelphia: Temple University Press, 1982.
Pempel, T. J., ed. *Policymaking in Contemporary Japan.* Ithaca, N.Y.: Cornell University Press, 1977.
Putman, Robert D. *The Comparative Study of Political Elites.* Englewood Cliffs, N.J.: Prentice-Hall, 1976.
Rōdōchōsa Kyōgikai. "Soshiki Rōdōsha No Seiji Ishiki Chōsa Hōkokusho." *Rōdō Chōsa*, April 1979, pp. 8–61.
Rōdōchōsa Kyōgikai. "Soshiki Rōdōsha No Shakai Seiji Ishiki." *Rōdō Chōsa*, March–April 1986.
Roth, Guenther. *The Social Democrats in Imperial Germany: A Study in Working Class Isolation and National Integration.* Princeton: Princeton University Press, 1963.
Sakamoto Mamoru. *Shakaitō Sōhyō Burokku.* Tokyo: Nihon Hyōronsha, 1981.
Sartori, Giovanni. *Parties and Party Systems: A Framework for Analysis.* Cambridge: Cambridge University Press, 1976.
Sartori, Giovanni. "Political Development and Political Engineering." *Public Policy* (1968), 17:261–298.
Sasada Shigeru. *Nihon Shakaitō.* 2 vols. Tokyo: San'ichi Shobō, 1960.
Sasaki Kōzō. *Shakaishugitekiteki Seiken.* Tokyo: Mainichi Shinbusha, 1975.
Satō Noboru. *Kakushin No Shinwa O Koete.* Tokyo: Gendai No Rironsha, 1978.

Satō Noboru. "Shakaishugi Kyōkai Hihan No Joshiki." *Shokun*, February 1978, pp. 50–66.

Satō, Seizaburō. "The Shifting Political Spectrum." *Japan Echo* (Summer 1984), vol. 11, no. 2.

Satō Seizaburō and Matsuzaki Tetsuhisa. *Jimintō Seiken*. Tokyo: Chūō Kōron Sha, 1986.

Satō Seizaburō and Matsuzaki Tetsuhisa. "The Liberal Democrats' Conciliatory Reign." *Economic Eye* (December 1985), 6(4):27–32.

Scalapino, Robert A. *Democracy and the Party Movement in Prewar Japan: The Failure of the First Attempt*. Berkeley and Los Angeles: University of California Press, 1962.

Scalapino, Robert A. *The Japanese Communist Movement, 1920–1966*. Berkeley and Los Angeles: University of California Press, 1967.

Scalapino, Robert A. and Junnosuke Masumi. *Parties and Politics in Contemporary Japan*. Berkeley and Los Angeles: University of California Press, 1962.

Schmidt, Steffen W., James C. Scott, Carl Lande, and Laura Guasti, eds. *Friends, Followers, and Factions: A Reader in Political Clientelism*. Berkeley and Los Angeles: University of California Press, 1977.

Shakaishugi Kyōkai. *Shakaishugi Kyōkai Tēze*. Tokyo: Shakaishugi Kyōkai Shuppan Kyoku, 1971.

Shimizu Shinzō and Ōta Kaoru. "Gendai Shakaishugi Ronsō." *Asahi Jānaru* (September 9, 1977), 19(36):30–37.

Sōma Masao. *Nihon No Sōsenkyo*. Tokyo: Mainichi Shinbunsha, 1969.

Sone Eki. *Watakushi No Memoāru, Kasumigaseki Kara Nagata-Chō E*. Tokyo: Nikkan Kōgyō Shinbunsha, 1974.

Stanley, Thomas A. *Ōsugi Sakae: Anarchist in Taisho Japan*. Cambridge: Council on East Asian Studies, Harvard University Press, 1982.

Steiner, Kurt, Ellis S. Krauss, and Scott C. Flanagan, eds. *Political Opposition and Local Politics in Japan*. Princeton: Princeton University Press, 1980.

Steven, Rob. *Classes in Contemporary Japan*. Cambridge: Cambridge University Press, 1983.

Stockwin, J. A. A. *The Japanese Socialist Party and Neutralism: A Study of a Political Party and Its Foreign Policy*. Carlton, Victoria: Melbourne University Press, 1968.

Suleiman, Ezra N., ed. *Parliaments and Parliamentarians in Democratic Politics*. New York: Holms and Meir, 1986.

Tachibana Takashi. *Nōkyō, Kyodai Na Chōsen*. Tokyo: Asahi Shinbunsha, 1980.

Tachibana Takashi. "Tanaka Kakuei Kenkyū—Sono Kin'myaku To Jin'myaku." *Bungei Shunjū* (November 1974), 52(12):92–131.

Takahashi Hikihiro. *Nihon No Shakai Minshushugi Seitō*. Tokyo: Hōsei Daigaku Shuppan Kyoku, 1977.

Takahashi Masao. *Shakaitō No Himitsu.* Tokyo: Chōbunsha, 1981.

Tamura Yūzō. *Sengo Shakaitō No Ninaitetachi.* Tokyo: Nihon Hyōronsha, 1984.

Tanaka, Kakuei. *Building a New Japan: A Plan for Remodeling the Japanese Archipelago.* Tokyo: The Simul Press, 1969.

Tanaka Naoki. "Shakaitō Seinenkon Wa Nani O Mezasu Ka." *Gendai No Riron* (April 1977), no. 159, pp. 116–124.

Tanaka Zen'ichirō. *Jimintō Taisei No Seiji Shidō.* Tokyo: Daiichi Hōki Shuppan, 1981.

Thayer, Nathaniel B. *How the Conservatives Rule Japan.* Princeton: Princeton University Press, 1969.

Tokyo Daigaku Shinbun Kenkyūjo. *Komyunitī Ishiki No Kenkyū.* Tokyo: Tokyo Daigaku Shinbun Kenkyūjo, 1977.

Tominomori Eiji. *Sengo Hoshutō Shi.* Tokyo: Nihon Hyōronsha, 1977.

Totten, George Oakley. *The Social Democratic Movement in Prewar Japan.* New Haven: Yale University Press, 1966.

Toyama Shirō. *Kōmeitō Giin Dan, Renritsu, Rengō Jidai No Chūdō Kakushintō.* Tokyo: Ikkōsha, 1975.

Tsujimura Akira. *Sengo Nihon No Taishū Shinri.* Tokyo: Tokyo Daigaku Shuppankai, 1981.

Uchida Kenzō. *Sengo Nihon No Hoshu Seiji.* Tokyo: Iwanami Shoten, 1969.

Uchida Kenzō, Shiratori Rei, and Tomita Nobuo. *Hoshu Kaiki—Daburu Senkyo To Minshushugi No Shōrai.* Tokyo: Shinhyōron, 1981.

Valeo, Francis R. and Charles E. Morrison, eds. *The Japanese Diet and the U.S. Congress.* Boulder Colo.: Westview Press, 1983.

Van Wolferen, Karel G. "The Japan Problem." *Foreign Affairs* (Winter 1986/87), 65(3):288–303.

Verba, Sidney, Norman H. Nie, and Jae-on Kim. *Participation and Political Equality: A Seven Nation Comparison.* Cambridge: Cambridge University Press, 1978.

Vogel, Ezra. *Japan as Number One.* Cambridge: Harvard University Press, 1979.

Watanabe Tsuneo. *Habatsu, Nihon Hoshutō No Bunseki.* Tokyo: Kōbundo, 1964.

Watanuki, Joji. *Japanese Politics: Changes, Continuities, and Unknowns.* Research Papers Series A-16. Tokyo: Institute of International Relations, Sophia University, 1973.

Watanuki, Jōji. *Nihon No Seiji Shakai.* Tokyo: Tokyo Daigaku Shuppankai, 1967.

Watanuki, Jōji. *Nihon Seiji No Bunseki Shikaku.* Tokyo: Chūō Kōron, 1976.

Watanuki, Jōji, Ichiro Miyake, Takashi Inoguchi, and Ikuo Kabashima, eds. *Electoral Behavior in the 1983 Japanese Elections.* Tokyo: Institute of International Relations, Sophia University, 1986.

White, James W. *The Soka Gakkai and Mass Society.* Stanford: Stanford University Press, 1970.

Yamakawa Hitoshi. "Kyōsantō To No Ketsubetsu." *Bungei Shunjū,* March 1950, pp. 49–59.

Yamakawa Kikue and Sakisaka Itsurō, eds. *Yamakawa Hitsoshi Jiden.* Tokyo: Iwanami Shoten, 1961.

Yamamoto Takeshi. *Kaisetsu, Seiji Shikin Kisei Hō.* Tokyo: Gyōsei, 1975.

Yamamura, Kozo, ed. *Policy and Trade Issues of the Japanese Economy: American and Japanese Perspectives.* Tokyo: University of Tokyo Press, 1982.

Yanada Hiroyoshi. *Gojūgonen Taisei To Nihon Shakaitō.* Tokyo: Ariesu Shobō, 1956.

Yomiuri Shinbun Seijibu. *Seitō.* Tokyo: Yomiuri Shinbunsha, 1966.

Yomiuri Shinbun Seijibu. " 'Nikaidō Kūdetā' Hōkai No Ketteiban." *This Is,* February 1985, pp. 8–24.

Yomiuri Shinbunsha. *83' Sandai Senkyo No Sōbunseki.* Tokyo: Yomiuri Shinbunsha, 1984.

Yomiuri Shinbunsha Yoron Chōsashitsu. *Senkyo O Tettei Bunseki Suru.* Tokyo: Yomiuri Shinbunsha, 1975.

Yoshida, Shigeru. *The Yoshida Memoirs.* Boston: Houghton Mifflin, 1962.

Yoshioka Yoshinori. *Kiki Ni Tatsu Shakaitō.* Tokyo: Shin Nihon Shuppansha, 1982.

INDEX

STUDIES OF THE EAST ASIAN INSTITUTE

THE LADDER OF SUCCESS IN IMPERIAL CHINA, by Ping-ti Ho. New York: Columbia University Press, 1962.

THE CHINESE INFLATION, 1937–1949, by Shun-hsin Chou. New York: Columbia University Press, 1963.

REFORMER IN MODERN CHINA: CHANG CHIEN, 1853–1926, by Samuel Chu. New York: Columbia University Press, 1965.

RESEARCH IN JAPANESE SOURCES: A GUIDE, by Herschel Webb with the assistance by Marleigh Ryan. New York: Columbia University Press, 1965.

SOCIETY AND EDUCATION IN JAPAN, by Herbert Passin. New York: Teachers College Press, 1965.

AGRICULTURAL PRODUCTION AND ECONOMIC DEVELOPMENTS IN JAPAN, 1873–1922, by James I. Nakamura. Princeton: Princeton University Press, 1966.

JAPAN'S FIRST MODERN NOVEL: UKIGUMO OF FUTABATEI SHIMEI, by Marleigh Ryan. New York: Columbia University Press, 1967.

THE KOREAN COMMUNIST MOVEMENT, 1918–1948, by Dae-Sook Suh. Princeton: Princeton University Press, 1967.

THE FIRST VIETNAM CRISIS, by Melvin Gurtov. New York: Columbia University Press, 1967.

CADRES, BUREAUCRACY, AND POLITICAL POWER IN COMMUNIST CHINA, by A. Doak Barnett. New York: Columbia University Press, 1968.

THE JAPANESE IMPERIAL INSTITUTION IN THE TOKU-
GAWA PERIOD, by Herschel Webb. New York: Columbia
University Press, 1968.

HIGHER EDUCATION AND BUSINESS RECRUITMENT IN JA-
PAN, by Koya Azumi. New York: Teachers College Press,
1969.

THE COMMUNISTS AND PEASANT REBELLIONS: A STUDY
IN THE REWRITING OF CHINESE HISTORY, by James P.
Harrison, Jr. New York: Atheneum, 1969.

HOW THE CONSERVATIVES RULE JAPAN, by Nathaniel B.
Thayer. Princeton: Princeton University Press, 1969.

ASPECTS OF CHINESE EDUCATION, edited by C. T. Hu. New
York: Teachers College Press, 1970.

DOCUMENTS OF KOREAN COMMUNISM, 1918–1948, by Dae-
Sook Suh. Princeton University Press, 1970.

JAPANESE EDUCATION: A BIBLIOGRAPHY OF MATERIALS
IN THE ENGLISH LANGUAGE, by Herbert Passin. New
York: Teachers College Press, 1970.

ECONOMIC DEVELOPMENT AND THE LABOR MARKET IN
JAPAN, by Koji Taira. New York: Columbia University Press,
1970.

THE JAPANESE OLIGARCHY AND THE RUSSO-JAPANESE
WAR, by Shumpei Okamoto. New York: Columbia University Press, 1970.

IMPERIAL RESTORATION IN MEDIEVAL JAPAN, by H. Paul
Varley. New York: Columbia University Press, 1971.

JAPAN'S POSTWAR DEFENSE POLICY, 1947–1968, by Martin E.
Weinstein. New York: Columbia University Press, 1971.

ELECTION CAMPAIGNING JAPANESE STYLE, by Gerald L.
Curtis. New York: Columbia University Press, 1971.

CHINA AND RUSSIA: THE "GREAT GAME," by O. Edmund
Clubb. New York: Columbia University Press, 1971.

MONEY AND MONETARY POLICY IN COMMUNIST CHINA,
by Katharine Huang Hsiao. New York: Columbia University Press, 1971.

THE DISTRICT MAGISTRATE IN LATE IMPERIAL CHINA, by
John R. Watt. New York: Columbia University Press, 1972.

LAW AND POLICY IN CHINA'S FOREIGN RELATIONS: A
STUDY OF ATTITUDE AND PRACTICE, by James C.
Hsiung. New York: Columbia University Press, 1972.

PEARL HARBOR AS HISTORY: JAPANESE-AMERICAN RE-

LATIONS, 1931–1941, edited by Dorothy Borg and Shumpei Okamoto, with the assistance of Dale K. A. Finlayson. New York: Columbia University Press, 1973.

JAPANESE CULTURE: A SHORT HISTORY, by H. Paul Varley. New York: Praeger, 1973.

DOCTORS IN POLITICS: THE POLITICAL LIFE OF THE JAPAN MEDICAL ASSOCIATION, by William E. Steslicke. New York: Praeger, 1973.

THE JAPAN TEACHERS UNION: A RADICAL INTEREST GROUP IN JAPANESE POLITICS, by Donald Ray Thurston. Princeton: Princeton University Press, 1973.

JAPAN'S FOREIGN POLICY, 1868–1941: A RESEARCH GUIDE, edited by James William Morley. New York: Columbia University Press, 1974.

PALACE AND POLITICS IN PREWAR JAPAN, by David Anson Titus. New York: Columbia University Press, 1974.

THE IDEA OF CHINA: ESSAYS IN GEOGRAPHIC MYTH AND THEORY, by Andrew March. Devon, England: David and Charles, 1974.

ORIGINS OF THE CULTURAL REVOLUTION, by Roderick MacFarquhar. New York: Columbia University Press, 1974.

SHIBA KŌKAN: ARTIST, INNOVATOR, AND PIONEER IN THE WESTERNIZATION OF JAPAN, by Calvin L. French. Tokyo: Weatherhill, 1974.

INSEI: ABDICATED SOVEREIGNS IN THE POLITICS OF LATE HEIAN JAPAN, by G. Cameron Hurst. New York: Columbia University Press, 1975.

EMBASSY AT WAR, by Harold Joyce Noble. Edited with an introduction by Frank Baldwin, Jr. Seattle: University of Washington Press, 1975.

REBELS AND BUREAUCRATS: CHINA'S DECEMBER 9ERS, by John Israel and Donald W. Klein. Berkeley: University of California Press, 1975.

DETERRENT DIPLOMACY, edited by James William Morley. New York: Columbia University Press, 1976.

HOUSE UNITED, HOUSE DIVIDED: THE CHINESE FAMILY IN TAIWAN, by Myron L. Cohen. New York: Columbia University Press, 1976.

ESCAPE FROM PREDICAMENT: NEO-CONFUCIANISM AND CHINA'S EVOLVING POLITICAL CULTURE, by Thomas A. Metzger. New York: Columbia University Press, 1976.

CADRES, COMMANDERS, AND COMMISSARS: THE TRAIN-
ING OF THE CHINESE COMMUNIST LEADERSHIP, 1920–
45, by Jane L. Price. Boulder, Colo.: Westview Press, 1976.

SUN YAT-SEN: FRUSTRATED PATRIOT, by C. Martin Wilbur.
New York: Columbia University Press, 1977.

JAPANESE INTERNATIONAL NEGOTIATING STYLE, by Michael Blaker. New York: Columbia University Press, 1977.

CONTEMPORARY JAPANESE BUDGET POLITICS, by John
Creighton Campbell. Berkeley: University of California Press,
1977.

THE MEDIEVAL CHINESE OLIGARCHY, by David Johnson.
Boulder, Colo.: Westview Press, 1977.

THE ARMS OF KIANGNAN: MODERNIZATION IN THE
CHINESE ORDNANCE INDUSTRY, 1860–1895, by Thomas
L. Kennedy. Boulder, Colo.: Westview Press, 1978.

PATTERNS OF JAPANESE POLICYMAKING: EXPERIENCES
FROM HIGHER EDUCATION, by T. J. Pempel. Boulder,
Colo.: Westview Press, 1978.

THE CHINESE CONNECTION: ROGER S. GREENE, THOMAS
W. LAMONT, GEORGE E. SOKOLSKY, AND AMERI-
CAN–EAST ASIAN RELATIONS, by Warren I. Cohen. New
York: Columbia University Press, 1978.

MILITARISM IN MODERN CHINA: THE CAREER OF WU P'EI-
FU, 1916–1939, by Odoric Y. K. Wou. Folkestone, England:
Dawson, 1978.

A CHINESE PIONEER FAMILY: THE LINS OF WU-FENG, by
Johanna Meskill. Princeton University Press, 1979.

PERSPECTIVES ON A CHANGING CHINA, edited by Joshua A.
Fogel and William T. Rowe. Boulder, Colo.: Westview Press,
1979.

THE MEMOIRS OF LI TSUNG-JEN, by T. K. Tong and Li Tsung-
jen. Boulder, Colo.: Westview Press, 1979.

UNWELCOME MUSE: CHINESE LITERATURE IN SHANGHAI
AND PEKING, 1937–1945, by Edward Gunn. New York:
Columbia University Press, 1979.

YENAN AND THE GREAT POWERS: THE ORIGINS OF
CHINESE COMMUNIST FOREIGN POLICY, by James
Reardon-Anderson. New York: Columbia University Press,
1980.

UNCERTAIN YEARS: CHINESE-AMERICAN RELATIONS, 1947–

1950, edited by Dorothy Borg and Waldo Heinrichs. New York: Columbia University Press, 1980.

THE FATEFUL CHOICE: JAPAN'S ADVANCE INTO SOUTH-EAST ASIA, edited by James William Morley. New York: Columbia University Press, 1980.

TANAKA GIICHI AND JAPAN'S CHINA POLICY, by William F. Morton. Folkestone, England: Dawson, 1980; New York: St. Martin's Press, 1980.

THE ORIGINS OF THE KOREAN WAR: LIBERATION AND THE EMERGENCE OF SEPARATE REGIMES, 1945–1947, by Bruce Cumings. Princeton University Press, 1981.

CLASS CONFLICT IN CHINESE SOCIALISM, by Richard Curt Kraus. New York: Columbia University Press, 1981.

EDUCATION UNDER MAO: CLASS AND COMPETITION IN CANTON SCHOOLS, by Jonathan Unger. New York: Columbia University Press, 1982.

PRIVATE ACADEMIES OF TOKUGAWA JAPAN, by Richard Rubinger. Princeton: Princeton University Press, 1982.

JAPAN AND THE SAN FRANCISCO PEACE SETTLEMENT, by Michael M. Yoshitsu. New York: Columbia University Press, 1982.

NEW FRONTIERS IN AMERICAN–EAST ASIAN RELATIONS: ESSAYS PRESENTED TO DOROTHY BORG, edited by Warren I. Cohen. New York: Columbia University Press, 1983.

THE ORIGINS OF THE CULTURAL REVOLUTION: II, THE GREAT LEAP FORWARD, 1958–1960, by Roderick Mac-Farquhar. New York: Columbia University Press, 1983.

THE CHINA QUAGMIRE: JAPAN'S EXPANSION OF THE ASIAN CONTINENT, 1933–1941, edited by James William Morley. New York: Columbia University Press, 1983.

FRAGMENTS OF RAINBOWS: THE LIFE AND POETRY OF SAITO MOKICHI, 1882–1953, by Amy Vladeck Heinrich. New York: Columbia University Press, 1983.

THE U.S.–SOUTH KOREAN ALLIANCE: EVOLVING PATTERNS OF SECURITY RELATIONS, edited by Gerald L. Curtis and Sung-joo Han. Lexington, Mass.: Lexington Books, 1983.

DISCOVERING HISTORY IN CHINA: AMERICAN HISTORICAL WRITING ON THE RECENT CHINESE PAST, by Paul

A. Cohen. New York: Columbia University Press, 1984.

THE FOREIGN POLICY OF THE REPUBLIC OF KOREA, edited by Youngnok Koo and Sungjoo Han. New York: Columbia University Press, 1984.

STATE AND DIPLOMACY IN EARLY MODERN JAPAN, by Ronald Toby. Princeton: Princeton University Press, 1983.

JAPAN AND THE ASIAN DEVELOPMENT BANK, by Dennis Yasutomo. New York: Praeger Publishers, 1983.

JAPAN ERUPTS: THE LONDON NAVAL CONFERENCE AND THE MANCHURIAN INCIDENT, edited by James W. Morley. New York: Columbia University Press, 1984.

JAPANESE CULTURE, third edition, revised, by Paul Varley. Honolulu: University of Hawaii Press, 1984.

JAPAN'S MODERN MYTHS: IDEOLOGY IN THE LATE MEIJI PERIOD, by Carol Gluck. Princeton: Princeton University Press, 1985.

SHAMANS, HOUSEWIVES, AND OTHER RESTLESS SPIRITS: WOMEN IN KOREAN RITUAL LIFE, by Laurel Kendall. Honolulu: University of Hawaii Press, 1985.

HUMAN RIGHTS IN CONTEMPORARY CHINA, by R. Randle Edwards, Louis Henkin, and Andrew J. Nathan. New York: Columbia University Press, 1986.

THE PACIFIC BASIN: NEW CHALLENGES FOR THE UNITED STATES, edited by James W. Morley. New York: Academy of Political Science, 1986.

THE MANNER OF GIVING: STRATEGIC AID AND JAPANESE FOREIGN POLICY, by Dennis T. Yasutomo. Lexington, Mass.: Lexington Books, 1986.

CHINA'S POLITICAL ECONOMY: THE QUEST FOR DEVELOPMENT SINCE 1949, by Carl Riskin. Oxford: Oxford University Press, 1987.

ANVIL OF VICTORY: THE COMMUNIST REVOLUTION IN MANCHURIA, by Steven I. Levine. New York: Columbia University Press, 1987.

SINGLE SPARKS: CHINA'S RURAL REVOLUTIONS, edited by Kathleen Hartford and Steven M. Goldstein. Armonk, N.Y.: M. E. Sharpe, 1987.

URBAN JAPANESE HOUSEWIVES: AT HOME AND IN THE COMMUNITY, by Anne E. Imamura. Honolulu: University of Hawaii Press, 1987.

CHINA'S SATELLITE PARTIES, by James D. Seymour. Armonk,
    N.Y.: M. E. Sharpe, 1987.
THE JAPANESE WAY OF POLITICS, by Gerald L. Curtis. New
    York: Columbia University Press, 1988.